POST-MEDIEVAL LANDSCAPES

Post-Medieval Landscapes

Edited by P. S. Barnwell and Marilyn Palmer

Landscape History after Hoskins

Volume 3

Series Editor: Christopher Dyer

WINDgather
PRESS

Post-Medieval Landscapes: Landscape History after Hoskins, Volume 3

Copyright © Windgather Press 2007

Published by: Windgather Press Ltd, 29 Bishop Road, Bollington, Macclesfield, Cheshire SK10 5NX

Distributed by: Oxbow Books, 10 Hythe Bridge Street, Oxford, OX1 2EW

British Library Cataloguing-in-Publication Data

A catalogue record for this book is available from the British Library

ISBN 978-1-905119-19-6

Designed, typeset and originated by Carnegie Book Production, Lancaster
Printed and bound by Cambridge Printing, Cambridge

Contents

List of Figures   vii

Abbreviations   x

Acknowledgements   xi

Series Foreword: Landscape History after Hoskins   xiii
    Christopher Dyer

1   Introduction: Post-Medieval Landscapes since Hoskins –
   Theory and Practice   1
    Marilyn Palmer

Part 1: Rural Landscapes

2   Hidden Boundaries/Hidden Landscapes: Lead-Mining
   Landscapes in the Yorkshire Dales   9
    Martin Roe

3   The Importance of Place: Placing Vernacular Buildings into a
   Landscape Context   23
    Adam Longcroft

4   The Estate: Recognising People and Place in the Modern
   Landscape   39
    Jonathan Finch

5   Landscapes of the Poor: Encroachment in Wales in the Post-
   Medieval Centuries   55
    Robert Silvester

6   The Grouse Moors of the Peak District   68
    David Hey

7   Hoskins and Historical Ecology   80
    John Sheail

Part 2: Urban Landscapes

8   New Markets and Fairs in the Yorkshire Dales, 1550–1750   93
     R. W. Hoyle

9   Rus et Urbe? The Hinterland and Landscape of Georgian
     Chester   107
     Jon Stobart

10 The Suburbanisation of the English Landscape: Environmental
     Conflict in Victorian Croydon   119
     Nicholas Goddard

Part 3: Landscapes Perceived

11 Wilderness and Waste – 'The Weird and Wonderful': Views of
     the Midland Region   137
     Della Hooke

12 Tally-ho! The Making and Representation of the Hunting
     Landscape of the Shires   151
     Nicholas Watkins

13 'An Angel-Satyr Walks these Hills': Landscape and Identity in
     Kilvert's Diary   169
     Philip Dunham

14 Ways of Seeing: Hoskins and the Oxfordshire Landscape
     Revisited   185
     Kate Tiller

15 Conclusion: Discovering the Post-Medieval Landscape – After
     W. G. Hoskins   201
     P. S. Barnwell

Contributors   205
Bibliography   208
Index   219

List of Figures

1. Stope, Danby Level, Arkengarthdale — 11
2. Stoped ground, Greenhow Rake Vein, Greenhow Hill — 16
3. Shaft hollows on Greenhow Rake Vein, Greenhow Hill — 17
4. Danby Level, Arkengarthdale — 20
5. Survey of shafts and other features above Danby Level — 21
6. Survey of Danby Level added to surface features — 21
7. Proportion of households taxed on one or two hearths, 1664/66 — 28
8. Soils in Norfolk — 28
9. One- and two-cell plans in Norfolk — 29
10. Proportion of households taxed on three to six hearths — 30
11. Three-cell plans in Norfolk — 31
12. Distribution of pre-*c.*1730 vernacular buildings in Norfolk — 33
13. The Carrmire Gate, Castle Howard — 44
14. Ray Wood and the Temple of the Four Winds, Castle Howard — 45
15. Early nineteenth-century watercolour by John Varley (1778–1842) of Harewood village — 48
16. A heated wall at Harewood kitchen gardens — 52
17. The Orangery, Burton Constable — 53
18. Aerial view of Moelfre City, Radnorshire (Powys) — 60
19. Part of the *cantref* of Maelienydd to the south-east of Llanbister, Radnorshire (Powys) — 61
20. Forden and Kingswood, Montgomeryshire (Powys) — 62
21. The middle Usk valley in Brecknock (Powys) — 63
22. Ffawyddog, Brecknock (Powys) — 64
23. Detail of P. P. Burdett's Map of Derbyshire (1791 edition) — 69
24. Gamekeeper's cottage, White Edge, Longshaw Moors estate — 72
25. Broomhead Moor shooting cabin — 73
26. Shooting butts on Bradfield Moors, Earl Fitzwilliam's estate — 73
27. Boundary stone between grouse moors — 76
28. The first of William Wilson's grouse drinking troughs on Stanage Moor, 1907 — 76

29.	Grouse drinking trough no. 33 in Wilson's second sequence	77
30.	Grouse drinking trough no. 25 in the third sequence	77
31.	Reeth in 1971	100
32.	Maps of Reeth in 1830 and in the late medieval period	101
33.	Leyburn, from an estate map of *c.*1730	104
34.	Leyburn, looking northwards	105
35.	Places mentioned in Chester newspaper advertisements, 1739–49	112
36.	Alfred Smee's garden in relation to Croydon, *c.*1872	124
37.	View of Beddington Church from Alfred Smee's garden, *c.*1872	125
38.	Duppas Hill, *c.*1900	128
39.	Park Hill recreation grounds, *c.*1900	129
40.	The Wandle, *c.*1925	132
41.	A view of the Stiperstones in Shropshire, from the west	140
42.	A view over the White Peak in Derbyshire	144
43.	Sherbrooke valley on Cannock Chase, Staffordshire	145
44.	A view over Axe Moor in the Dark Peak	148
45.	The view from Mortimer's Way over the Vale of Wigmore, Herefordshire	149
46.	Detail from *Southern and Wales Showing the Fox Hunts, Baily's Hunting Directory 1921–1922*	152
47.	Sir Alfred Munnings, *The Prince of Wales on Forest Witch*, 1921	153
48.	Lionel Edwards, *Sheepthorns*, 1928	156
49.	Henry Alken Senior, *The Leicestershire Covers*, 1824	157
50.	John Ferneley Senior, *The Quorn Hunt scurry at Billesdon Coplow*, 1831	160–1
51.	Sir Alfred Munnings, *Frank Freeman on Pilot*, 1925	164
52.	Sir Alfred Munnings, *Changing Horses*, 1920	165
53.	John Ferneley Senior, *The Hon. George Petre with the Quorn at Rolleston*, 1814	168
54.	'Kilvert Country': the Radnorshire/Herefordshire Borderland	171
55.	The Black Mountains, from Clyro Hill	173
56.	Pastoral Visits by the Diarist, 1870	176
57.	The Rev. Francis Kilvert, *c.*1869	177
58.	Bird's Nest Lane, Clyro, as it is today	181
59.	Steeple Barton Vicarage, built in 1856 to the designs of S. S. Teulon	186
60.	The area chosen by Hoskins to discuss the imprint of communications on the landscape	188

List of Figures

61. The contrasting characters of Sandford St Martin and Middle Barton   192

62. Villages replanned, from the 1944 north Oxfordshire survey *Country Planning*   193

63. A USAF F-111 swing-wing fighter at RAF Upper Heyford   196

64. Archaeological sites in the Cherwell Valley   197

Abbreviations

AONB   Area of Outstanding Natural Beauty
CCA   Cheshire and Chester Archives
HMSO   Her Majesty's Stationery Office
NYRO   North Yorkshire Record Office
RCHME   Royal Commission on the Historical Monuments of England
SCR   Sheffield Clarion Ramblers
TNA:PRO   The National Archives, Public Record Office
YASRS   Yorkshire Archaeological Society Record Service

Acknowledgements

The conference on which this book is based was organised by a committee drawn from the School of Archaeology and Ancient History and the Centre for English Local History in the University of Leicester, with David Palliser as a representative of the Royal Historical Society, and Tony Brown for the Society for Landscape Studies. It attracted support and sponsorship from English Heritage, the British Academy, the Friends of the Centre for English Local History, the Historical Geography Research Group, the Medieval Settlement Research Group, Oadby and Wigston Borough Council, Oxbow Books, the Royal Historical Society, the Society for Landscape Studies and Windgather Press. The excursions were led by the late Harold Fox, Graham Jones and Charles Phythian-Adams. Impeccable organisation was provided by Barbara Johnson, with help from David Johnson and Mike Thompson. Publication of the papers in a series of three volumes has depended on the services of the editors: P. S. Barnwell, Andrew Fleming, Mark Gardiner, Richard Hingley, Marilyn Palmer and Stephen Rippon. An anonymous referee gave valuable service. All of the editors and contributors are indebted to Richard Purslow of Windgather Press for his help and support in producing this series, and to Sarah Harrison, who prepared the index for each volume. Financial help for the costs of publication from the Aurelius Trust is gratefully acknowledged.

Christopher Dyer

Landscape History after Hoskins,
Series Editor, Christopher Dyer

Volume 1
Prehistoric and Roman Landscapes
edited by Andrew Fleming and Richard Hingley

Volume 2
Medieval Landscapes
edited by Mark Gardiner and Stephen Rippon

Volume 3
Post-Medieval Landscapes
edited by P. S. Barnwell and Marilyn Palmer

Landscape History after Hoskins

Christopher Dyer

This book celebrates a great scholar; it emerged from an inspiring occasion; and it reflects the vigour of an enthralling subject, the history of the landscape. It contains a selection of the papers presented to a conference called *W. G. Hoskins and the Making of the British Landscape*, held at the University of Leicester on 7–10 July 2005 to mark the fiftieth anniversary of the publication of *The Making of the English Landscape* by W. G. Hoskins. A Devon man, Hoskins spent the early part of his life as a student in that county, and returned to it in retirement. He held the post of Reader in Economic History at Oxford in 1951–65, and he lived in London when he held a wartime post in the civil service. Leicester was the appropriate place for a conference to honour his work in landscape history, as he had developed his approach to local history and topography in his time on the staff of the University College in the 1930s and late 1940s (he briefly returned as Professor in 1965–8). He was active in the Leicestershire Archaeological Society, and contributed some notable articles to that Society's *Transactions*. He attracted an enthusiastic following to his adult education lectures at Vaughan College. His books on Leicestershire included *The Midland Peasant* and, for a wider readership, the Shell Guide. While at Leicester he founded the University's Department (later Centre) of English Local History.

The Making of the English Landscape appeared in 1955 and had a major impact on the reading public, as it was well written, accessible, and revealed a new way of looking at the past. Hoskins showed that our everyday surroundings – roads, hedges, trees, buildings – had an historical significance, and he was tapping a new source of evidence. The Ordnance Survey map became in his hands a vital document, and he asserted that the landscape was 'the richest historical record we possess'. *The Making* was admired by academics as well as a wider readership, and went through a number of versions, including a Penguin paperback and a Folio Society edition. It was followed by a series of studies of individual counties, which made good progress but was not completed. The book produced a rather delayed response in academia, in the sense that the discipline of Landscape History did not grow rapidly until the 1970s and 1980s, when it was widely practised by archaeologists and geographers, rather than historians. It gained a society and journal with the foundation of the Society for Landscape Studies in 1979, which has published *Landscape*

History ever since. So much research and writing was being done on the subject, and it attracted so much interest from the public as well as professional scholars, that a second journal, *Landscapes*, was launched in 2000.

At the 2005 Leicester conference sixty papers were given in two parallel sessions under ten themes: prehistoric/Roman landscapes; rural settlement; towns; industry; buildings; designed landscapes; environments; ritual; perceptions; and techniques of mapping. The conference was attended by 250 people, and indeed the need to limit the numbers in each lecture room meant that latecomers had to be turned away. Plenary talks were given at the beginning by Christopher Taylor (a landscape archaeologist who knew Hoskins well), Elisabeth Zadora Rio (who provided a continental European perspective), and Fiona Reynolds of the National Trust, who had been influenced by *The Making* when she read it as a student. Three receptions were held, and excursions on three alternative routes occupied one afternoon. The beginning of the conference on 7 July was overshadowed by the London bombings but, in spite of this setback, a cheerful and positive atmosphere prevailed, helped by the sunny weather, good hospitality and attractive surroundings.

Those who gave papers at the conference were encouraged from the beginning not to think of the event as a memorial or a retrospective. W. G. Hoskins was the starting point, and almost every speaker made some reference to the pioneer, but they were focused on recent research and future developments. A number of themes covered subjects which Hoskins himself did not consider in much detail and used techniques that have emerged since 1955. The organisers had hoped that the conference would attract representatives of different disciplines, and would promote interdisciplinary contacts, and this was achieved. Younger scholars were encouraged to attend and to contribute, and a good number responded. The papers in this book, only a selection of those presented at the conference, reflect the progress in landscape history after Hoskins, and readers will gain an impression of the liveliness of the discipline, the new thinking, and the wide range of subject matter.

Christopher Dyer
Professor of Regional and Local History and Director of the
Centre for English Local History
Chair of the Conference Organising Committee

CHAPTER ONE

Introduction:
Post-Medieval Landscapes since
Hoskins – Theory and Practice

Marilyn Palmer

....

This, the third book resulting from the University of Leicester conference *Hoskins and the Making of the British Landscape*, is concerned with the post-medieval period. It is generally accepted that the great turning points both economically and politically after the High Middle Ages were the Black Death and its aftermath, and the Reformation, both of which affected systems of land tenure, social structures, extent of settlement and types of building. In *The Making*, despite his great interest in the antiquity of English villages, Hoskins devoted more than half the book to this period, and many other students of the landscape since, such as Tom Williamson, have acknowledged that 'the formation of the landscape archaeological record … is primarily a product of the post-medieval period' (Everson and Williamson 1998, 7).

This book, then, reflects some of the most recent work in landscape studies concerning the period since 1500, the range of which is commented on by my fellow-editor, Paul Barnwell, in his Conclusion. My own thoughts here are more concerned with the great range of disciplines which now contribute towards the study of the British landscape and particularly to my own field of archaeology. Like Hoskins, some of whose lectures I attended while studying History at the University of Oxford, I too became conscious of the importance of physical remains in understanding the past, not just those buried beneath the surface but also the earthworks, hedge patterns, trackways and buildings in the present landscape. In this, my academic career was fostered by the growth of extra-mural education in the 1970s and 80s, where Hoskins's work perhaps found its most fertile ground, and particularly in this county of Leicestershire, where adult groups have carried out systematic fieldwalking for decades under the leadership of local authority archaeologists such as Peter Liddle, Bob Rutland and Fred Hartley. Two other renowned field archaeologists, Tony Brown and Christopher Taylor, contributed to these extra-mural programmes and it is not their fault that in the end I became an industrial archaeologist – indeed, the ideas and techniques I learnt from them have enabled me to help bring industrial archaeology into the academic as well as the extra-mural sphere. The work carried out now by many archaeological units, particularly those of Cornwall and the University of Manchester (see Nevell 2003), indicates the extent to which it is now accepted that industrial sites contain useful evidence of past human activity, something explored by Roe in this volume.

Hoskins, though, perceived archaeology to be about 'digging up the past' – a misconception regrettably popularised by television producers. In the Introduction to the 1976 edition of *The Making*, Hoskins acknowledged the increasing contributions made by archaeologists to our knowledge of the antiquity of the present landscape, especially in the form of 'rescue digs' which uncovered at speed 'a vast amount of evidence which might have remained buried for ever or discovered only at long intervals or by accident'; a description equally applicable to modern developer-funded archaeology. However, he went on to say that the borderline between landscape history and archaeology is a fine one but that he himself had striven to analyse what can be seen on the surface today: 'the visible landscape offers us enough stimulus and pleasure without the uncertainty of what may lie beneath.' The major difference fifty years later is that archaeologists regard the surface remains themselves as being within their province of study and do not always feel compelled to delve beneath them. Hoskins certainly appreciated the significance of earthworks in his study of deserted medieval villages, for example, but would not, I think, have recognised the term 'landscape archaeology'. The work of the former Royal Commission on the Historical Monuments of England (RCHME), fostered by Christopher Taylor, moved on from studies of individual sites and buildings to consider relict landscapes as a whole. Paul Everson has pointed out how, in the case of industrial landscapes, for example, the 'field remains are sometimes physically and always functionally interlinked in some way – by transport networks, power sources or the flow of materials' (Everson 1995). Landscape archaeology focuses on scales of analysis much wider than individual sites or buildings and makes use of non-destructive techniques, made more possible in recent decades by the introduction of electronic survey techniques and the systematic application of aerial photography (see Bowden 1999). Yet, certainly in the post-medieval period, landscape archaeologists seek to make sense of patterns observed in field survey by recourse to documents. There is, perhaps, not a great deal of difference between the terms 'landscape archaeology' and 'landscape history', except perhaps the order in which the types of evidence are approached.

Of course, disciplines other than history and archaeology have made distinctive contributions to the understanding of the post-medieval landscape. As John Sheail points out in this volume, one of the Nature Conservancy's first regional officers, Eric Duffey, was also strongly influenced by Hoskins's teaching both in Adult Education and in the University at Leicester and went on to take part in research which demonstrated that the Norfolk Broads were derived from medieval peat workings; while Hoskins's interest in dating hedgerows was enthusiastically taken up by other historical ecologists such as Max Hooper, based at the Monks Wood Experimental Station. Historical geographers, too, have contributed extensively to the understanding of field systems (see Baker and Butlin 1973), while Hoskins's great interest in buildings in the landscape was taken up and developed by the work of the Vernacular Architecture Group and the RCHME, notably in Eric Mercer's highly influential *English Vernacular Houses* (Mercer 1975), J. T. Smith's work in Hertfordshire (RCHME 1992) and Sarah Pearson's in Lancashire and Kent (RCHME 1985; Pearson 1994).

What *The Making* shows, of course, as did Maurice Beresford's *History on the Ground*, published only two years afterwards (Beresford 1957), is the importance of the human role in shaping the landscape. All studies of past landscapes – and none more so than those of industrial landscapes – involve an appreciation of the interaction between natural features, such as geology and topography, and human agency. For the industrial archaeologist, the location of industry in the landscape is determined partly by the presence of minerals, the availability of water for power and the gradient of the land, which influences the siting of processing plants and transport networks, but partly also by human choice: the distribution of iron furnaces in south Derbyshire in the late eighteenth century, for example, bore more relation to the estate boundaries of the Hastings, Burdett and Ferrers families than to purely geological considerations (Palmer and Neaverson 1998, 18). One of the more challenging developments in landscape studies has been to explore further, in more theoretical terms, the role of people in both the formation and the perception of landscapes. Perhaps inspired by Chris Tilley's *A Phenomenology of Landscape* (Tilley 1994), more thought has been given to how people encounter places and invest those places with significance. This involves attempting to understand how people perceived the world in which they lived and how they moved through it: as Tim Ingold has said, 'the landscape is the world as it is known to those who dwell therein, who inhabit its places and journey along the paths connecting them' (Ingold 2000, 193). Philip Dunham's chapter in this volume deals with Francis Kilvert's encounter with what he thought of as a 'borderland' and explores the way in which he tried to experience and record particular moments of encounter with the Clyro countryside. Central to this way of thinking is the concept of a sense of place, an understanding of what places meant to people and how they lived in them – something that is important not just in the prehistoric landscapes discussed by Chris Tilley but also in more modern industrialised landscapes in which senses of community and identity have enabled people to come to terms with often less than idyllic surroundings. A case in point is the exploration by Kathleen Stewart of the 'senses of place' in the Appalachian hills of West Virginia, devastated by a now-vanished extractive industry and occupied by people seeking to come to terms with their changed surroundings: as she says, 'the detritus of history piled high on the local landscape has become central to a sense of place emergent in re-membered ruins and pieced-together fragments' (Stewart 1996, 137). Cultural geographers, ethnographers and social anthropologists have their own contributions to make to the increasingly complex field of landscape history and archaeology.

Such theoretical explorations of landscape have resulted in cultural definitions of the environment which have found practical expression in government policy both internationally and nationally. Cultural landscapes, as defined by UNESCO, represent 'the combined works of nature and man … illustrative of the evolution of human society and settlement over time, under the influence of the physical constraints and/or opportunities presented by their natural environment and of successive social, economic and cultural forces, both external and internal'. An example of a World Heritage site inscribed under these criteria is the Hallstatt-Dachstein/Salzkammergut alpine region, known for its salt mines and described as 'an outstanding example of a natural landscape of great beauty and scientific interest which also contains evidence of a fundamental human economic activity, the whole integrated in a harmonious and mutually beneficial manner'. Nationally, such cultural definitions of the environment have resulted during the past decade in a considerable change not just in terminology but in the scope of what is regarded as worthy of preservation in the contemporary landscape. The term 'historic environment' is now generally in use: Sites and Monuments Records have become Historic Environment Records and counties now have Historic Environment Services. Devon County Council defines the term as encompassing 'all those material remains that our ancestors have created in the landscapes of town and countryside. It covers the whole spectrum of human activity from the largest – towns, cathedrals and motorways – to the very smallest – signposts, standing stones or flint tools. Because of unceasing human activity through the ages, virtually all the rural landscape of England, as well as its towns and villages, forms part of the historic environment.' This wide-ranging concept was perhaps first given public expression in *Power of Place* (English Heritage 2000), which placed emphasis on the need to understand the character of places and the value and significance that people ascribe to them. Although this clearly means the value people living in the contemporary landscape ascribe to their surroundings, it obviously encompasses past perceptions which are communicated to the present by the survival of buildings, monuments and landscapes. The relationship between people and places, people and their heritage, is central to current government thinking on this topic. Characterisation projects on various scales bring together as many aspects of places as possible and try to understand the experience of being in them. The most ambitious of these projects, a paper on which was presented during the Leicester Conference, is English Heritage's Historic Landscape Characterisation (HLC) programme, which is designed to create an appreciation of the time-depth of human landscapes aligned with scenic or ecological considerations (see Clark *et al.* 2004); while, at the same time, the Countryside Agency is carrying out Landscape Character Assessments. Modern mapping techniques, particularly the availability of digitised historic maps and the use of GIS, have enabled considerable complexity and time-depth to be included in the assessments. These are, of course, not just pieces of research but management tools for trying to deal with processes of change in ways which, hopefully, will help to minimise the loss of landscape character, a process which Hoskins so deplored: the significance of his words 'since the year 1914, every single change in the English landscape has either uglified it, or destroyed its meaning or both' (Hoskins 1988, 237) is explored by Kate Tiller in the final contribution to this volume. Such publicly funded programmes designed to understand the historic nature of the landscape and to try to manage its future, for all the limitations that such large-scale projects inevitably have, are a clear vindication of the importance of Hoskins's approach and a measure of how far we have come in the fifty years since *The Making* was published.

PART ONE

Rural Landscapes

CHAPTER TWO

Hidden Boundaries/ Hidden Landscapes: Lead-Mining Landscapes in the Yorkshire Dales

Martin Roe

In *The Making of the English Landscape* (1955), Hoskins discusses industrial landscapes in a chapter entitled 'The Industrial Revolution and the Landscape'. He suggests that in the sixteenth century, in the time of Leland and Camden, there 'was nothing that could be called specifically an industrial landscape', thus enshrining the concept that industrial landscapes are primarily a product of industrial growth in the late eighteenth and the nineteenth centuries. Still widely followed, this idea is, however, untrue, for industries such as lead mining have shaped the landscape for much more than 300 years. Indeed, although Leland lived in a world that had not yet produced the term 'landscape', the relationship between industry and landscape was probably not unfamiliar to him. Writing about Swaledale in the Yorkshire Dales, he stated that 'The market [at Grinton] is of corn and linen cloth for men of Swaledale, the which be much used in digging lead ore. On each side of Swaledale be great hills where they dig' (Leland 1535–48, 26). Maps of the former lands of Marrick Priory dated 1592[1] depict both areas of mining and the locations of several bale smelting sites, confirming the presence of an industrial landscape prior to 1600. Nor is this unusual: some lead-mining landscapes have been worked from prehistoric periods to the twentieth century, many being documented from the early medieval period.

Many people still believe that mining destroys its own past. Raistrick, writing about the West Riding of Yorkshire as part of the 'Making of the English Landscape' series edited by Hoskins, categorically states that 'it is the fate of almost all extractive industries that their early workings are removed in later work or buried underneath later spoil so that only the remains of the nineteenth and occasionally of the eighteenth century are visible ... this is particularly true of lead mining where nearly the whole of the mining scene belongs to the nineteenth century' (Raistrick 1970, 119). As will be demonstrated, this is not the case: just as Hoskins was able to demonstrate that landscapes are composed of elements from many different periods, with the basic form often established long before the age of parliamentary enclosure, this chapter will show how evidence survives from many different phases of the development of lead-mining landscapes.

Within lead-mining areas the boundaries of both natural features and human intervention are the key to understanding the landscape. The form of human interventions and the time at which they occurred vary across the Yorkshire Dales, as do the social and economic triggers for them, though full discussion of the latter is beyond the scope of this chapter. The boundaries are rarely obvious, frequently hidden in what are big and often complex landscapes. In addition, although mining is fundamentally an underground activity and much evidence is therefore concealed below the ground, the subterranean landscape has rarely been recorded and interpreted in the same way as that on the surface. This chapter explores the physically hidden belowground landscape and the poorly understood surface features, and argues that the landscape of Dales lead mining is of much greater antiquity than usually thought.

Geology: the foundation of the landscape

Geology is the foundation which gives a landscape its character. Understanding the nature of that character is a vital precondition for an examination of the human activities which have shaped the landscape through time to produce the landscapes present today. It is geology that has defined the location and nature of lead mining, and geological features which have produced inter-regional variations reflected in the mining landscapes. This is as true for the other, non-ferrous, ores – copper and tin – as for lead, as all are most commonly found deposited in near-vertical mineral veins, so that much of the following discussion has implications for a context wider than the mining of lead ores in the Yorkshire Dales.

Lead mining has been confined to the eastern side of what is now the Yorkshire Dales National Park, and extends eastwards into the Nidderdale AONB. The geology in most of the Yorkshire Dales ore field consists of a rhythmic sequence of sedimentary rocks, mainly limestones, cherts, gritstones and shales, known as the Yoredale Series. These beds have been subject to faulting or fracturing, and mineral-rich solutions have entered these fissures and crystallised to form mineral veins. Where the fissures pass through harder or brittle beds of limestones and cherts and some gritstones, they are more open, allowing the formation of ore bodies which can be economically exploited (Figure 1). The result is that mining is mainly confined to the hard or brittle beds, historically termed 'bearing beds'. This very important principle has eluded many writers, who have not understood that it introduces varied physical zones within each vein which have affected the way in which miners exploited the resource and, therefore, the development of the landscape. In the Yorkshire Dales, even though the mineral veins can be several hundred

FIGURE I.
Stope, Danby Level, Arkengarthdale. The cavity reflects the size of the ore body.

metres deep, economically attractive ore is only located in well-defined zones usually less than 30 m tall, separated by barren beds. This is very different to other areas, such as Cornwall, where some veins are continuously mineralised from the surface to great depths.

Hidden landscapes – the underground workings

Post-Medieval Landscapes: Landscape History after Hoskins Volume 3

Underground may seem to be a separate landscape, even an alien one, and it is certainly one that few experience. Even those who do experience it can easily treat it as remote from the surface landscape. To the miners, however, both landscapes would have been part of the same world and, therefore, to enable correct interpretation and understanding it is important to think in terms of a landscape that includes both visible and hidden elements, on and below the surface. This is perhaps a concept more familiar to the archaeologist than the historian. Archaeologists, particularly prehistorians, view landscapes of the past from the present. Certain elements of these landscapes have changed or disappeared and therefore have to be reconstructed in the mind. Other aspects, such as the spiritual or cultural significance of landscape, are much less tangible, yet they are accepted as important elements in the understanding of the past. In comparison with those approaches, the problems of understanding the underground and surface elements of mining landscapes, and of mentally combining them, are relatively straightforward, though they require those investigating such landscapes to revise their approach. The rewards are an enhanced understanding often radically different to the interpretations advanced by well-known writers thirty to forty years ago and still quoted today without critical discussion.

To understand the underground mining landscape it is helpful to consider two main types of component. The first consists of features related to gaining access to the mineral resource, such as shafts and levels, often driven from the surface, which may run through barren rock before reaching an ore body. Such features not only permit access to a mineral resource, but also serve to get men and materials to and from working places, and to move ore, and sometimes waste, back to the surface. They may also provide drainage and ventilation, and form an infrastructure on which the whole working of the mine depends. In addition, they are often the only link to the surface landscape, representing not just a physical entrance but also the link between the visible and the hidden landscape. The second component is serviced by the first, and comprises the working places or stopes – the cavities created by the mining process. They have often been backfilled with waste material and can be unstable and inaccessible, and thus their interpretation may have to be based on the evidence of the surrounding infrastructure rather than on researchers' visual experiences of them. These two elements combine to form the physical 'structures' that define the underground workings, and therefore the underground landscape. The 'structures' are in fact cavities excavated in natural geological 'structures', but can conceptually be treated as structures in their own right (Roe 2000).

As with the surface landscape, careful observation and recording of features underground can demonstrate different events, changes and modifications which can be used to suggest development sequences which often cannot be identified on the surface. The amount of evidence for a particular phase can vary, and is usually fuller in the infrastructure part of the underground landscape than in the stopes, because reworking of the latter destroys most of the evidence of earlier phases. Nevertheless, the underground landscape can act as a significant source of additional information, and its contribution should not be underestimated.

The physical characteristics of shallow mining

If understanding the development of mining landscapes depends on a careful observation of the above- and below-ground field remains, it can be assisted by surviving documentation. The usefulness of documents is variable, and the level of detail they contain means that they are often only a supporting form of evidence, the landscape having the status of the primary text. Examination of the landscapes often results in conflict with, and contradiction of, those previous writers who have based their research on written records. In particular, the evolution of the landscape is frequently much more complex than documentary sources would suggest.

A good place to test the work of previous writers is where mineral veins outcrop. It is rarely possible to examine what is happening beneath the lines of small shaft mounds, pits and open-cut trenches which mark the course of mineral veins, and this has resulted in some misunderstandings, both of what those features themselves represent and of the order in which different types of feature appeared in the landscape. At Duck Street Quarry, Greenhow Hill, quarrying has removed the top from a line of small shaft mounds on Greenhow Rake Vein, exposing both the underground workings and the remains of several shafts, and providing enough clues to enable the formulation of a hypothesis concerning the way in which these landscape features developed (Figure 2). It appears that shafts were sunk directly onto the vein, and irregular drifts driven between the shafts at different depths, so cutting the mineralised ground into blocks like a vertical form of pillar and stall mining. As with that pillar and stall working in coal, there may have been be a later phase in which the pillars were removed to produce a large stope cavity, which, if close to the surface, could be opened to the sky and become an open cut. Application of this interpretation to other sites suggests that previous interpretations which described these features as bell pits were wrong. Bell pits are usually described as discrete shafts sunk and then worked outwards from the foot; once abandoned, another shaft would be sunk nearby, and it has been suggested that the spoil from the second would be used to fill the first. Clearly this is not the case in the Dales lead mines, as the shafts are connected. Another often-repeated statement is that open cuts are a sign of early workings, but the evidence presented here suggests that they represent an end stage of mining which removed vein pillars which had probably been left in place to support the workings – an activity that can only sensibly take place at the end of the life of a mine.

In the parts of the Yorkshire Dales where the outcropping veins are found on steep hillsides, the phase of opening up the stopes to form open cuts was replaced by hushing. This is a form of hydraulic mining in which a dam is built at the top of a hill so that water could be periodically released to send a stream down the hillside which would scour off the topsoil and any loose material (Forster 1883, 165). This has also been considered an early form of mining, possibly even Roman, but careful reading of the landscape is demonstrating that, in the Yorkshire Dales, hushes on the veins, like the open cuts, represent a final stage in the mining of outcropping veins which took place mainly in the eighteenth century.

These observations of physical properties, which arise from an analysis of both surface and underground features, are, however, only part of the picture. As mentioned earlier, the landscape is full of boundaries, even though they are frequently hidden. Remembering that minerals are a resource that has been owned and controlled since before records began, it is worth considering whether that control affected the development of the landscape.

The administration of mining fields

This administration of mining is a complex subject of which only an overview, focusing on those aspects that can be identified in the landscape, can be given here. Studies of the prehistoric landscape of Swaledale have suggested the presence of a territory or kingdom in the upper valley west of Grinton. The area is defended by a post-Roman dyke system and there are earlier defended sites, including the Maiden Castle hillfort which Andrew Fleming considers may indicate political control over the area in the Iron Age, if not the Bronze Age (Fleming 1998). If one asks what resources upper Swaledale possessed that would be have been worth controlling and defending, one option is the mineral resources, and it is possible that early earthworks provide evidence for the controlled exploitation of lead mining as long ago as the prehistoric era.

Working under customary mining law

The earliest known form of administration of individual sites that appears to be identifiable in the landscape is a system found with regional variations across the country, known as customary mining law. It is thought to have originated before the Norman Conquest, and continued to be used until the post-medieval period. In contrast to later leases, miners took grants of ground on a single vein and were able to work it for as long as they wanted, provided that they worked the ground continuously. If the ground stood idle for a specified length of time it could be taken over by other miners (Gill 1989).

Where customary mining law prevailed, the ground along each vein was divided into rectangular blocks called meers. In the Yorkshire Dales lengths of 30 and 32 yards (27.5 to 29 m) were most common (Gill 1988). Strictly, the meer is a linear measurement: to form a block of ground a space known as a 'quarter cord', which, as its name suggests, was quarter of a meer, was allocated on either side of the vein. Some recorded mining laws state that miners were expected to confine all their activities within the quarter cord, and were allowed to use it to stack their waste, dress ore and construct buildings (Hooson 1747; Rieuwerts 1998). Although such a clause is absent in Yorkshire, as mining law was based on an oral tradition, it is possible that the provision was accepted as so normal that it did not need to be recorded when the laws were eventually written down. A survey carried out on West Craven Moor, Appletreewick, in 2000 identified a clear zoning of material around Fielding Vein which shows that development waste and most of the ore dressing waste is confined to a narrow strip of ground on either side of two large open-cut trenches. This has been interpreted as evidence of meer-working, in which mining and dressing activities were confined to the quarter cord (Roe and Davies 2002). Subsequent work has shown that this is a widespread phenomenon.

On nearby Grassington Moor the first mining grants were recorded in 1732 and mining was carried out under customary law with meers 30 yards (27.5 m) long with a quarter cord of 7½ yards (7 m) either side of the vein. The official in overall control of the day-to-day running of a mining area under customary law was the barmaster, and at Grassington the survival of many of the barmasters' ledgers allows detailed examination of the way in which meer grants were established and later changed hands. This shows that, once established, the position of the individual meers remained constant, even if the ownership changed and the overall pattern of the grants was altered (Gill 2000, 48). Field survey on the western part of Grassington Moor has since confirmed that the vast majority of the mining activity was confined to the quarter cord; where this is not the case other factors provide explanations. Although the quarter cords can be located, it does not appear to be possible to identify the boundaries of individual meers, even on well-documented sites.

At Greenhow Hill, customary law is likely to have been practised from the medieval period, for a legal document of 1225 refers to 'exploring' a pit 'to the bounds of the mine' (Gill 1998, 12). This may refer to the custom of chasing, or proving, the vein along the length of one meer before moving on to another (Hooson 1747), which is a further element of customary mining law. It may also help to explain the close spacing of shafts and pits which mark the course of the outcropping veins (Figure 3), as well as the underground connections previously mentioned. Further evidence of customary mining survives in the form of place-name evidence. Prim-Gap was formerly the name for High View Farm, close to the Prim Gap Vein: a Prim Gap is 'a length of vein less than half a meer between two mine titles or separate jurisdictions' (Rieuwerts 1998, 123).

Some caution has to be applied before blindly accepting that all outcropping veins were worked under customary law. Mapping zones of mining activity can demonstrate that such law is confined to small areas which relate to the outcrop of the limestone, but how far mining methods were affected by the method of administration – as opposed to the underlying geology – is not completely clear. As far as the geology is concerned, the ore-bearing parts of

FIGURE 2.
Stoped ground,
Greenhow Rake Vein,
Greenhow Hill. The
figure is positioned in
a former shaft.

FIGURE 3.
Shaft hollows on
Greenhow Rake Vein,
Greenhow Hill, typical
of veins worked under
customary mining law.

the veins are close to the surface, so that only shallow excavation was needed
to reach them. Such shallow excavation would result in shaft mounds of a
small diameter, unlikely to extend beyond the boundary of the quarter cord.
This would cast doubt, therefore, on the idea that areas of customary mining
can be identified by the confinement of activity within the quarter cord. This
changes, however, when the location of ore dressing areas is examined, as on
many sites ore dressing took place in close proximity to the shaft and was also
contained within the quarter cord (Roe 2003a).

The change to leases: expanding the boundaries
Customary law was abandoned in Swaledale at the end of the seventeenth
century, earlier than in the rest of the Dales, when time-limited leases of
small areas were introduced (Gill 1988). As would later occur at Grassington,
the length of leased areas continued to be defined by meers, but the quarter
cord was expanded to allow the working of several veins at once. The areas
leased gradually increased in size, often as a result of the consolidation of
smaller grants into ever larger areas which eventually became defined by topographical boundaries such as streams and watersheds. A process of this kind is
documented at Appletreewick in Wharfedale in the 1760s, and is postulated
to have occurred at Greenhow Hill earlier in the eighteenth century.

It was not until 1774 that customary mining law at Grassington was abandoned: the earlier grants were replaced by leases of larger blocks of ground

formed by extending the quarter cord out to 75 yards (68.5 m) of ground (Gill 1993, 24), though some elements of the earlier system survived, as the length of the grant was still calculated in meers. The boundaries of the new areas were marked by meerstones bearing the initials of the lessees. Sadly, many of the meerstones have subsequently been removed, but the few that survive help to fit surviving plans of the moor, such as Samuel Brailsford's 1781 plan showing the boundaries of the new grants, to the current landscape. In 1820 John Taylor and Company took over the administration of the mines and several of the smaller grants were consolidated into bigger units to encourage new development. This prompted the capital investment needed for longer-term development work and saw deeper working from shafts equipped with horse gins and, in some cases, shafts wound and pumped by a system of waterwheels (Gill 1993).

Apart from the few surviving meerstones, the most significant archaeological remains of this phase of mining are a series of shallow trenches and several lines of small shaft mounds running at right angles to the veins. The purpose of these features would appear to have been exploration of the ground between known veins and the new boundaries to identify the presence of new ore resources; it can therefore be argued that they date from the sideways expansion of the meer grants in 1774. At least one of the trenches is cut by the Dukes Water Course, a major water leat system constructed in the early 1820s, which confirms that they pre-date the consolidations carried out by Taylor (Roe 2003b).

These long prospection trenches are similar to features found on the west side of Arkengarthdale, where Dam Rigg Cross Hush, a prospection hush, runs down Whaw Edge across the known course of the mineral veins. On the opposite side of the ridge a shallow trench, reminiscent of those at Grassington, runs down to Wetshaw Bottom. Although on a larger scale, if Arkengarthdale followed the same pattern of development as seen at Grassington, these features would suggest a similar phase of prospection following an expansion of previous boundaries, the ends of the trench and the hush therefore defining a new boundary.

The maturing of mining landscapes

The introduction of fixed-term leases encouraged the capital investment needed to follow outcropping veins where they disappeared. Where the bearing beds outcrop the surface archaeology reflects the underlying geology. Once the bearing beds reach a moderate depth single shafts tend to work several veins and the relationship between the ore bodies and the location of surface features is no longer obvious. These shafts could attain moderate depths. At the Old Gang Mine in Swaledale, for example, shafts sunk in stages reached down 100 m to the main limestone in 1684. Later, from the second quarter of the eighteenth century, the staged shafts were replaced by deep straight-sided shafts equipped with horse-powered winding engines, known variously as gins, whims or whimseys. The number of horse gins is suggested by the 114 shafts in the Yorkshire Dales which include the element gin, engine or whim in their name.[2] The true number could be considerably higher: on Grassington Moor, for example, there are at least twenty-four shafts with physical remains of horse gins where this is *not* reflected in their names. Owing to a lack of suitable local coal, steam power never really replaced the gin in the Dales.

As has already been shown, with the introduction of leases of larger areas, activities no longer need to be confined to a narrow strip of ground alongside the veins. Field evidence suggests that ore dressing could be concentrated centrally within the newly established lease areas rather than directly at individual shafts as previously, although there are exceptions to this rule. With this phase, the wider mining landscape reaches maturity. The next developments resulted in a change of focus to a small number of sites, and the virtual abandonment of the wider landscape.

Abandonment and fossilisation

Possibly the most significant change to the mining landscapes occurred at the beginning of the nineteenth century, when, if the topography was suitable, level networks were developed. These consisted of tunnels driven from the valley sides which provided both drainage and haulage routes, so that ore from many veins could be brought out to centralised dressing floors which were often adjacent to smelt mills. Although drainage levels, or adits, are known from the medieval period, the early nineteenth century saw them equipped with wooden and iron rails and made large enough to admit horses – hence their alternate name of 'horse level' (Figure 4). Because a horse pulling a rake of wagons could move considerably more ore in a day than could be raised by a horse gin, this resulted in increased productivity. This, along with the installation of up-to-date mechanised ore-processing plants at the mouth of the levels, allowed the exploitation of what had been previously marginal ore resources. Field survey shows that in almost every case the levels intersect veins just below the main bearing beds, which were accessed from rises developed upwards from the levels. The driving of levels was, therefore, a very well-planned operation based on a detailed knowledge of the underlying geology. It also strongly suggests that the nineteenth-century miners were often reworking veins to extract ore considered uneconomic by earlier miners.

The significance of levels can be demonstrated by looking at part of the Arkengarthdale mines. The west side of the valley is divided into two areas, Moulds Side and Danby Side, which had been worked *via* shafts from at least the sixteenth century. In 1800, Frederick Hall, a principal shareholder and mine manager, set about reorganising the mines (Tyson 1995). Instead of hauling ore up numerous gin shafts he replaced the shafts with a small number of levels, such as Danby Level, placed so as to intersect several previously worked

FIGURE 4.
Danby Level,
Arkengarthdale, a
typical horse level
driven in the early
nineteenth century.

veins and designed to bring ore to centralised and mechanised dressing floors (Figure 5).

Examination of the surface archaeology above the level reveals that three veins (Stoddart Vein, Martin's Vein, and Dam Rigg Vein) had been worked extensively from shafts. The underground evidence gives a very different picture (Figure 6). The level entrance is located part-way up a steep hillside, not at the bottom as might be expected if the level were to provide access to and drain the full height of the veins. The level is driven dead straight until just past Dam Rigg Vein, with branches driven onto veins, as well as several rises indicating where mineralised features have been investigated. The main part of the level turns left and right on the Dam Rigg Vein, which strongly suggests that this was the main target of the level when it was begun. Beyond, the level was driven towards the boundary with the neighbouring Surrender Mine. At least nineteen veins were examined from it, most in the section leading towards Surrender Mine: though some may have proved unproductive, this demonstrates that levels could be an effective method of prospection for veins that did not outcrop on the surface. With one exception, the level cuts the veins either at the base of, or just below, the main limestone which is the main bearing bed in the area.

This example, which can be paralleled elsewhere, reinforces the fact that examining only the surface archaeology can be misleading, giving a false impression of the scale of mining. Because levels generally made the earlier shafts redundant, the evidence of a 'gin' name indicates that the feature with which it is associated dates from before the levels. In addition, as the levels focused activity onto a few sites on the valley sides, the larger mining landscape was for the most part abandoned and fossilised, left to the wasteworkers who made a meagre living from reworking dressing waste. Activity

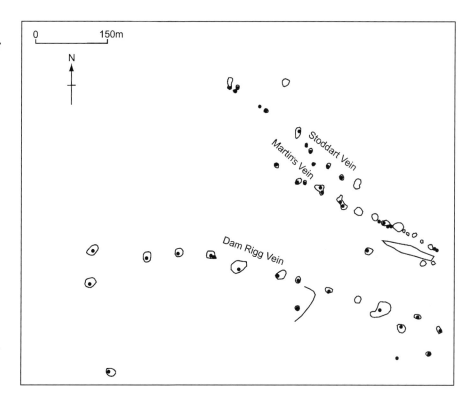

FIGURE 5.
Survey of shafts and
other features above
Danby Level.

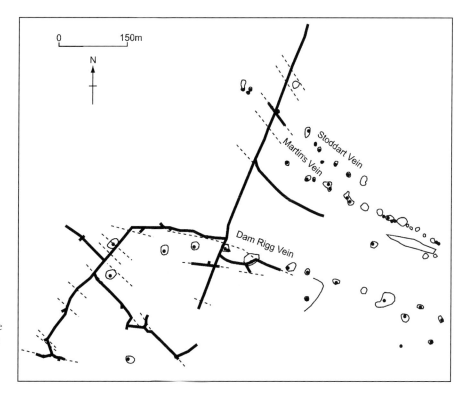

FIGURE 6.
Survey of Danby
Level added to surface
features. Dotted lines
indicate the position
of veins.

underground, however, expanded: levels were often driven to the boundaries of a mine to prospect for further veins, therefore performing the same role as prospection trenches found on the surface.

Summary

Integrating the evidence from the hidden underground landscape of mining with that derived from the study of surface features considerably aids understanding of the whole mining landscape, and modifies the conclusions of earlier investigators. In particular, the sequence of development which can be reconstructed contradicts Raistrick's assertion that 'nearly the whole of the mining scene belongs to the nineteenth century'. In fact, the opposite is true: only a few sites at the margins of areas of mining activity date from so late a period; the vast majority of the landscape represents activities that reached a peak in the eighteenth century or earlier. The developments of the seventeenth to the nineteenth century can be quantified, though the chronology varied across the Yorkshire Dales in response to changing social and economic conditions; these are matters which need further exploration. One of the most exciting possibilities is that the recognition of areas exploited under customary mining law could ultimately lead to the identification of mining landscapes of the medieval period or even earlier. The longevity of the system may, however, pose difficulties for interpretation, and the best that can be claimed at this stage is that understanding hidden surface boundaries makes it possible to identify a medieval style of administration.

Notes

1. Leeds University Library, Brotherton Collection, Marrick Priory Archive 3/1/80–3/1/84.
2. Records of the Northern Mine Research Group.

CHAPTER THREE

The Importance of Place: Placing Vernacular Buildings into a Landscape Context

Adam Longcroft

It is hardly controversial to point out that vernacular buildings reflect the area in which they are built. This is, after all, one of the key characteristics that separates vernacular architecture, which is characteristic of a locality, from supra-vernacular or 'polite' architecture, which draws on wider and more overtly intellectual influences. However, in this chapter it will be argued that vernacular architecture specialists too often overlook the full implications of the intimate relationship which once existed between 'building' and 'place', and, in doing so, have created an unhelpful divide between the built environment and the wider historic landscape. Using the county of Norfolk as a case study, it will be shown that variations in historic housing stocks, as well as modern distributions of vernacular buildings, can only be fully understood by placing both into a meaningful landscape context. It will also be argued that individual houses can only be fully understood through an examination of their precise local context: in particular, the local economy which they were designed to accommodate, the size and status of the resident household and – crucially – the landscape setting, which often determined the disposition of structures within the farmyard, and the presence or absence of decorative elements.

The importance of place

During our lives most of us develop a sense of place. Sometimes we might find it difficult to articulate this abstract concept. For some, place is about relationships with others: with family, friends and colleagues. For many it emerges through an active interaction with the local environment: with its weather, relief, and unique disposition of woods, roads, greens, heaths, fells, hedges and fields. Perhaps one of the most important factors in developing a sense of place is the built environment – the particular combination of materials, styles and periods of building which lend localities their unique character. Before the arrival of efficient high-speed transport systems, which enabled building materials and styles of building to be rapidly and cheaply conveyed between and within regions (irrespective of their appropriateness) this sense of place was, perhaps, even more profoundly reflected in the buildings in which people lived and worked. It is odd, therefore, that historians of vernacular architecture – that type of architecture which is more wedded to place than any other – often find themselves giving detailed consideration to the plans of buildings yet none or little to the landscape within which they are located. Studies of vernacular architecture often touch briefly upon factors such as geology in providing materials suitable for construction in a given district, county or region. And yet – with some notable exceptions (Hall 1983; Pearson 1994; Harrison and Hutton 1984; Penoyre and Penoyre 1978; Penoyre 2005; RCHME 1985; RCHME 1986) – they rarely attempt to relate historic housing stocks (or modern patterns of survival) to historic variations in soil quality, or to consequent variations in farming regimes and social structures. This criticism could be levelled even at recently published studies of vernacular architecture (Roberts 2003; Jennings 2003; Moran 2003) which, whilst excelling in relaying the minutiae of structural forms and materials, are often less successful in examining or explaining the economic and social factors which prompted buildings' creation and allowed their survival. Indeed, the discipline of vernacular architecture studies continues to be dominated by traditional approaches which focus primarily (and often exclusively) on the structural forms of those buildings which still stand in the modern landscape, despite Chris Currie's warning that it is dangerous to assume that the surviving houses of a given area are truly representative (Currie 1988, 6). Shortly before his death, Eric Mercer argued that the obsession with structural forms (which he termed 'Formalism') had resulted in the study of structural detail becoming an end itself rather than a means to an end, and that this had, in turn, undermined the development of a healthy dialogue and interaction with historians and archaeologists working in separate but related fields of enquiry. As a result, he argued, the wider implications of vernacular architecture studies had remained largely unfulfilled (Mercer 1997, 9–12), an argument which has been reinforced by recent research by Chris Currie, which clearly demonstrates that little progress has been made in advancing interdisciplinary studies of vernacular architecture in the past forty years (Currie 2004, 1–11). Mercer also drew attention to a concept which he labelled 'Generalised Regionalism' – an obsession with a division of the country into Highland and Lowland zones, 'each with its age-old elements giving rise to traditions seen almost as Laws of Nature, eternal and unchanging' (Mercer 1997, 11). As Mercer was acutely aware, this over-simplified division obscured the fact that within each region there were major variations in landscape and building traditions; the similarities between areas in different zones were often greater than the dissimilarities. Consequently, Mercer pleaded for research 'into those differences and variations within the zones which might be of value to wider readers' (Mercer 1997, 11). In the first half of this chapter, an attempt will be made to respond to both of Mercer's pleas: first, that we should make greater use of alternative sources of evidence in the study of vernacular buildings; and second, that we should explore how housing stocks were affected by the existence of subtle yet important variations in soils, farming economies and social structures, even over relatively small areas.

The hearth tax

In order to develop a clearer understanding of the development of vernacular architecture we need to investigate not only those buildings which have survived, but also those which have not. This process involves the examination of historic housing stocks alongside modern patterns of survival and demands that we look beyond the physical evidence of standing buildings and seek other sources of evidence which might shed light on earlier patterns of building. The approach adopted here is a historical one, and will draw on a hitherto under-utilised documentary source: the hearth tax. The hearth tax assessments for the county of Norfolk will be exploited in order to examine variations in the historic housing stock (that which existed in the past) and to explore possible causes of these variations. It is not the author's contention that the hearth tax is the only source of valuable information for this type of analysis – it is merely used here to provide others with a straightforward example of how historical variations can be reconstructed at the 'macro' or county level.

The hearth tax, which was introduced by Act of Parliament in 1662, was intended to help the newly restored monarchy to meet a deficit of £200,000 in Crown revenues and was the first of what was to become a new breed of luxury taxes. The tax was levied at the rate of 2 shillings per year for each hearth, collections being made twice in each year, on Lady Day (25 March) and at Michaelmas (29 September). All individuals whose houses were worth more than 20 shillings a year were liable, as were those who contributed to the church and poor rates in their parish (Webster 1988, xxv). Norfolk has three published volumes of hearth tax assessments. The first two relate to Michaelmas 1664 and Lady Day 1666 (Frankel and Seaman 1983; Seaman 1988). These provide the data on which the current study is based. The third (Seaman 2001), which focuses only on exemption certificates for the four key urban centres in the county, has not been used.

Utilising the hearth tax as the basis for an analytical study is not without its problems, which have been rehearsed on a number of occasions by other historians (Spufford 1990); this is not the place in which to do so again. However, it might be helpful to readers to draw attention to key aspects of the Norfolk assessments. Firstly, neither of the two published assessments for 1664 and 1666 is complete. Fortunately, the two assessments dovetail well – missing fragments in one can usually be made good by referring to the other. Secondly, lists of households exempted from payment are patchy. Where they survive, exempted persons appear to account for 41 per cent of the county population. This is significantly higher than the figure for its East Anglian neighbours Suffolk (36 per cent) and Essex (35 per cent) (Arkell 2003, 148–74) and probably reflects the fact that Norfolk possessed a smaller area of 'wood-pasture' clayland than its neighbours – a distinctive landscape given over largely to a pasture-orientated economy which, as will be seen, supported a more egalitarian social structure in the seventeenth century, in which extreme poverty was less of a problem. Tax evasion is another unknown quantity. William Fenery of Badwell Ash, Suffolk, refused point blank to pay the tax of 2 shillings on his two hearths in 1662 because it was 'un-concionable high' (Colman 1971, 173). Although we can never be sure how many of Fenery's neighbours followed his example, Tom Arkell has shown that evasion in some areas was rife (Arkell 2003, 159). These factors combine to ensure that the true value of the hearth tax assessments lies not so much in the insights they provide into the houses of individuals or individual communities, but, instead, in the opportunity they provide to investigate historical patterns over a wider area. The percentage figures which appear on the maps presented here are based solely on those who paid the tax; exempted persons, by necessity, have been omitted from the calculations. This means that the maps reveal variations in the housing stock of all but the poorest members of society (who had insufficient wherewithal to pay the tax).

Variations in historic housing stocks

Spufford was one of the first historians to realise the potential of the mapping of hearth tax assessments. In her seminal book *Contrasting Communities*, she used the assessments for Cambridgeshire to explore variations in the rural economy. By plotting the Cambridgeshire assessments in map form she identified, amongst other things, a small group of parishes bordering on the fens in the north of the county which had 'clearly developed differently, economically, from those in the rest of the county' and possessed 'an abnormally high proportion of the middlingly-prosperous' (Spufford 1974, 44).

Since Spufford's pioneering work, hearth tax assessments have been plotted and analysed in similar ways for other areas. Pound, for example, has shown that wealth in Norwich (as reflected in the hearth tax) was concentrated within particular wards, such as Middle Wymer ward and St Peter's ward, where the proportion of houses with six hearths or more was largest. In poorer wards, such as South Conesford (centred on King Street), households taxed on a single hearth accounted for nearly three-quarters of the total (Pound 1988, 44). Colman has revealed similarly stark contrasts within the Hundred of Blackbourne in Suffolk (Colman 1971, 171), while Giles has discovered considerable variation within the Calder Valley in west Yorkshire (RCHME 1986, 121–5). Working in the Midlands, Alcock found 'notable differences … between different parts of Warwickshire in the number of hearths and by implication in the size of houses'. Alcock argues that these variations – especially the number of those exempted from the tax – reflect economic diversity: 'a dependence on mining led to a high proportion of cottagers, while pastoral farming (in the Arden) had the opposite result' (Alcock 1993, 201). When Webster compared the number of hearths with the number of taxpayers in Nottinghamshire he came to a similar conclusion:

> The lowest mean values were in the north of the county, the centre-east and south east and the west. Those areas would seem to have been areas of poorer housing, and presumably of less wealth, which suggests that while the density of taxpayers was greatest along the arable clayland belt, it was not matched by wealth since this was a relatively poor area. (Webster 1988, xxviii)

In the Lancashire Pennines, Pearson discovered an interesting link between the survival of houses and the number of hearths listed: 'most of the identifiable [surviving] houses fall within the top 17 per cent and half of them are in the top 9 per cent of houses assessed in the area' (RCHME 1985, 105). In a more recent study of the hearth tax assessments for Kent, Pearson has shown that the distribution of hearths largely failed to correspond with the main soil divisions in the county; it revealed, instead, a series of bands of similar wealth aligned in a north–south fashion which cut across the east–west aligned soil divisions which reflect the underlying geology of the county (Harrington *et al.* 2000, xxxiii–xxxv). Fortunately, a national programme dedicated to publishing hearth tax assessments on a county by county basis, coordinated by Roehampton University and the British Records Society, is now well advanced and should ensure that the hearth tax becomes one of the most accessible of all English taxation records.

When the Norfolk hearth tax returns of 1664 and 1666 are plotted in map form, distribution patterns emerge which strongly imply regional variations in the quality of the contemporary housing stock. If we take, for example, the proportion of households taxed on one or two hearths (Figure 7) it is evident that these were concentrated in north Norfolk, suggesting that householders living in small cottages formed a greater proportion of the tax-paying population here. If we consider how this distribution relates to soil variations across the county (Figure 8), it immediately becomes apparent that cottages and smaller houses clustered in areas characterised by light soils – areas associated, in turn, with a 'sheep-corn' economy in which open-field agriculture was combined with the grazing of large flocks of sheep. These were areas where large estates were beginning to emerge in the 1600s (Williamson 1993, 18), and the existence of strong lordship here facilitated the creation of vast sheepwalks (Yaxley 1995, 311–14). The hearth tax returns strongly suggest that it was in the sheep-corn districts that economic polarisation within society was most advanced by the middle of the seventeenth century and where communities predominantly comprised cottagers with small, unsophisticated dwellings. Spufford identified a similar concentration of parishes with a high proportion of cottages on the chalk ridge of south-east Cambridgeshire between Balsham and Woodditton (Spufford 1974, 44).

But what types of houses are we talking about? What would they have looked like? Fortunately, in order to answer this question we are not entirely

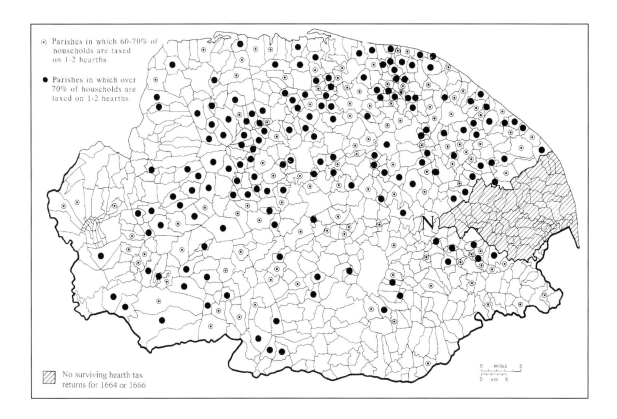

- ⊙ Parishes in which 60-70% of households are taxed on 1-2 hearths
- ● Parishes in which over 70% of households are taxed on 1-2 hearths

N

- ▨ No surviving hearth tax returns for 1664 or 1666

```
0      miles      5
0       km       5
```

- ▤ Peat and silt
- □ Light loams
- ▨ Medium clays
- ▦ Heavy clays
- ⣿ Acid sands and gravels

```
0              15km
```

dependent on documentary sources; Norfolk is blessed with a surprisingly large number of small vernacular houses which survive from the seventeenth century or even earlier. Tiny cottages with only a single ground-floor room and a solitary fireplace include Apple Cottage, Stiffkey, and Pip Cottage, Stiffkey. Slightly larger houses, with two ground-floor rooms and two hearths, include 3–5 Bridge Street and 38–40 Wells Road, Stiffkey. The former possessed a cross-passage plan with a gable-end chimney stack, the latter a lobby-entry and a centrally positioned stack (Figure 9).

Returning to the hearth tax, there are areas within the county notable for their low proportions of houses with one or two hearths. These include the silt fenlands around Terrington St Clement, the extreme north-west of the county around Sedgeford and Docking, parishes lying on the greensand ridge between Dersingham and Congham, and the claylands of south Norfolk. It is in precisely these areas that the proportion of substantial houses (many presumably inhabited by well-to-do yeomen) with between three and six hearths is correspondingly high (Figure 10). The concentration of these medium-sized farmhouses is especially pronounced in south Norfolk, in particular within a triangle between Roydon in the south-west, Norwich in the north and Gillingham in the south-east. Houses with between three and six hearths are particularly common along the south-facing slopes of the Waveney Valley and along the valley of the River Tas. In both areas such concentrations are likely to be the result of economic prosperity based on fertile soils, plentiful river-bottom meadows, and extensive areas subject to common grazing rights. As historians have shown (Williamson 1995b; Wade Martins and Williamson

FIGURE 7.
Proportion of
households taxed on
one or two hearths,
1664/66.

FIGURE 8.
Soils in Norfolk.
Williamson 1993;
reproduced by kind
permission of the
author

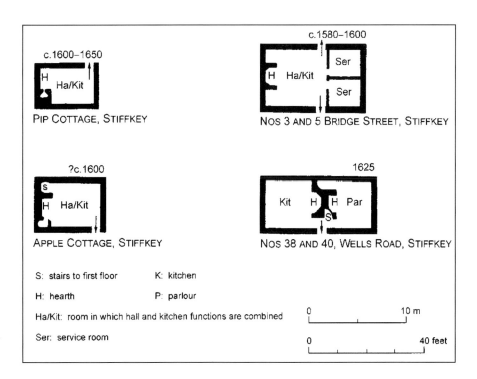

c.1600–1650

PIP COTTAGE, STIFFKEY

c.1580–1600

NOS 3 AND 5 BRIDGE STREET, STIFFKEY

?c.1600

APPLE COTTAGE, STIFFKEY

1625

NOS 38 AND 40, WELLS ROAD, STIFFKEY

S: stairs to first floor   K: kitchen

H: hearth   P: parlour

Ha/Kit: room in which hall and kitchen functions are combined

Ser: service room

0   10 m

0   40 feet

FIGURE 9.
One- and two-cell
plans in Norfolk.
Surviving houses
of sixteenth- and
seventeenth-century
date in Stiffkey.

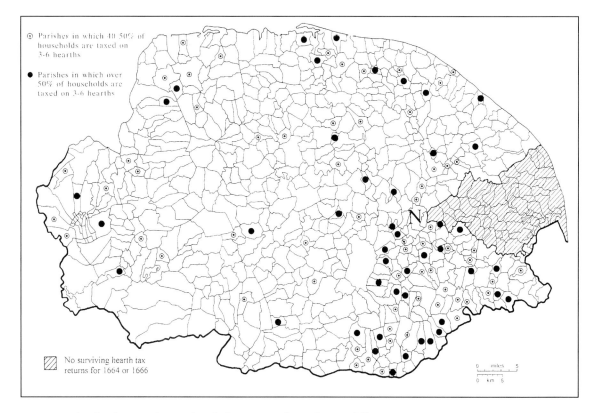

FIGURE IO.
Proportion of
households taxed on
three to six hearths.

1999, 21–5), the heavy clay soils of this part of south Norfolk gave rise to a pastoral economy based on dairying. Weakly manorialised, with a preponderance of free tenures and rural industries such as linen and worsted weaving (Evans 1993, 150–1), wood-turning and tanning (Barringer 1993, 152–3), this area became a focus for rural prosperity in the sixteenth and early seventeenth centuries. More importantly still, villages were more egalitarian in their socio-economic make-up, with large numbers of small to middling-sized farms supporting moderately prosperous yeoman farmers living in substantial farmhouses most of which, by the mid-1600s, boasted elaborate brick chimneys and multiple hearths. In the south of Norfolk high population densities and an egalitarian social structure provided ideal conditions for the creation of large numbers of multiple-hearth houses in the late sixteenth and early seventeenth centuries. High levels of wealth are reflected in significant concentrations of houses with crow-stepped gables, most of which were erected before 1650 (Tolhurst 1993, 112–13). Crucially, brick was also used to construct substantial axial brick chimney stacks, many of which were endowed with multiple flues. This resulted in a proliferation of multiple hearth houses from the late sixteenth century, most of which possessed either a cross-passage or a lobby-entry plan. Juniper House, Ketteringham, and Waterloo Farm, Garveston, are good examples of the former, while The Old Ram Inn, Tivetshall, and Fir Grove Cottage, Morley St Botolph, are fine examples of the latter (Figure 11).

In contrast, many communities in the north of the county had become socially and economically polarised by the early 1600s, the gap between the rich and poor becoming wider with each new generation. As Williamson and Wade Martins, and others, have demonstrated, it is here that the increasing size and 'improvement' of farms is most notable during the eighteenth and nineteenth centuries (Wade Martins and Williamson 1999, 76–81; Dymond 1985, 214–28). Building traditions here took a different course to those in the south of the county, with brick and flint the favoured walling materials. As a result, chimneys were more likely to be incorporated within a gable wall (probably for reasons of economy). Larger houses usually had two gable-end chimney stacks and, after 1650, were often endowed with curvilinear 'Dutch' gables. Large farmhouses with axial stacks were certainly not unknown in this part of the county, but surviving buildings of this type are now thinner on the ground than is the case in south Norfolk. By far the most numerous surviving houses in north Norfolk are small structures with either one or two rooms on the ground floor. These rarely possessed more than two fireplaces. The evidence suggests that the small two-cell house with one or two hearths remained the most common type across north and west Norfolk throughout the early modern period. Though some survive, far more were swept away by later phases of rebuilding in the late eighteenth and nineteenth centuries.

The hearth tax clearly shows that smaller houses with only one or two hearths exhibited a different distribution to that of medium-sized farmhouses with between three and six hearths. The former proliferated in arable areas – in particular, across a broad area of north Norfolk – whilst medium-sized

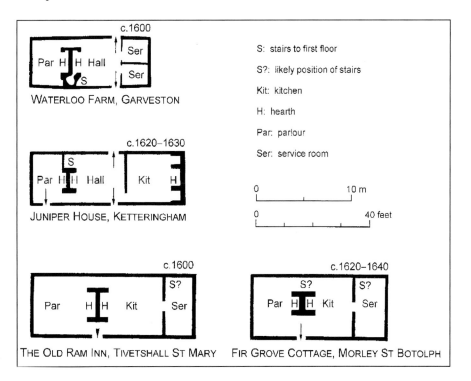

FIGURE 11.
Three-cell plans in Norfolk. Surviving houses of sixteenth- and seventeenth-century date in south Norfolk.

farmhouses with multiple hearths seem to have been more plentiful in areas which were dominated by cattle grazing – in particular, on the heavier clays of the south Norfolk plateau. It seems likely that two key factors affected the distribution of hearths in Norfolk. The first was soil quality. Variations in soil quality inevitably resulted in the development of distinctive farming regimes and subsequent geographical variations in rural wealth, both in respect to total wealth and the way in which this wealth was distributed within communities. In economically polarised communities in which wealth became concentrated into the hands of a few and the gap between rich and poor widened, large, multi-hearth farmhouses were thinner on the ground. In more egalitarian areas, where wealth was distributed more evenly within society, they appear to have proliferated. It is argued here, therefore, that differences in farming regimes which reflected variations in soils gave rise in turn to distinctive social structures which profoundly influenced the development of the historic housing stock at regional and sub-regional levels. The second key factor was the emergence of divergent vernacular building traditions. Across the north of the historic county of Norfolk a flint building tradition had emerged by the sixteenth century. This favoured, for reasons of economy, the use of gable-end chimney stacks. In communities where most people could only afford houses with one or two rooms on the ground floor, a single gable stack incorporating one or possibly two hearths usually sufficed. Here the proliferation of hearths occurred within a small group of affluent yeoman farmers who were relatively sparsely distributed in comparison with numbers in pasture-orientated areas like south Norfolk. In the latter area, the large number of surviving sophisticated multi-hearth houses reflects not just the concentration of wealth within a dominant and very large class of moderately prosperous yeoman farmers, but also a well-established tradition of timber-framed construction which favoured the adoption of multiple-flue axial stacks. In south Norfolk, the plan incorporating an axial stack (within the main body of the house) remained the dominant type until changing architectural tastes in the second half of the seventeenth century dictated the adoption of plans with double gable end chimney stacks, which were more aesthetically in tune with the times but less efficient in their use of brick. Early examples of this type of plan, like Dairy Farm, Tacolneston (*c*.1640), appear at the time of the Civil War, but are more commonly found after the Restoration, as at Cross-ways Farm, Chedgrave (*c*.1669) (Carson 1976, 26; Mercer 1975, pl. 101).

If we compare variations in the historic housing stock as reflected in the hearth tax assessments with the modern distribution of vernacular houses dating from before 1730, as mapped by Tolhurst in the early 1980s (Tolhurst 1982) (Figure 12) some important themes are thrown into stark relief. Tolhurst's map indicates that the largest number of surviving pre-1730 houses is to be found in the southern claylands of Norfolk – precisely where, as we have seen, houses with three to six hearths proliferated in the seventeenth century. Their survival cannot be fully explained by their size since evidence from probate inventories indicates clearly that yeoman houses in north Norfolk, though fewer in

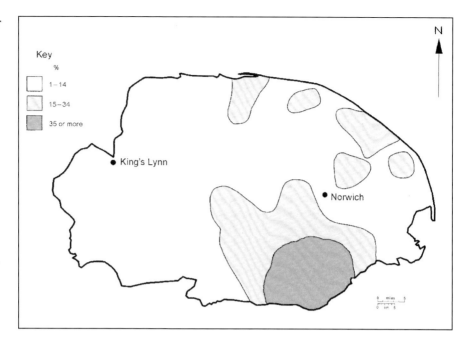

FIGURE 12.
Distribution of pre-
c.1730 vernacular
buildings in Norfolk.
Tolhurst 1982;
reproduced by kind
permission of the
author

number, were larger. Moreover, houses in both areas were built using durable materials. The density of surviving houses in south Norfolk is less likely to reflect constructional superiority than the fact that this area of Norfolk failed to benefit from later phases of rebuilding which resulted from massive investment in new farming methods in the predominantly arable areas. Tolhurst's map also suggests that small houses suffered a much higher attrition rate than larger ones. This may be due, at least in part, to the 'improving' activities of large landowners in the north of the county during the eighteenth and nineteenth centuries. There are many estate villages across north Norfolk where the hand of the resident landlord is all too apparent in the almost complete absence of surviving 'early' houses and cottages. The high attrition rate amongst smaller houses may also, however, reflect the fact that they were simply less well-suited than larger houses to subsequent adaptation in later periods.

The local context

In the first half of this chapter it was argued that regional and sub-regional variations in the historic and modern distributions of vernacular houses can only be properly understood through an examination of the implications of variations in soils, farming regimes and social structures. Yet understanding the landscape context within which vernacular buildings were erected is as important at what might be termed the 'micro' level as it is at the 'macro', or county, level. At micro level – at the level of the parish or even the individual property – vernacular houses often exhibit characteristics which reflect their physical location or their role within the local economy. Crucially, these 'characteristics' are frequently more than just a reflection of the availability of different building materials and are, instead, often the product of a complex set of factors. Foremost amongst these factors is the type of farm attached to a farmhouse. Though it is glaringly obvious, historians often overlook the fact that farmhouses were more than just houses – they were also units of production in which agricultural produce was stored, processed, finished and often (in the case of beer) sold on the premises.

As Holderness has shown, certain types of agriculture allowed farmers sufficient flexibility on a day-to-day basis to engage in part-time industrial activities (Holderness 1984, 199). Though discouraged by central government, the process of rural industrialisation accelerated dramatically during the sixteenth and seventeenth centuries and increasingly it became the norm for craftsmen in rural areas to operate a farm, and for farmers to engage in industrial manufacture. For farmers, part-time engagement in industry provided a useful supply of ready cash. The wares produced in rural areas were often of a lesser quality (the best stuffs being made in the towns and marketed to a wealthier clientele) but as levels of rural wealth increased so too did the demand for such goods. Arable farming was too labour intensive and left little time for part-time employment, but in pastoral areas rural industries such as weaving found what Thirsk has termed a 'congenial home'. In such areas, 'people had time on their hands that could be devoted to industrial work, and … they also had the freedom, and the land, to attract additional workers if their industry flourished …'. (Thirsk 1978, 110–11). In the 'wood-pasture' areas of East Anglia, where pasture farming and dairying, in particular, were dominant, Evans found that part-time employment in rural industries was a key factor in maintaining the prosperity of the local economy: 'The importance of by-industries as one of the main factors which made it possible for wood-pasture regions to support a high density of small farms which provided their owners with a comfortable standard of living, cannot be over-emphasised' (Evans 1984, 309). In the south Norfolk claylands many farmers supplemented their farm incomes by engaging in by-industries – a fact which is reflected in the number of spinning wheels and looms recorded in their probate inventories. The development of dual-income strategies inevitably had implications for the way in which houses were organised. There is some evidence, for example, to suggest that the provision of double butteries in this area reflected the increasing importance of commercial brewing amongst yeoman farmers. In a similar vein, attics with dormer windows made an early appearance in south Norfolk farmhouses. This subtle yet important change may reflect the use of attics as a weaving facility – a scenario which was all too commonplace in the city of Norwich. These idiosyncrasies should be taken into account when interpreting surviving houses in south Norfolk, and, of course, in other areas of the country where a pastoral economy resulted in a tendency towards dual occupations.

Williamson has recently argued that much more research also needs to be focused on the relationship between the size of farmhouses and the size of farms attached to them (Williamson 2004, 56). This relationship might be a complex and an indirect one and is likely to be confused by factors such as the extent of common grazing enjoyed by farmers, but establishing broad estimates is arguably an achievable objective in areas where good documentary sources exist. Research in Norfolk has demonstrated that farm size is often a crucial factor in the survival of farmhouses. In a study of eight parishes in the county a consistent relationship emerged between the survival of pre-1750 properties and the size of the farms attached to them (Longcroft 1998): indeed, survival was far more dependent on farm size than on tenure. Even in a region such as East Anglia, where free tenures were far more prevalent than in most other parts of the country, copyhold was the norm in the eight parishes in question and very few surviving early houses were owned by free-holders. Owner-occupation appears not to have been an important factor in survival. On the contrary, surviving houses tended to be sub-let. Continuity of function, however, was as important as farm size in ensuring survival – properties which continued to function as farmhouses into the nineteenth century were far more likely to survive into the twentieth century than those which had lost their farmhouse status. By merit of their continuing status as the foci of generally large working farms and their function as a 'draw' for well-heeled tenants, they escaped the fate of subdivision and down-grading which awaited many other properties (Longcroft 1998, 309–13). These findings reinforced earlier research by the author which revealed that a direct relationship existed between the complexity of messuage plots as depicted on early maps of sixteenth- and seventeenth-century date and the survival of these messuages as residential plots. Messuages of simple type containing only a farmhouse and no other ancillary agricultural buildings were far less likely to survive as residential plots into the twentieth century than complex messuages with two or more structures (Longcroft 1989, 67–77). These discoveries suggest that there is much to be gained from the placing of individual buildings and larger groups of buildings into a meaningful and geographically specific economic and social context. They also support Currie's assertion that survival is determined less by variations in housing quality at the time of construction than by a selective processes of attrition in later periods (Currie 1988).

The status of owners is another key consideration. Some gentlemen, for example, were able to disengage from farming and, instead, sub-let their land to others for a cash rent, or loan money at interest within the local credit network. Hugh Painter, yeoman, and Thomas Chieney, gent., of East Dereham, both farmed holdings of between 80 and 100 acres (32–40 ha) and had possessions of similar value. However, whilst livestock and crops made up nearly 50 per cent of Painter's wealth, they accounted for only 10 per cent of that of Chieney, who had invested over 80 per cent of his entire worth in the local credit market. Thus, one worked for his living while the other had his capital do it for him (Carter 1986). Gentleman farmers like Chieney could afford to do without the plethora of service rooms required by 'hands-on' yeomen like Painter and their houses looked very different. Yeoman houses were, in turn, often quite dissimilar to those of husbandmen. A study of service rooms listed in Norfolk probate inventories has shown, for example, that service rooms appear in yeoman inventories which do not appear in those of husbandmen or labourers – these include larders, wool houses, quern houses, store houses, brew houses and sculleries (Longcroft 1995, 41). These peculiarities within the Norfolk housing stock may appear inconsequential but, in fact, have significant implications for the way in which household activities were organised and on the development of historic housing stock more generally.

Another Norfolk peculiarity is the number and function of parlours recorded in the probate inventories. In areas like Oxfordshire and Berkshire parlours were rare. Those houses which did possess a parlour tended be the larger houses of well-to-do yeomen. In these houses parlours served as ground-floor sitting rooms (Portman 1973, 160; Currie 1972, 266). In Norfolk, however, a large-scale study of inventory evidence by the author has demonstrated that parlours featured in well over three-quarters of all husbandman and yeoman farmhouses between 1590 and 1730. The vast majority of these rooms also contained beds as well as tables and chairs and obviously served as bedsits, suggesting that a tradition of having the best bedroom on the ground floor persisted in Norfolk into the eighteenth century, in contrast to other parts of the country, where this practice had been abandoned by the early 1600s (Longcroft 1998, 63–4). An awareness of subtle regional peculiarities of this kind, and their inevitable impacts on plan forms, is something which scholars of vernacular architecture need to take into account when studying buildings at a local level (Longcroft 2002). Peculiarities in local economies also occasionally result in peculiar buildings. Recent research in the medieval town of New Buckenham has demonstrated, for example, the impact which a distinctive urban economy could have on plan forms. Here some distinctive plan forms emerged which, although well-suited to the needs of a group of urbanites with little or no engagement in agriculture, were also highly idiosyncratic and apparently without parallel elsewhere (Longcroft 2005, 56–64).

Greater attention needs also to be given to the original landscape setting within which buildings were erected, as these have often changed a great deal over time as a result of processes such as parliamentary enclosure and modern development. As Williamson has pointed out:

> … if we are interested in understanding the impact which their appearance made on visitors or passers-by – clearly an important aspect of a building's social role – we need to remember that the configuration of public and private spaces was often changed dramatically over the centuries. Most houses, especially on the southern [Norfolk] clays, originally stood on the edges of commons and were often viewed at close quarters – and from different and a greater range of, perspectives – than now. Such patterns of movement and access need to be reconstructed if we are to appreciate, for example, the different treatments given to the different façades of a house. (Williamson 2004, 58)

Understanding the original disposition of features such as routeways, gardens, home closes and farm buildings is also crucial in reconstructing the landscape setting of farmhouses. How important, for example, was the spatial arrangement of service rooms (butteries, dairies, pantries, bakehouses, etc.), living rooms and outbuildings for the smooth and efficient operation of the farm economy? Was a particular spatial proximity favoured between house and barn and, if so, why? Recently, historians of vernacular architecture have begun to give greater attention to the use of social space inside vernacular houses through the application of archaeological techniques such as planning analysis (Martin 2003), yet the study of how houses relate to farmyards and the secondary structures within them has been neglected. We might also consider the importance of wider environmental factors. One recent study from Herefordshire has demonstrated that a close relationship often existed between the orientation of hall houses and prevailing winds in the Middle Ages (James 2003, 20–31). To what extent was this the norm within other localities, however, and to what extent did environmental factors like these continue to influence the orientation of farmhouses once the open hall and cross-passage had disappeared? The case for developing a greater understanding of the 'micro' landscape context of vernacular buildings is a compelling one and one which vernacular architecture specialists need to engage with on a more systematic basis.

Summary

In this brief study I have attempted to illustrate the importance of placing vernacular buildings into a landscape context at both local and county level. It has been argued that vernacular buildings can only be properly understood by relating them to the farms and local economies which gave them meaning, and by reconstructing the original landscape settings which governed the way they were used by their owners and the ways in which they were viewed by others. Moreover, it has been argued that understanding variations in farm size and messuage complexity, and later changes in the function of farmhouses, is central to understanding why some buildings have survived and some have not. Understanding place and the myriad variables between one place and another is thus an essential prerequisite for understanding individual buildings and groups of buildings within the landscape. In developing this new sensitivity to the importance of place, scholars of vernacular architecture will need to look more regularly over the garden fences and hedgerows surrounding the buildings they study to the wider landscape beyond, and to delve into the rich documentary records of their local record office. As Hoskins pointed out a very long time ago, 'There is no opposition between fieldwork and documents' (Hoskins 1967, 183). Developing a sense of place is just as important, however, when attempting to interpret historic housing stocks and modern patterns of survival at county and regional level. That scholars of vernacular architecture need to understand how individual buildings evolve physically over time is indisputable. But it is argued here that they should also seek to understand the 'larger picture' – those subtle variations caused by differences in soils, farming regimes and patterns of social organisation which are discernable across larger districts, counties and regions and which, as I hope I have demonstrated in this chapter, are manifested in the contemporary documentary records as well as in surviving buildings. It is my contention that vernacular buildings only make sense when studied in relation to local and regional variations in soils, social structures and economic organisation. They are also, of course, about people – something which Hoskins himself frequently emphasised – and reflect an infinitely variable set of priorities and pressures, from the concern of a farmer to build a house fit for purpose, to the needs of a community to control or safeguard precious resources such as timber, reed or clay for building. Developing a sense of place is thus inevitably an attempt to understand how our ancestors interacted with and responded to the unique set of social, economic and physical constraints placed upon them by their communities and environment. As I hope I have shown, these interactions and responses manifested themselves in Norfolk in fascinating variations in both the historic housing stock and in the modern pattern of surviving buildings – variations which one suspects were and are repeated, perhaps in even more dramatic ways, in other counties.

CHAPTER FOUR

The Estate:
Recognising People and Place
in the Modern Landscape

Jonathan Finch

The landscape that has developed since the sixteenth century is often assumed to be too familiar, too well documented, and too well trodden to require abstract theorisation and serious investigation by landscape historians and archaeologists. The latter are particularly prone to characterise the modern landscape as a sheer veil, through which the contours and shadows of ancient landscapes can be traced. It is the understanding and reconstruction of those ancient landscapes that has been the focus of the most innovative approaches to landscape theory and interpretation over the last decade. Prehistorians have articulated cognitive geographies of the past by exploring the dynamic relationships between monuments, settlements and land use (Bradley 1998; Edmonds 1999; Ingold 2000; Tilley 1994). Drawing on anthropological models of the complex relationships between landscapes and the processes of inhabitation, they have sought to people the prehistoric landscape. One of their key aims has been to connect and contrast individual, subjective and fleeting lives with the long-term processes that structured the material conditions with which those people engaged, in order to reconstruct the experience of past landscapes (Barrett 1994, 1–3; Gosden 1999, 154).

Such approaches have, however, failed to make a significant impact upon our interpretation and understanding of the historic or modern landscape for two reasons. Firstly, there is the assumption, mentioned above, that the social institutions and economic climate, and even perhaps the mentalities that shaped the landscape, are familiar and understandable: they are part of what defines 'modernity' and, as such, they are perceived as lacking the 'otherness' that demands critical and imaginative engagement with the material remains. Secondly, there is a strong tradition of empiricism within historical landscape studies that aims to 'read the landscape', reinforcing a dualism between physical and cultural landscapes by emphasising the former over the latter rather than recognising their indivisibility. Features of the modern landscape are therefore (easily) recognised and classified: once they are 'read' and understood the interpretive process comes to a halt. As a result, the modern landscape is rarely imbued with an active or symbolic role in social processes, and is seen instead merely as a reflective medium. This has, in turn, perpetuated the belief that an economic rationale was the determining agent of change. There are, of course, exceptions to this generalisation: for example, designed or ornamental landscapes in both Europe and North America have been extensively studied and interpreted in the light of changing social relationships, power and aesthetics (Bermingham 1987; Daniels 1988; Leone 1984; Williamson 1995a). Yet many of these studies are not concerned to people those landscapes. Indeed, it might be argued that ornamental landscapes have proved such a popular area for some because they were depopulated, uninhabited landscapes. Studies could thus concentrate on ideological or symbolic landscape meanings without having to integrate complex social dynamics or multiple perspectives.

Yet the wealth of material, documentary and visual evidence from the period suggests that it should be a rewarding area within which to pioneer the concept of a socially integrated landscape. Theory and practice should be used together to reassemble the material conditions of life in the past, discerning significance from what people did in the landscape and where they did it, in order to articulate a 'cultural logic and structure of action' through which we can understand how landscapes were used and perceived in the past (Gosden 1999, 158). This chapter, therefore, seeks to explore how economic, social, political and aesthetic values were placed and perceived within the landscape, endowing it with a power that was both recognised and exploited by contemporaries of all social groups. By using documentary sources alongside the physical landscape, buildings and material culture to build up a picture of how the landscape was encountered in the past, it is possible to identify processes of change and continuity that both link and distance those landscapes from our own cultural experience.

This chapter is based on a pilot project in Yorkshire, conducted with the cooperation of the curators and owners of seven of the region's country houses: Burton Constable Hall, Brodsworth Hall, Castle Howard, Harewood House, Lotherton Hall, Nostell Priory and Temple Newsam (Ridgway and Warren 2005). Each house has its own distinct biography, ranging from those built from the ruins of the Dissolution to nineteenth-century mansions. Today they also represent various forms of administration and management, from national bodies such as English Heritage and the National Trust, to local authorities, educational trusts, charitable foundations and private ownership. Importantly, the houses also demonstrate a range of relationships with their historic estate land – some are now administered by separate businesses, some by different departments in the same institution. Only at Castle Howard are the house and estate managed together in a manner that demonstrates continuity with their historic relationship.

The estate landscape: definitions and scope

The study of estates has been pioneered by historical geographers who have tended to use a core/periphery model to interpret the landscape, and dualistic lord/peasant models for the social hierarchy within (Fuller 1976; Mills 1980). In his study of the Yarborough estates centred on Brocklesby Hall, Lincolnshire, for example, Charles Rawding argues that the landscape exhibits a declining level of investment, ornamentation and symbolism the further one moves from the house at the centre (Rawding 1992). Similarly, Heather Clemenson defines the 'home' or 'principal' estate as the consolidated landed area surrounding the house and its ornamental landscape, usually located within the confines of a single county (Clemenson 1982, 33–8). Beyond the principal estate Clemenson identifies 'secondary estates' and 'peripheral land' – those at some distance from the principal seat, possibly in another county, yet substantial units in their own right (Clemenson 1982, 34–8). In its basic form this model has tended to marginalise the importance of the estate in relation to the designed landscape and the country house itself. This has served to emphasise the park pale as the boundary between lord and peasant, the physical realisation of the deep class divide.

Yet the estate sustained the country house and framed the lives of the estate workers who worked within the house and grounds, permeating the physical barriers in the landscape. The household drew on the landscape as an agricultural, industrial, ornamental, urban and sporting resource without which its social and economic functions soon broke down. This was apparent in the post-war period, when houses and land were frequently sold off separately under mounting political and economic pressures (Cornforth 1998). It is important, therefore, to redefine our model of the estate in a manner that recognises its role and significance as a socially and symbolically constructed landscape, both locally within the lives of the landowning family, the workers and tenants, but also nationally and internationally in terms of political structures and the development of a global economy.

Estates were landscapes imbued with social meaning, action and performance, which might be conceptualised as several tiered but inter-related *locales* – bounded, meaningful, physical contexts within which 'institutionally embedded social encounters and practices take place' (Giddens 1984, 118–19). The highly stratified groups and communities that lived within these *locales* created a range of distinctive, variegated landscapes. Within the principal estate, boundaries, axes, vistas and entry points attracted considerable attention and investment, whilst maps, surveys and paintings served to represent and connect quite disparate *locales*. Indeed, in the age of colonial expansion, ownership and management could connect landscapes around the globe within the portfolio of a single estate.

Four themes have been chosen to demonstrate the impact, role and extent of the estate in various aspects of lives and landscapes. In an effort to move away from the compartmentalisation of the modern landscape and the prioritisation of single causal factors as determining change, links and continuities have been made between the themes. The aim is to recognise the active role of the landscape in the way people inhabited the past, linking the fleeting impact of the individual lives at the local scale to the longer-term cultural developments on the global stage.

Agricultural aesthetics

The agricultural landscape has been interpreted predominantly in terms of profit, although recent studies have suggested that large landowners were not at the forefront of innovative or successful agricultural improvement during the late eighteenth century (Wade Martins 2004). Economic improvement was, instead, achieved on landscapes characterised by smaller farming businesses, such as the fenlands and heavy clays of the eastern and home counties (Williamson 2002, 83). There were perhaps fewer imperatives for large landowners to take risks with agricultural innovation, since they enjoyed the protection of economies of scale and more diverse holdings. Nonetheless, most were sensitive to Nathaniel Kent's remark that agriculture was a public duty at a time of national anxiety and wars in Europe and North America:

> A competent knowledge of Agriculture is the most useful science a gentleman can attain; it … becomes a duty, which they owe not only to themselves but to the community, as it behoves every man to make the most of his property, by every laudable means' (Kent 1775, 7–8)

During periods of domestic and international tension, wheat and bread prices were closely linked to social order, connecting the productive process to the temperature of national politics. The range of labour-intensive tasks associated with arable landscapes also served to keep rural communities employed at times of potential unrest. There were, therefore, socio-political reasons for large landowners to participate in the process of 'improvement' that transformed the agricultural landscape, since decisions about land management might be made for many reasons other than efficient farming.

At Castle Howard in North Yorkshire, for example, the 3rd Earl of Carlisle exploited the symbolic juxtaposition of unimproved agricultural and ornamental landscapes to great effect. The gothick, fortified wall and gateway that Hawksmoor built across the main approach avenue in about 1730 (Figure 13) marked the threshold from the working landscape into the newly completed Arcadia beyond. For fifty years after its completion, the transition was accentuated by the fact that the Carrmire Gate was approached across an unenclosed open-field system, complete with ridge and furrow. Beyond the turreted gate, the land rose up dramatically to a ridge with the mature oaks of the medieval deer-park silhouetted against the sky; the horizon was punctuated by pyramids and temples. Within sight of the new palace, however, Carlisle had been assiduously putting the arable down to grass since his arrival at the turn of the century, and the two temples of Venus and Diana on the eastern side of the grounds afforded views out over pasture that preserved the ridge and furrow as a relict of former times, presenting a very different message about progress and harmony in the agricultural landscape from that experienced as one approached the entrance at the Carrmire Gate (Figure 14) (Finch 2007).

Further east, on the poor, light soils of the Yorkshire Wolds, Sir Christopher Sykes of Sledmere is often credited as an heroic agricultural improver who, towards the end of the eighteenth century, transformed the landscape through enclosure. He was, however, directly involved in relatively few enclosure acts, and his motives combined aesthetic as well as economic concerns. Sykes drew up detailed accounts setting out the value of unenclosed land at Sledmere, its value at enclosure, and its value fifteen years later, when returns of three or four times their initial value were expected. Despite the eventual increases in value, however, the enclosure of Sledmere was clearly related to the enlargement of the park around the house. Aesthetic concerns also motivated Sykes's involvement in the enclosure of Garton-on-the-Wolds, where his stated aim was to create a ride of some 6 miles (*c.*10 km) through his estate towards the market town of Beverley (English 2000, 186–90).

As part of the transformation of the Sledmere landscape through enclosure, Sykes took the opportunity to build eight large farmsteads, each of which served as an architectural eye-catcher within the environs of the house and its approach routes (English 2000, 186–90). As well as demonstrating the landowner's commitment to the process of agricultural and aesthetic 'improvement', new farms on consolidated holdings served to attract tenants who were wealthy and influential individuals in their own right, and who would be expected to invest, innovate and improve the land still further (Wade Martins 2004). The redistribution of farms within the newly enclosed landscape also redefined social relationships. Estates such as Birdsall, also in the East Riding, used the architectural design of the new farmsteads to divide the living and working spaces of the 'polite' farmer from that of the live-in labourers, as well as to segregate male and female workers (Hayfield 1998, 120–1). The debate about the proletarianisation of the rural workforce, the decline in numbers of farm servants, and the capitalist modernisation of post-enclosure agriculture has been conducted largely beyond the context of the estate landscape, despite its obvious relevance (e.g. Moses 1999). However, it is clear that whether it hindered or promoted the development of socio-political consciousness, the impact of the estate ethos or moral economy needs to be explored within the context of landscape transformation.

It is also clear from these examples that there was no clear line between the 'designed' and the 'agricultural' landscape. Just as it has been shown that the ornamental landscapes were far from unproductive (Williamson 1995a), so the aesthetics and symbolism of the arable fields, both enclosed and open, played a part in constructing meaning in the landscape. For the large landowner, the decision whether or not to enclose could be as much about being seen to engage with a national process as it was about economics or aesthetics, or

FIGURE 13.
The Carrmire Gate: the
fields in front of the
Carrmire Gate (*c.*1728–
30) were working open
fields until enclosure
in 1779. Beyond, the
land rises in a series of
ridges – Hawksmoor's
Pyramid (1728), on
St Anne's hill, marks
the first. To the east
(right), the dome of
the mausoleum (begun
1728) can be seen.

constitution and social roots – some in Yorkshire and elsewhere, for example, were set up by tenant farmers – most large estates were connected to hunts or kennelled hounds. Some landowning families maintained a long tradition, such as the Yarboroughs at Brocklesby in Lincolnshire, whilst others contributed during their time as Master of Fox Hounds, supported by neighbouring landowners (Carr 1976). Foxhunting provided a very public occasion to demonstrate the ties between tenant farmers and their landlord through a ritualised pastime that evolved in tandem with the agricultural landscape. In the Midlands, where modern hunting reinvented itself as a fast and furious extreme sport in the late eighteenth century, it was the move to pasture and improved drainage associated with enclosure that created firm grassland over which the field could gallop and which would better hold the scent of the fox. In landscapes where the enclosure of open fields or commons had redefined or denied traditional rights of access and routeways through the landscape, hunting provided a conspicuous spectacle predicated on access across newly privatised enclosures (Finch 2004). This privileging of sport and the necessary manipulation of the landscape over production was emphasised further by the promotion of a healthy population of vermin for the purpose of the hunt – a fact that was somewhat anomalous within the supposedly rational, capitalist, post-enclosure landscape. Field corners were fenced and planted with gorse or blackthorn to provide cover for the earths and protection from 'bagmen' who stole foxes to sell to those restocking their country. Larger regular areas were taken out of productive fields and planted with trees and shrubs, or enclosed

FIGURE 14.
Ray Wood and the Temple of the Four Winds (centre): to the east of Castle Howard, the trees of Ray Wood – a medieval woodland – crowd behind the bastion wall. The Temple of Diana (1724), now known as the Temple of the Four Winds, affords views out over ridge and furrow preserved beneath the pasture.

land that had not been managed was bought by the hunt or rented for use as fox-coverts. The effect of this piecemeal afforestation could be dramatic in areas of little woodland: in the first thirty years of the nineteenth century the area of gorse coverts in the Quorn country in Leicestershire increased tenfold (Bovill 1959, 51). Despite much continuity of use and place-name evidence, these coverts are rarely acknowledged as such by those outside the hunting fraternity. Historic Landscape Characterisation schemes, for example, recognise them as nineteenth-century woodland, but unlike defunct or relict medieval deer-parks, their role within the landscape as part of the heritage of hunting is not being systematically acknowledged or recorded.

Foxhunts also featured amongst set-piece 'community' celebrations such as those at Harewood in November 1845 to celebrate the coming of age of Lord Viscount Lascelles. The festivities included a tenants' dinner for 400 held in an 'apartment' erected on the west terrace, decorated with agricultural and sporting devices, at which the Earl of Harewood toasted the assembled tenantry and pledged 'to co-operate with his tenants in the improvement of their farms, and to assist by every means in his power the encouragement of agriculture'. In his turn, Mr Sturdy, a tenant of some thirty years, responded that they were happy not to live under a 'cotton-lord' who raised rents when the tenants improved their profits. The third day was devoted to outdoor sports, including a foxhunt, and was 'more especially devoted to the entertainment of the cottagers, labourers, and workpeople engaged on the estate'. The landscape became an arena for the demonstration and assertion of ties between the various social levels within the estate. The lawns to the north of the house were opened up to the celebratory events, much as they are utilised for events today, and *The London Illustrated News* wrote approvingly:

> The principal object was to afford amusement to all classes; from the peer to the peasant ... Thus the Nobility and gentry had their gay and glittering ball; the tenantry their well spread table; the rustics their ludicrous revels.

Such events, when boundaries were removed or transgressed, served to reinforce paternalist bonds between landowner and tenants through the use of landscape and create a sense of unity within the estate community, whilst reinforcing the fact that access was usually denied or restricted.

Settlement and community

A range of communities whose lives were framed by the landscape inhabited the estate. The settlements and social structures of estates have usually been interpreted within the debate about 'open' and 'closed' parishes and the impact that patterns of landholding exercised over demographic characteristics and settlement change (Banks 1988; Holderness 1972; Mills 1980; Spencer 2000). It is important not simply to polarise the social dynamic between those on either side of the park pale, however – social tensions existed within and between different social groups, not just between landowner and tenants. Furthermore, the advantages of living within an estate in terms of employment, accommodation, even education and pensions, suggest that the boundary of the wider estate was as significant as the more obviously delineated park pale. During the nineteenth century the legacy of carefully controlled development within estates could result in rural slums in adjacent parishes which accommodated the expanding workforce often dependent on the estate for employment.

On estates where extractive industries such as coal mining were developed entirely new communities were sometimes created. These communities were new both in the sense that settlements were created to house them, often near to the point of extraction rather than within the established settlement pattern, but also new in the sense of the migrant workers who lived within them. On the Brodsworth estate in west Yorkshire, for example, the appointment of a colliery overseer from Stavely, in Derbyshire, prompted an influx of workers and their families from the same area. 'Tin Town' rapidly grew up to accommodate them, and was in turn replaced during the early twentieth century by the Woodlands development. Such regional migrations and regional skills were well established by the nineteenth century, but they were often implemented or encouraged by large landowners transferring or importing communities from one area to another when new opportunities to utilise them arose.

Within the traditional, agriculturally based communities, the later nineteenth century saw an increase in the levels of paternalism directed towards tenants, and this was strongly represented in the architectural identity of many estates. Using architectural style to articulate power and status had long been a characteristic of the estate – indeed, it was the main way in which the extent of a landed estate was signalled. Model villages, such as that built outside the gates of Harewood House in the second half of the eighteenth century to designs by John Carr of York (Figure 15), provided a grand approach to the park and demonstrated the close relationship between the villagers and the estate core. By the mid-nineteenth century investment extended to the systematic rebuilding of workers' accommodation right across estates, rather than simply piecemeal maintenance or showpiece villages. The main burst of investment in cottage provision nationally appears to have taken place in the decade between 1865 and 1875 (Clemenson 1982, 86–91). Activity on the Castle Howard estate came earlier – in the 1840s – as a direct result of Lord Carlisle taking 'a greater interest in the management of the estate and in the social condition of the resident population than he had previously done', as his agent John Henderson reported a decade later.[1] It is unclear what motivated this personal interest; it may have been sparked by outbreaks of typhoid and cholera, or it may have been related to Carlisle's increased participation in national politics, perhaps demonstrating the link between practical intervention on the estate and political debates taking place on the national stage. The concerted campaign of estate improvement that followed included demolishing cottages that were considered inadequate to make room for more commodious modern dwellings. Some thirty years later, during the 1870s, another period of

investment saw around £9500 spent on fifty-three cottages, lodges, a reading room and a school-house in the six core parishes of the principal estate. By 1883 there was a detailed inventory of all the cottages, which listed rent, tenant, number of bedrooms, occupation and remarks about the condition of the properties: 57 per cent (177) were in good repair, whilst 29 per cent (90) were in bad repair or were damp. A fifth (63) were still thatched.[2]

This rich vein of documentation allows us to build up a picture of settlement change alongside a detailed demographic and occupational profile of those who dwelt within the estate. For example, in 1883 one-fifth of the households in Coneysthorpe, just north of Castle Howard and visible from the north front, were occupied by pensioners, widows or retired estate workers, with other residents including the Clerk of Works, the organist and chaplain, a school mistress, and Dr Robert Spence, a naturalist.[3] Clearly Coneysthorpe had a particular role within the estate, as home to favoured staff, both past and present; distinguished professionals; and those involved through education or religion with what might be termed the moral welfare of the estate. Accounts also reveal that there were dynasties of tenants who continued over several generations. At Burton Constable, in the East Riding, several of these dynasties shared an extra link with the Constable family – that of religion – as there was an unusually high proportion of Catholics on the estate.

The documentary evidence also allows detailed biographies of people and

FIGURE 15.
Harewood village: This undated early nineteenth-century watercolour by John Varley (1778–1842) shows two earlier buildings surviving alongside John Carr's classical rebuilding. The triumphal entrance arch into the park (1801–5) can just be seen in the centre. Reproduced by kind permission of the Earl and Countess of Harewood and the Trustees of Harewood House Trust

48

places, which include insights into the material conditions of life within estates, to be built up. For example, the inventory of the gamekeeper's cottage from 1856, again at Castle Howard, opens a window into the private world of a key estate worker: one who could be called upon to forcibly defend the landowner's rights of access and ownership within the landscape against armed poachers. His parlour was furnished with a mahogany bookcase, six mahogany chairs, two armchairs and an oak table. On the walls were two prints of the Holy Family and prints of the 5th, 6th and current Earl and Lady Carlisle, as well as a large print of Castle Howard with its fountain. The fireplace was decorated with a variety of ornaments, as well as polished fire irons and two screens. There was a writing case, a box of mathematical instruments and a barometer.[4] Material culture is thus transformed into personal effects through a link with place and lifecycle, and allows us to see how personal identities were constructed through a close relationship with the estate, its landscape and its owners.

Colonialism and consumption

Despite the importance of the expanding world market and colonialism in defining the historical dimensions of the modern age, the landed interests of the élite are rarely conceptualised as extending beyond the British Isles. Yet many families held estates that were administered in a quite distinct manner and which were located in dramatically different landscapes to their seats in England. Irish estates, for example, exhibited a set of social dynamics and tensions relating to the history of the English in Ireland, the role of Irish estate managers in place of the absentee owners, and the distinct nature of Irish topography and agriculture (Orser 1996, 144–58).

The Irish estates owned by the Gascoignes of Lotherton Hall, West Yorkshire, were brought into the family through marriage by Richard Oliver of Clonodfoy, Co. Limerick, during the first decade of the nineteenth century (White 2004, 69). Social relationships between tenants and landowners only improved, paradoxically, from the mid-nineteenth century, when management passed from Oliver's brother and Irish kinsmen to the new joint heiresses – Mary Isabella and Elizabeth Gascoigne. They invested heavily in the Irish estate for the first time, rebuilding the main house as 'Castle Oliver' in the Scottish baronial style and paying regular extended visits, until Elizabeth eventually resided there after her marriage to the Anglo-Irish peer, Lord Ashtown. When the potato famine struck hard in 1845/6 the sisters embarked on an extensive construction programme in order to provide employment for the destitute tenants of their own, as well as of neighbouring estates: new corn, flax and carding mills were built at Kilfinnane. In doing so, however, it can be argued that the sisters played their part in a wider process that saw the communities of western Ireland transformed through the institution of patterns of production and social relations closer to the English and Scottish models than those established in the region – structures which redrew the landscape in both physical and tenurial terms (White 2004, 71–2; Whelan 1997, 88–91).

Landscape transformations were also undertaken in the further reaches of the colonies, where aristocratic and mercantile families held land. The Lascelles of Harewood, for example, owned eighteen sugar plantations by the end of the 1780s accounting for over 9,500 acres (3845 ha) of land on four islands – and hundreds of slaves. Henry Lascelles (d. 1753) settled in Barbados between 1712 and 1734 to secure the family's business enterprise and Barbados became the centre of their interests, with Lascelles House outside Hopetown and plantations at Bell, Thicket and Fortesque. The landscape of the eastern Caribbean had been subject to dramatic change since the permanent settlement of European colonists in the late seventeenth century: the forest was cleared from fertile areas and river valleys in order to lay out geometric holdings defined by hedges and fences – suggesting the imposition of European models of intensive agriculture with land held in severalty (Pulsipher 1994, 202). With the establishment of commercial mono-cropping focused on exotics such as sugar and coffee, estates were laid out in a manner that reflected 'both idealised notions of the way an estate ought to look and constraints imposed on that idea by the natural environment' (Clement 1997, 94).

The spatial arrangement of plantations demonstrated segmentation into 'task specific zones' (Delle 1999, 146), with the estate staff inhabiting the area around the planter's house and gardens, all of which were usually at a greater elevation than the production areas, and were often within view of neighbouring plantation houses in order to engender a feeling of solidarity within the planter class (Clement 1997, 99). The fertile grounds, often in river valleys with good sources of water or wind power, were devoted to cultivation, with slave accommodation in positions peripheral to the main complex. The overseer's house and office were sometimes positioned so as to mediate between the polarised spatial arrangements of the planter's house and the zones of production. Dell Upton analysed movement around and between zones on Virginian plantations, demonstrating that the manipulation of space ensured that planters and slaves had very different experiences of the same landscape (Upton 1988). However, the slave 'villages' express a variety of relationships to the wider plantation landscapes. At Courland, Tobago, for example, Clement has argued that the plantation's role as the premier estate on the island is reflected in a greater axial coherence of the whole complex, including the positioning of the 'estate village' next to the house (Clement 1997, 101). The enslaved communities began to have an impact on the landscape from the eighteenth century. Provision grounds of between a quarter and three-quarters of an acre (0.1–0.3 ha) were provided by the planters for each slave to produce their own food, but there is contemporary evidence that they cultivated the forest and ravines of the wider hinterland to supplement their land allowance and to provide a refuge and place of assembly beyond the eye of the overseer or owner (Delle 1999, 140–1; Pulsipher 1994).

The transformation of the distant plantation landscapes was intimately connected to the landscape in England through the flow of capital for investment. Within a decade of Henry Lascelles' death, his sons were able to spend around £75,000 on land in Yorkshire and embarked on a lavish building programme that included the principal seat of Harewood House and extended to secondary houses at nearby Goldsborough and Plumpton (Walvin 2003). Even the abolition of the slave trade brought with it further windfalls. It is notable that the last major phase of building work at Harewood House and the construction of an Italianate terrace on the south front to designs by Sir Charles Barry in 1840 were embarked upon only a few years after the Lascelles received government compensation for losses incurred by the abolition of slavery.

The exploitation of the colonies was also linked to the domestic landscape through the importation of exotic plants, shrubs and trees. The greenhouse, stovehouse, or hothouse became an integral part of larger estates and gardens from the end of the seventeenth century, when the first fruits of the colonies began to arrive back in England. The investment in new technology to grow exotic flowers, shrubs and fruit was extraordinary. Orangeries were built at houses such as Burton Constable, East Yorkshire (Figure 16), to house fruiting citrus trees and coffee plants, which would be moved outside in tubs during the summer (Woudstra 2003). Elsewhere in the kitchen garden, fermenting tanners' bark was used to create raised hot-beds and the walls of kitchen gardens were built with flues through which hot air from stoves circulated to keep frosts off delicate trees such as peaches and apricots and to aid ripening in the autumn (Figure 17). The most exotic flowers were nurtured in stovehouses that required constant attention. Philip Miller's popular *Gardener's Calendar* (1760) recommended lighting six to eight candles in the greenhouse every night throughout January, with the stoves lit and tended from October through to March. The prize of the stovehouse was, of course, the pineapple, which was by far the most expensive fruit to cultivate. The names of the preferred varieties make their provenance explicit – the Brown Antigua, St Vincent's, Black Jamaica. John Urry has argued (1995) that the economic exploitation, scientific investigation and visual and physical consumption was about 'consuming places' framed by colonialism – gardens became 'living maps' of the exotic. Significantly, given the scientific imperative of the Enlightenment, which sought to categorise and regularise nature itself, Miller added a new section to the twelfth edition of his *Gardener's Calendar* in 1760 – a short introduction to the science of botany 'in the present fashionable system of Doctor Linnaeus'.

When the landscape gardener Humphry Repton stayed at Harewood in the early nineteenth century, he visited the kitchen garden intent on seeing the 'celebrated' hothouses, of which one was devoted solely to the highly perfumed Heliotrope, another to the only passionflower in the country upon which the fruit actually ripened. Yet in amongst these more spectacular plants Repton and his party – which included the abolitionist William Wilberforce – also happened upon 'an evolved leaf of the most beautiful tender green, just

rising out of a garden pot … it was a young sugar cane plant' (Gore and Carter 2005, 81–2). Here the cultivation of the colonies was brought right into the heart of the estate, linking place and power through distant and contrasting, yet related, landscapes.

Conclusion

This brief overview of how the estate landscape might be approached embraces W.G.Hoskins's conviction that the landscape was about people, and about place. It was an estate over which Hoskins chose to stage his modern nightmare, with 'black-hatted officers of This and That' swarming over the house whilst the parkland was filled with 'overspill' or flattened by the timber merchant (Hoskins 1955, 231). Peter Mandler and others have subsequently documented the extraordinary rate at which country houses and their estates were being demolished and dismembered during the 1950s, when Hoskins was writing his personal view of both the history and the future of the English countryside (Mandler 1997; Cornforth 1998). However, whilst the country house was reinvented as the nation's favourite heritage attraction, the dissolution of their landscapes – the wider estate – and the subsequent rate of change within those landscapes has gone relatively unnoticed, even within landscape studies.

FIGURE 16.
The Orangery, Burton Constable: Remodelled by Thomas Atkinson 1788–9, the orangery faces south-west onto a level lawned area where exotic plants would have been displayed in tubs during the summer. William Constable (1721–91) was a noted plant collector and scholar, who employed the best botanical illustrators to document his collection.

FIGURE 17.
A heated wall at
Harewood kitchen
gardens: the restoration
of this eighteenth-
century wall shows two
parallel flues running
the length of its upper
section. Each is half-
filled with soot and
ash from the fires. The
south face of the wall
is just a single brick
(right) to maximise
heat exchange. This
prevented frost damage
to fruit blossom in the
spring and promoted
ripening in the
autumn.

The challenge that faces those studying the historic landscape is to develop an integrated 'idea of landscape': one that assesses relationships between physical and perceptual landscapes, and maps cognitive geographies of different social groups within a broad understanding of the landscape as an active constituent within social processes. The goal is to recognise the modern landscape as an inhabited social construct, utilising the full range of sources available. By using paintings, poetry, accounts, diaries and newspapers alongside the physical remains of field boundaries, cottages, hothouses and fox-coverts, we can approach a 'thick description' of the landscape: an understanding of the social actions that took place within the landscape and the reciprocal relationship between the landscape and the meaning of those actions for the actors involved (Geertz 1993, 27). Archaeologists and landscape historians – following the lead of historical geographers and historians – might usefully adopt a more holistic approach to the estate as an important cultural landscape. There has not been space here to discuss the enormously important impact of industrial development within the estate landscape, but just as industrial archaeologists have sought to bring together the social and the technological aspects of the recent past in a 'framework of inference', so those studying the historic landscape must unite the economic with the cultural, the social, the perceptual (Palmer 2005). By studying the estate as a cohesive element within the landscape – and more specifically by exploring it as an inhabited social landscape – we might reach a better understanding of the complex forces that lie behind the formation of the modern landscape – a landscape we inhabit, manage and enjoy today.

Notes

1. Castle Howard Archives, CH F598, 27 Feb 1854.
2. Castle Howard Archives, CH F5/83.
3. Castle Howard Archives, CH F5/83.
4. Castle Howard Archives, CH F5/69.

CHAPTER FIVE

Landscapes of the Poor: Encroachment in Wales in the Post-Medieval Centuries

Robert Silvester

It is all too easy to dismiss Wales as little more than a single undifferentiated upland landmass, appended to the western side of England. Rackham's much cited division of England into 'ancient' and 'planned' countryside, for instance, conveniently labelled Wales as Highland Zone – excepting Anglesey, off its north coast, and a thin coastal strip in the extreme south – suggesting that it shared upland traits with much of northern England and the southwestern peninsula (Rackham 1986, 3). That there is a more subtle complexity to the country is signalled by the truncation of several of Roberts and Wrathmell's provinces and sub-provinces by a boundary defined for little more than political convenience in the mid-sixteenth century (Roberts and Wrathmell 2000, fig. 1), and more explicitly in even the smallest-scale maps prepared by Welsh geographers such as Howe and Thomas (1968, fig. 2).

It is implicit, however, in Rackham's mapping that his zone of 'ancient countryside' along the western side of England should be carried over into Wales, and there is considerable justification for such an extension. Nevertheless, Wales is a country of diverse geomorphology which has influenced human activity over the centuries in ways both varied and complex. But while it might be assumed that the landscape of Wales has been long established, the underlying theme in this chapter is that some of the components of that landscape as we see them today are of no great age. This in itself, of course, comes as no surprise. It was alluded to by W. G. Hoskins in his discussion of parliamentary enclosure in *The Making of the English Landscape* (1955, 177) and has been addressed by other writers in recent times (e.g. Whyte 2003, 4).

Some of the agencies of landscape change during the last four centuries are obvious. Parliamentary enclosure has incised large chunks of the Welsh uplands, around 160,000 ha in the later eighteenth and nineteenth centuries (Chapman 2004, 82). In contrast, the extent of informal or unilateral enclosure is almost impossible to assess, other than at a local level (Silvester 2004, fig 5.3), but there can be little doubt that in places it was extensive.

Thomas, for instance, saw the sixteenth century and its immediate aftermath as a crucial stage in the evolution of the local landscape in Merioneth, with enclosure playing a fundamental role (Thomas 1967, 153). Industry, and particularly extraction, has also had a dramatic and permanent effect on large tracts of upland Wales, particularly the Glamorgan uplands in the south and the hills of the north-east, as well as more localised impacts in places such as Parys Mountain on Anglesey. Then there are the designed landscapes of the gentry, though in general these are less extensive and in many cases less dramatic than their counterparts in England.

There are two other factors that ought to be included. Modifications, sometimes comprehensive, to some long-farmed landscapes were imposed in the nineteenth century, in extreme cases leading to a complete redesign not only of the field patterns but also of the other features associated with the landscape infrastructure. It is a landscape change which we are just beginning to appreciate, and can again only be gauged, initially, at the local level (see, for instance, Britnell *et al.* forthcoming), just as it is in England (Turner 2004, 30). Finally, there is the subject of this chapter: the widespread movement of the landless and the poor – variously called cottagers, squatters, settlers, encroachers and the like – on to the commons and the waste. The term 'encroachment' is adopted here to describe this movement of people, and to distinguish it from the general process of enclosing tracts of land where no settlement was involved, but it ought to be stressed that no such distinction was uniformly made by contemporary or indeed modern commentators. The phenomenon of encroachment in Wales has been studied by social and economic historians, and there is a useful body of literature on it (see, for instance, Davies 1976; Howell 2000), but much less attention has been paid to it by archaeologists and landscape historians. Yet it was a widespread and pervasive phenomenon which modified some landscapes and transformed others, albeit sometimes only temporarily.

The physical form of encroachment

Certainly from the seventeenth century, and particularly in the eighteenth and early nineteenth centuries as the general population level rose, growing numbers of landless people resorted to the commons and the waste, erecting dwellings for themselves and carving smallholdings from the open uplands. Taking advantage of lax control by landowners, not least of whom was the Crown, and sometimes encouraged by local parishes that had no wish to maintain them, the squatters invaded the open ground and established themselves with varying degrees of success. A decisive landowner, concerned with the loss of grazing and the potential threat from uncontrolled communities, might have had men demolish newly built dwellings, yet on the other hand such encroachment might be actively encouraged, particularly where a landowner was attempting to exploit the mineral wealth of his uplands.

The extent of encroachment was considerable and its impact on local thinking immense. When Sir John Vaughan of Crosswood, one of the major landowners in Cardiganshire in west Wales, had his lands surveyed in 1768/9, encroachment was revealed as the most urgent issue that needed to be addressed on the estate, and the prevailing view in some circles was articulated in a subsequent survey towards the end of the eighteenth century, which stated that 'there are several valuable commons attached to [the] estate, but they are now built upon, enclosed and colonized by the very scum of the earth, and I can venture to assert that these rascals by this Encroachment have injured these estates to the amount of £200 per annum' (Davies 1976, 105). Later, in the nineteenth century, some of the largest landowners in Wales, such as Sir Watkin Williams Wynn, determined to enclose their commons in the anticipation that it would rid them of the encroachments that were reducing their value (Howell 1977, 40).

Much of this encroachment in upland Wales appears to have been embedded in the traditional concept of the *ty unnos*, the overnight house, whereby it was believed that if a family, with the help of friends and relatives, could erect a dwelling of turves or timber during the night and have smoke coming out of the chimney by daybreak, they could legitimately take up residence. They could also claim a small amount of surrounding ground, this to be defined by how far from the dwelling the new owner could throw an axe (Sayce 1942; Howell 1977, 29). In time, the rapidly constructed 'clod dwelling' would be replaced by something more durable. Inevitably, most *tai unnos* have disappeared, except perhaps as earthworks, but their stone-built successors may well remain (Wiliam 1995, 37).

We need not dwell on the conviction amongst those who built *tai unnos* that they had a traditional right to do this. Active landlords instructed their agents to clear away such dwellings, but many others survived, and after they had been there for at least twenty years they acquired a degree of protection from interference which can be detected, for instance, in nineteenth-century enclosure acts, though on the commons of the Crown Manors the term before protection was acquired was reportedly sixty years (Barnes 1970, 125; Howell 1977, 29).

The physical features or elements that constitute a typical encroachment landscape display relatively little variation. There are one or more cottages or houses; initially these were single structures, though in some cases they developed into farms with all the ancillary accoutrements. The small enclosed plots around the cottages usually covered little more than a couple of acres initially, and formed irregular patterns. A track served each property, and usually each encroachment was severed from the enclosed farmlands by at the very least a thin strip of common land, thus creating islands on the common which provided visual indicators of independence.

In places these developing settlements had other attributes that left their mark on the landscape. In mining and quarrying areas, for instance, the cottages, often numerous, are set within the extensive remains of quarries, shafts, spoil tips and the like (Barnes 1970, 125). Where convenient peat deposits could be used – and prior to the nineteenth century this was virtually the only accessible source of fuel in many uplands – the peat cuttings remain as scars in the landscape. And in Radnorshire, in central Wales, some encroachers took up rabbit farming, with over forty individual, or groups of, pillow mounds now recognised on the commons (Silvester 2004, 64).

Upland encroachments

Whatever the form of the encroachments, they altered the appearance of the landscape, breaking up the large expanses of unenclosed upland pasture with pockets of improvement and cultivation. Even in 1970, Radnorshire, the historic county that is now part of modern Powys and which borders the western fringes of Shropshire and Herefordshire, still had some 47,000 ha of common land, all but a very small portion of it in the uplands. In the late eighteenth century, the commons and waste were estimated to extend over 80,000 ha (Silvester 2004, 54). The northern part of this region fell within the *cantref* – equivalent to the English hundred – of Maelienydd. Encroachments here were commonplace.

Some encroachments consisted of solitary cottages in their own enclosures. Others tended to aggregate, giving a cartographic image comparable to frogspawn. The underlying reasons for such concentrations are not always clear. Probably the better soils on a common were exploited (Wiliam 1995, 24), and inevitably there may have been familial ties in some of these communities that encouraged nucleation. Moelfre City, in the parish of Llanbister (and note the irony, which was fairly commonplace in the names given to encroachments), was one such concentration, and it retains its identity today (Figure 18). The tithe survey in the mid-nineteenth century shows twelve cottages, seven of which remain today within a patchwork of small and haphazardly ordered fields. It lies on a saddle of ground between three higher hills; two streams pass through it. Overall, the enclosed area spread across little more than 42 ha, but it is a major component in this local landscape, even though its encroachment identity has been diluted by its incorporation with the later nineteenth-century farmland enclosures that spread up the valleys from the west and east. Smaller groups of encroachments lie to the south-east, and the field patterns to the north-west hint at further encroachments which even at the time of the tithe survey had already been incorporated into the surrounding farming landscape.

Moelfre City is unusual only for the number of cottages concentrated in a restricted area. In Maelienydd, a survey of the crown lands in 1734 revealed 421 encroachments on the commons and another 363 instances where land had been enclosed; 154 cottages had no land attached and only 21 had more than 4 acres (1.6 ha) (Howse 1955, 29). A century later the tithe maps for the *cantref*, which predominantly date from 1840–2, depict approximately 520 cottage encroachments isolated on the commons or already subsumed into the enclosed land around their edges, but which still exhibit the tell-tale traces of small appended enclosures (Figure 19). Of that large number, over 300 appear now to have disappeared or have been abandoned as dwellings, sometimes leaving a fingerprint, a residual pattern of small fields whose presence is only a minor inconvenience in the modern stock-keeping economy. Indeed, over 210 had gone by the end of the nineteenth century, an indication of how transient many of these cottages were.

Encroachment was not a constant. Some commons appear largely to have escaped such intrusion altogether, perhaps as a result of varying factors; the most obvious of these are the controls exerted by the local landowner, and the physical environment which deterred even the most determined squatter. For there can be no doubt that some commons were inhospitable, and that while a minority of cottagers preferred to live in isolated and out of the way spots, perhaps because these were felt to be less vulnerable to interference, most cottagers settled within a relatively short distance of the periphery of their common. The extensive commons in the multi-township parish of Beguildy, which lies beside the upper Teme where it forms the border with England, illustrate both tendencies. Here on the remote northern edge of an upland known as the Black Mountain were the dwellings of New Invention, Wernyginog and one known simply as Black Mountain Cottage. But more, including Green Hollow, Golden Grove and Hyde Park, sheltered around the edge of the common within an accessible distance of the tracks down to the valley and the main settlements. In the extensive and largely unbroken tracts of open upland in the west of the county beyond the upper Wye only a handful of encroachments emerged.

Lowland encroachment

The hallmarks of encroachment are evident not only in Radnorshire but throughout most of Wales where uplands form sizeable portions of the landmass. This much is familiar to any archaeologist working in the Welsh hills, yet there is rather more to the phenomenon than the unregulated occupation of the commons. When we start to examine the valleys of some of the major Welsh rivers, corridors that have witnessed occupation from the prehistoric era onwards, it becomes apparent that tracts of unenclosed land, not just lowland commons, but also afforested areas and more poorly drained valley floors were formerly more prevalent than is generally appreciated, though generally they were both smaller in extent and more likely to disappear at an earlier date than the upland commons. They are, too, less predictable in their occurrence, and it is the landscape patterns, and often the encroachments, which can assist in their identification. Examples from three river catchments indicate the variety.

South of Oswestry, the convergence of the River Vyrnwy and its parent, the Severn, has a created a low-lying tract of land spanning the Montgomeryshire/Shropshire border, much of the area being less than 60 m above sea level. The floodplain is extensive and winter inundations still occur despite the presence of modern flood defence banks. Equally there is good farmland here, and church foundations, and perhaps associated settlement, go back into the early medieval era at places such as Llandrinio and Llandysilio.

It is a map of 1748, now in the Powys County Archives, by the renowned surveyor John Rocque, showing the lands in the lordship of Deuddwr, which formed an extensive tract across what was northern Montgomeryshire, that depicts the enclosed grounds interspersed with an extensive and irregular network of commons. South of the settlement of Llandysilio, fossilised medieval open-field strips survived into the middle of the eighteenth century, and south-eastwards, towards the confluence of the rivers, the relict open fields around Llandrinio were even more obvious before their wholesale enclosure in 1799. But intercalated with these medieval agricultural remnants were the commons or heaths, which also persisted from medieval times. South-west and south-east of Llandysilio were Domgay Common, Llandrinio Rhos Common, Tretherwen (Trederwen) Common, Gwern-y-go Common and others for which no names were given. Every one of these commons disappeared at the time of enclosure at the end of the eighteenth century, almost all being converted to enclosed farmland. Not so Llandrinio Rhos Common, which had developed its own distinctive topography. On Rocque's map two small encroachments were depicted in the centre of the common, and during the following 100 years these were joined by others to create a characteristic spread of at least fifteen cottages with appended small enclosures which largely filled the common, and almost all of which are still extant today. This pattern of

FIGURE 18.
Moelfre City, Radnorshire (Powys). Aerial view from the south-east: unenclosed common lies to the north-west and north-east and later nineteenth-century enclosures are just visible to the south-west. © Clwyd-Powys Archaeological Trust: 09-C-225

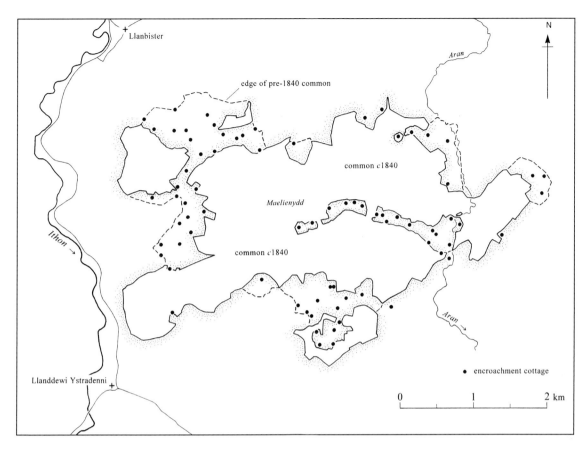

FIGURE 19.
Part of the *cantref*
of Maelienydd to
the south-east of
Llanbister, Radnorshire
(Powys), showing
cottages around the
upland common in
the mid-nineteenth
century.

small and irregular fields remains today, and the name *rhos* (= English 'moor')
has been retained as a modern label.

Fifteen kilometres further down river in the valley of the Severn, just to the
south-east of Welshpool, is the seemingly modern settlement of Kingswood.
Its origins are not readily discernible from the present Ordnance Survey map
and on the ground part of it now has the appearance of a recently planted
dormitory enclave. The tithe map of 1843–4, however, reveals a different aspect
of its history. In an area of little more than 40 ha were over thirty cottages,
with the network of small and haphazardly laid-out enclosures that signal a
closely set cottage settlement. Lying on the edge of one of the townships in
the historic parish of Forden, this was a typical setting for a common, and
by the early nineteenth century it had metamorphosed into an encroachment
landscape.

Less than 2 km south along the road towards Montgomery was the settlement of Forden itself. It had a medieval church until drastic Victorianisation
in 1867, and the churchyard's original curvilinear form might well indicate
a pre-Conquest origin. Forden spreads across an undulating rise at around
110 m above sea level on a gradually narrowing spur of land between the Severn and its tributary, the Camlad, while Kingswood lies further back along
the same spur (Figure 20).

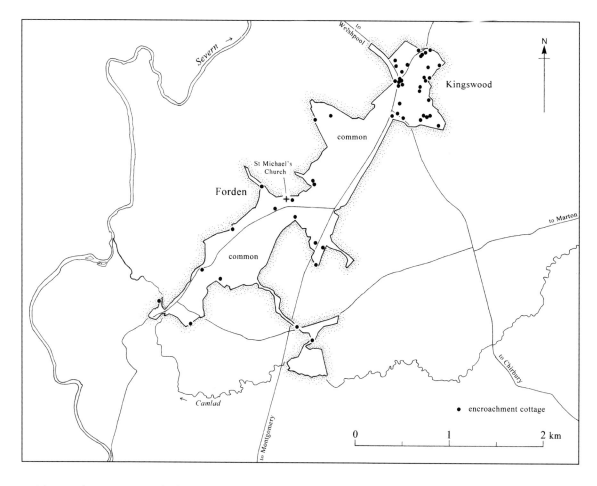

FIGURE 20.
Forden and
Kingswood,
Montgomeryshire
(Powys). The
sporadic pattern of
encroachments in
Forden contrasts with
the more nucleated
distribution in what
was to become
Kingswood.

The settlement around the church is undistinguished and rather sparse, typical of the upper Severn Valley except that it is rather smaller than most of the other nucleations along this particular reach of the river. An estate map of 1783, however, clarifies some of the subtle variations in the settlement pattern. The church was shown on an 'island' – the churchyard – in the middle of a group of conjoined commons that straggled over about 170 ha, four times the size of that at Kingswood. Upwards of nineteen squatters' dwellings were mapped, a few in the vicinity of the church, others located apparently randomly around the periphery of the commons. The historical context here is a pre-Conquest one. The putative early medieval church foundation at Forden aside, Offa's Dyke defines the eastern boundary of the largest common, and less than 200 m to the east of the church is the motte and bailey of Nant-cribba, which, it has been argued, had an early medieval origin (Musson and Spurgeon 1988, 104). Hem Farm, sandwiched between two arms of the common, is undoubtedly pre-Conquest and, as with Forden itself, was one of the few manors in Montgomeryshire to be recorded in *Domesday Book*. Altogether this is an unlikely place to find under-utilised land on the scale shown in the late eighteenth century, though the map does reveal that the different commons were allocated to the various townships of Forden, suggesting it was an exploited and managed resource. Clearly, however, this did not stop the encroachers. In 1783 the image of an encroachment landscape was obvious, but parliamentary enclosure followed in 1803 and by the time of the tithe survey additional settlement elements had coalesced to a degree where the encroachment origins had been largely obscured.

The final examples are drawn from the Usk valley in Brecknock. Over a linear distance of no more than 13 km and within a short distance of the river is a series of relatively small cottage landscapes which illustrate how the chronology of encroachment can vary from area to area (Figure 21). For some of the insights here we are indebted to an excellent series of maps, starting with the so-called Badminton Manorial Survey of the manors of Crickhowell and Tretower of 1587, now in the National Library of Wales, which is claimed to be the earliest British atlas of estate maps compiled to a uniform scale.

The area of settlement now known as Ffawyddog, on the end of an upland ridge, was in the Middle Ages the location of the forest of Pennalte, a small wooded promontory on the south side of the Usk in the parish of Llangattock. The forest was a small one, seemingly of less than 40 ha and evidently of little significance to the Earls of Worcester, who acquired the manor of Crickhowell

FIGURE 21.
The middle Usk valley
in Brecknock (Powys),
showing areas of
encroachment.

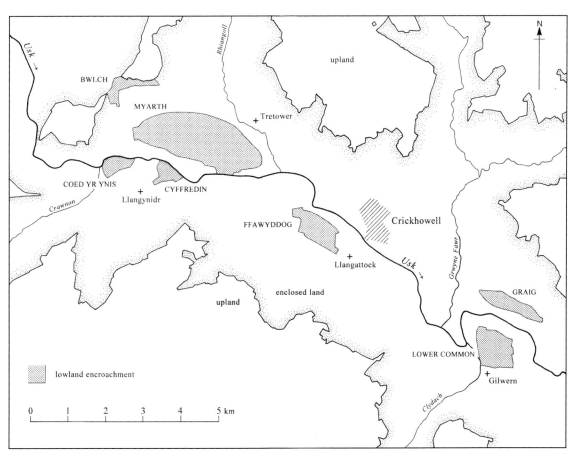

63

in which it lay in 1463. Nine cottages were already in existence by 1587, strung out around the forest edge, and two buildings that are assumed to have been dwellings lay at the forest's centre. Some of these may have been legitimate leaseholds, for the survey indicates that some tenants were paying rent on the Ffawyddog at that date. But in 1606 the Crickhowell manorial court was presented with a list of twenty-one cottagers who had recently erected dwellings on the Ffawyddog, and a year later the number had risen to twenty-five (Redwood and Redwood 2002, 33). Encroachment then levelled out, for an estate survey which can be attributed to the period around 1760 reveals no more than twenty-six dwellings. These were spread across the former forest, leaving small patches of open common, a situation that continues to the present. Ffawyddog stands out from the surrounding farmland because of the density of its houses (Figure 22).

The origins of Bwlch, 6 km to the north-west and on the opposite side of the valley, are more difficult to establish, for it lay beyond the lands that were mapped in 1587. Whether this was simply because it was open and unoccupied common at the end of the sixteenth century, or because it was held in a different ownership at that time, is unclear. The settlement lies on a saddle between Buckland Hill, in a loop of the Usk, and Cefn Moel, one of the Black Mountain ridges, the saddle forming a natural conduit for traffic running along the north side of the valley; this is reflected in its name, the Welsh *bwlch* translating as 'pass'. By the later eighteenth century the farmed lands had pushed up the lower slopes out of the river valley, and just beyond this, in corona-like fashion, ribbon encroachment followed two lanes skirting Cefn Moel, with a

FIGURE 22. Ffawyddog, Brecknock (Powys). The scattered encroachments in the former forest occupy the centre of the photograph. The river Usk arcs across the top and beyond it is the medieval town of Crickhowell. © Clwyd-Powys Archaeological Trust: 05-C–211

similar if less marked pattern around the edge of Buckland Hill. Only later did the main route itself through Bwlch also become a focus for settlement.

Three kilometres to the south-east, occupying another isolated hill of around 300 ha beside the Usk, was the forest of Myarth, which retains tree cover to the present day, although this is now in the form of conifer plantations. In 1587 it is evident that there were a number of small assarts around its edge, but in 1610 more than twenty people were presented in court for encroaching on the Myarth and by 1760 more than fifty smallholdings were shown on the lower slopes (Llangynidr Local History Society 2000, 57). Such a pattern would certainly have been recognisable as encroachment had it survived into modern times, but the handful of present-day farms and the hotel close to the river give no sign of the phenomenon. An active policy of closing down the smallholdings appears to have been adopted on Myarth, probably in the nineteenth century.

On the south bank of the Usk in Llangynidr parish were two small commons. Coed yr Ynys (Welsh *coed* = wood) covered about 20 ha and in 1587 had sixteen cottages scattered around its perimeter. By the late eighteenth century it has been completely transformed, with the erection of around twenty-five dwellings and the division of the common into smallholdings interspersed with small tracts of open ground, much as on Ffawyddog, although, unlike the latter, the open ground has now been absorbed into large fields and many of the cottages have disappeared. No more than a kilometre to the east, on the other side of Llangynidr village, was another small riverside common of just over 5 ha at Cyffredin, where there were further cottage encroachments.

Lower down the Usk, between Crickhowell and Abergavenny, is a steep hillside called the Graig, now covered in Forestry Commission woodland. Beneath it are the valley farms and on the plateau above it there are further enclosed lands. Disguised in the woodlands on the slope are the dispersed ruins of at least twenty cottages with ancillary structures, garden plots and artificial terraces levelled up for agriculture. Some of these cottages had already fallen out of use by the 1880s, but when the first encroachments were made is unclear. A beginning in the early eighteenth century is implied by a solitary datestone of 1746 (Jones 2003). Completing this group, on the far side of the Usk, and directly opposite the Graig, was Lower Common, which lay in a loop of the river below the village of Gilwern.

Even without the estate maps of the late sixteenth and eighteenth centuries, these encroachment settlements would in general be recognisable from their modern layout – they form pockets of settlement more closely set than the otherwise dispersed pattern of farms, and thus form discordant elements in the general farming landscape of the Usk Valley. Their histories remain to be properly researched, but enough is known to suggest varying chronologies. For Ffawydog and Myarth, encroachment came early: the late sixteenth and particularly the very early seventeenth century seem to have been critical to their development. Bwlch, Coed yr Ynys and perhaps the Graig seem to have expanded at a later date.

Conclusions

What are the general points to emerge from this? The most obvious is the broad canvas across which encroachment activity spread. The examples presented here are taken entirely from the three historic counties that make up modern Powys, but every Welsh county was to a greater or lesser extent affected by the movement of otherwise landless people on to the commons, the waste and the forests. These encroachers might settle with the tacit permission of the lord of the manor – this was certainly the case for many of those who worked in the extractive industries – slate, stone, lead, coal and the like – but the activity was less legitimate amongst those who were general labourers or aspired to their own smallholdings. Regardless of the legitimacy of the encroachments, their physical form was broadly the same and their appearance in the landscape fairly consistent. Anyone familiar with Everitt's chapter on common land in *The English Rural Landscape* (Everitt 2000) will recognise the parallels here: England and Wales share much, and in this respect as in so many others the political boundary between the two countries is largely an irrelevance. Everitt, we may also recall, expressed his surprise about the extent of common land across England prior to the twentieth century. Wales, in this respect, was little different.

Secondly, it is normally the encroachments of the eighteenth century that are the focus of attention, particularly for social historians. Yet, in as much as this was a single, definable phenomenon, some of the examples cited here take us back into the later part of the sixteenth century, and it is evident too that in some of the more remote areas encroachment continued, albeit on a reduced scale, until almost the end of the nineteenth century (Howell 1977, 29). The phenomenon thus spread over a period of some 300 years.

Every episode of encroachment introduced new elements into existing landscapes and in some localities generated completely new landscapes, whether in the sixteenth century or later. In the uplands, encroachment carried settlement to altitudes and remote locations which had last seen occupation in the prehistoric era, marginal land where permanent settlement was always likely to founder, leaving behind relict landscapes. Conversely, even the more densely utilised river valleys, such as the Severn and the Usk, had tracts of ground that were unenclosed and thus acted as a magnet for illegal settlement when controls were lax. Obviously though, as the examples of Four Crosses and Forden show, encroachment was feasible or permissible only intermittently. Why Llandrinio Rhos Common was so attractive to cottagers whilst other neighbouring commons in the same lordship seem not to have witnessed a comparable degree of encroachment activity has yet to be explained.

The recognition of such encroachment settlements is not invariably straightforward, and to a degree is dependent on whether the settlement was dispersed or more nucleated. And, of course, the initiation of encroachment was wholly dependent on the presence of commons, and these too cannot always be easily recognised. The picture from Forden is instructive. The encroachment landscape of Kingswood would be readily discernible from early Ordnance Survey mapping regardless of the enclosure that occurred in 1803. In contrast, the sporadic encroachment around the edges of the commons in the vicinity of Forden itself would be difficult to identify without the late eighteenth-century estate map, and even detailed morphological analysis of the field systems in the parish would probably fail to recapture all the detail of the layout of those commons, let alone the encroachments. This raises a further issue, for the commons themselves were not static and those around Forden in the second half of the eighteenth century may be only a portion of what was open land a century earlier, with informal enclosure eating away at the edges. Thus the two arms of the common lying to the south-west of the church give the impression of being residual survivals of a common that originally spread across the intervening area and may even have had its own encroachments.

Nor is there a straightforward correlation between the uplands and solitary encroachments on the one hand, and the lower commons and more nucleated settlement on the other. Such was the extent of the upland commons and waste over much of central Wales that for those who led a subsistence existence, relying on their stocks and crops, there was little positive benefit from living cheek by jowl with their neighbours, for the surrounding common itself offered a resource which could be utilised. That this was not invariably the case is revealed by such complexes as Moelfre City; here, other factors must have come into play. The geographically limited commons in the Usk Valley saw tight-knit encroachment communities developing, no doubt because land accessible for such incursions was limited. But the differential patterns in the Severn Valley – with a nucleation at Kingswood yet well-spread cottages around some of the other Forden commons – indicates that there is no general rule that can be invoked and that each area has to be treated on its own merits.

It was E. G. Bowen, one of the foremost historical geographers in twentieth-century Wales, who pointed out that 'the proliferation of squatter settlements marked the final phase in the expansion of the single farm [in Wales]' (Bowen 1971, 192). Equally, his observation in relation to the *tai unnos* that 'these crude dwellings became in time more permanent homesteads with little to distinguish them from the traditional *tyddynnod* or single farms' (Bowen 1971, 191) serves to confirm that it is in fact the landscape patterning of these encroachments that acts as virtually the sole marker of the process.

There is, finally, a conspicuous social dimension to encroachment. These are, in essence, 'landscapes of the poor', in contrast to the other types of transformation referred to at the beginning of this chapter, which tended to be at the instigation and to the benefit of the wealthier classes. Possibly these are the only landscapes to which such a label can be pinned. And while many survive in mutated form, many others have gone, removed through parliamentary enclosure or absorbed with their fields into wider agrarian landscapes. Just as these landscapes were created by the lowest social groups, so it is that they are perhaps less likely to survive intact than the landscapes of their wealthier counterparts.

CHAPTER SIX

The Grouse Moors
of the Peak District

David Hey

Grouse moors form a distinctive, managed landscape that is unique to the British Isles. Red grouse (*Lagopus lagopus scoticus*) is a subspecies which is confined to these islands (McKelvie 1985, 56–86). If the desire to shoot enormous numbers of grouse had not taken such a hold in the nineteenth and twentieth centuries, our moorland landscapes would now look very different and important archaeological sites from the prehistoric, medieval and post-medieval periods would have been destroyed. Many moors would be clothed with conifers and others would have been much reduced in size by new pastures and meadows.

Upland moors form a major part of the English landscape, yet the role of grouse shooting in freezing moorland landscapes has attracted research only recently. Indeed, a pioneering article on the Yorkshire Dales (Done and Muir 2001) has been the sole detailed study and recognition of the importance of this theme is relatively new in more general works (Hey 2000; Simmons 2003). What were commonly regarded as 'wastes' before the era of parliamentary enclosure became carefully controlled landscapes, where the public were denied access so that exclusive groups could pursue a sport during a strictly limited season. In upland parts of England grouse shooting had a greater effect on the landscape than did foxhunting or the shooting of pheasants or partridges in lowland England, topics that have attracted more attention.

The Peak District moors that are still used for grouse shooting are instantly recognisable from the typical patchwork effect that has been created by burning the heather in rotation – rather like the felling cycle in a coppice wood – in order to encourage the growth of fresh shoots for the grouse to feed upon while providing patches of thick heather for nesting out of sight of predators. Burning heather was an ancient practice, for sheep, too, enjoyed eating young shoots, but it was developed on a large scale only from the 1860s, when shooting butts were introduced on the moors. The heyday of grouse shooting was the late Victorian and Edwardian period. It is now a pale imitation of its former self (Figure 23).

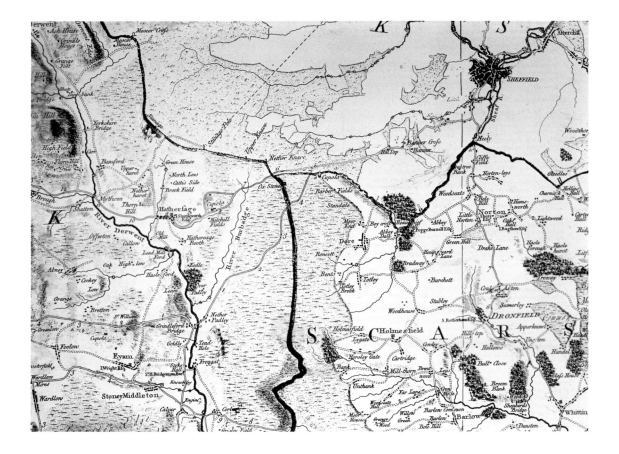

FIGURE 23.
Detail of P. P. Burdett's *Map of Derbyshire* (1791 edition), showing the moors referred to in the text before their enclosure. The Big Moor, which came to be owned by the Duke of Rutland, is in the centre. Stanage and Moscar Moors are shown at the top.

Early grouse shooting

Grouse were once known as moor fowl or moor game. A survey of the manor of Sheffield in 1637, for example, noted 'moore game in abundance, both blacke and red, as moorcocks, moorehenns, and young pootes [half-grown birds] upon the moores' (Ronksley 1908). About 100 years later, a local gentleman, Godfrey Bosville of Gunthwaite Hall, wrote in rhyming couplets about the moors (Hunter 1828–31, vol. 2, 198):

The moor-game's feathers glitter in the sun.
A bird in better countries never known;
The curious black-game, in this dreary place,
Seeks a lone refuge from the human race.

Black grouse were once widespread in the Peak District, but they were already in decline by the early nineteenth century (Farey 1817, vol. 3, 99). A few years ago only a few pairs were left on the Staffordshire Moorlands near Longnor.

George Walker's portrait of 'The Dog Breaker' in his *The Costume of Yorkshire*, published in 1814, is accompanied by the comment that 'young dogs should be put into the breaker's hands to be tried with partridges in the spring, and taken to the moors towards the end of July, when the young broods of moor game are beginning to take wing' (Walker 1814, pl. IV). Before the Restoration, moor game, partridges and pheasants were caught chiefly by hawking and netting. The use of the flintlock gun to shoot birds on the wing was a fashion imported by aristocrats and gentry who had been exiled on the Continent during the Civil War. In south-west Yorkshire the eighteenth-century antiquary John Wilson, of Broomhead Hall, claimed that his ancestor, who had died in 1687, was the first local person to shoot game on the wing (Hunter 1828–31, vol. 2, 183). In Derbyshire, similar claims were made for a Mr James Tunstead, a captain of dragoons in the Royalist army and Warden of the Peak Forest, who in 1661 had an annuity of £50 'for taking the King's game of heath poults in Derbyshire and other parts north of the Trent' (Brighton 1981, 47). This practice involved healthy exercise tramping across the moors with a dog and a guide who carried the game bag and the ammunition, and grew in popularity in the late eighteenth century, when the success of the day's sport began to be measured by the size of the 'bag' recorded in game books. Similar trends can be seen in the shooting of partridges and pheasants. As early as 1773 'wastes' in Yorkshire were rented 'for the purpose of shooting Moor Game' (Munsche 1981, 35–6). In the Peak District, a Baslow boundary perambulation of 1787, taken well before the parliamentary enclosure of the moors, mentions a point 'where the Game cabin now stands' (SCR 1947–8, 100–1).

The shooting of game was regulated by Parliament in numerous Acts passed between 1671 and 1831 (Munsche 1981, 8–9, 35–6, 173–4). The 1671 Act prevented legal hunting of hares, pheasants, partridges and moor fowl by anyone other than freeholders of more than £100 per annum or long leaseholders of more than £150. Sons and heirs of esquires and other persons 'of higher degree' were permitted to hunt, while all lords of manors 'not under the degree of an esquire' were authorised to appoint gamekeepers with the right to seize guns and dogs and search suspected poachers. From 1693 penalties were imposed on those who burnt heather between 2 February and 24 June, and from 1762 the seasons in which game could be legally killed were defined. In 1772 the present dates were agreed. The grouse-shooting season was established as 12 August to 10 December and anyone caught shooting outside that season was fined heavily.

Parliamentary enclosure and the Game Act (1831)

It is well known that the parliamentary enclosure of commons and wastes enabled great landowners to form compact moorland estates for the principal purpose of shooting grouse. For example, after the Duke of Rutland acquired vast acreages from enclosure as lord of the north Derbyshire manors of Barlow, Baslow, Brampton, Holmesfield, Dore, Totley and Hathersage, he built Longshaw Lodge in about 1830 in mock-Jacobean style as a shooting lodge with accommodation for his guests and even a chapel. The turnpike road was pushed back to a discreet distance and drives were constructed for wheeled vehicles. At the same time, the Duke ordered the erection of gamekeepers' lodges, two of which survive in lonely positions on the moors (Figure 24). The keepers shot foxes, crows and other predators and encouraged the rearing of young grouse, but the moors were not yet managed intensively.[1]

The 1831 Game Act took the power over game from lords of the manor and conferred it upon the owners of land. This had the effect of raising the rental value of moorland estates to four times their previous level, though this was not without some comic effects. A visitor to Kinderscout in the summer of 1880 wrote:

> The owners of the moor are jealous to the last degree of their rights, and quarrel over the few birds which by some accident are still left as though the cause of empires were at stake. This arises from the foolish way in which the district has been parcelled out among a number of small holders, in patches not much larger than a table-cloth. One man's allotment is actually under two acres in extent, and his only chance of getting a shot is on the days when his neighbours are out shooting, and the grouse are driven over his field. Then he stands waiting for a chance … On an average during the season, there are about three guns out to each bird, and in one case a gentleman who pays £50 a year for his bit of moor only got two birds all last season. (Jennings 1880, 106–8)

The 1831 Act also led to the formation of shooting clubs such as the Bradfield Game Association, whose fifteen members paid £10 per annum for their printed ticket and whose treasurer, Mr Elmhirst, a local gentleman descended from an old yeoman family, had sole charge of management and the prosecution of poachers. Elmhirst and his keeper employed forty men to protect the moor on the opening day of the season.[2] In the 1840s the absentee owner of the neighbouring Midhope Moors let his shooting rights to a similar group, which was led by a corn miller and then by a solicitor. The seventeen members of this group were drawn from the local middle classes. The solicitor, John Dransfield, was also a local historian, and wrote of a day's sport, which was followed by a substantial dinner at the Club Inn, Midhope:

> One of the most enjoyable days we had for many years on Midhope Moors was one old sportsman christened the 'Duffers' Day'. I invited annually a number of friends who were not regular shooters and had not otherwise the opportunity of showing their skill on the moors to a day's driving. (Dransfield 1906, 510)

The first day of the shooting season attracted widespread interest. In 1869 the local historian the Revd Alfred Gatty wrote:

> On the 12th of August the moors attract crowds from Sheffield as spectators, who come by thousands, and but for the wild space over which they are distributed, they would mar the sport. But there is a good-humoured

FIGURE 24.
Gamekeeper's cottage,
White Edge, Longshaw
Moors estate. Now a
National Trust holiday
home, it was built in
mock-Jacobean style
c.1830 on the Duke of
Rutland's grouse moor.

view to be taken of this motley invasion; and as all vehicles, varying from the costermonger's donkey cart to the four-horsed omnibus, are strictly kept on the roads, those who have the enjoyment of shooting need not grudge or resent, which they do not, the universal interest felt in this locality in all which concerns the sportsman's recreations.

At first the 'bags' were modest: Gatty thought that 'a good shoot on the 12th of August may kill forty or fifty brace of red grouse' (Hunter 1869, 11–12).

Guns and butts

Dransfield wrote that in the 1830s his uncle walked 8 miles (13 km) from his home to the grouse moor, shot all day with a twelve-inch bore muzzle loader weighing twelve pounds, then walked home at night. It was, he thought, rather different from sitting in a grouse butt all day (Dransfield 1906, 512). This new method of shooting came about with successive improvements in gun manufacture, particularly the invention of the breech-loading shotgun. Several thousands of these were in use by the early 1860s (Carr 1981, 475–87; Thompson 1981, 457–74; Simmons 2003, 139). It was then that the management of the moors, particularly the burning of sections on a rotation basis, began in earnest in order to provide enough birds to shoot. Other improvements included the digging of drains in the wettest parts of the moors to encourage heather at the expense of cotton grass, bog-moss and purple moor

FIGURE 25.
Broomhead Moor
shooting cabin. The
best-fitted cabin on the
Peak District moors
and one of the few still
in use, it was erected
in 1903 by the
brothers John and
Reginald Henry
Rimington-Wilson.

FIGURE 26.
Shooting butts on
Bradfield Moors,
Earl Fitzwilliam's
estate. Lines of butts
such as these became
normal from the
1860s onwards as gun
technology improved.

grass; the digging of ditches to prevent the spread of fire; the construction of pony and cart tracks and of single-storeyed, single-roomed, stone cabins for shelter at lunchtime (Figure 25). Rhododendrons were planted near some of these cabins for the delight of the shooters.

The most radical change came with the introduction of shooting butts, or 'driving holes' as Dransfield called them. These were made of stone or wood, disguised by turf up to waist level (Figure 26). The shooter was accompanied by a loader or two to keep up the rate of firing. Whereas in the past birds had been shot as they flew away, they were now driven by beaters towards the butts. This method – the *battue* – had been introduced from France in the late eighteenth century for pheasant shooting and then for partridges. The beaters were local countrymen employed to rouse the birds by shouting, shaking rattles and firing guns into the air. By the 1880s the 'bags' shot each day were enormous. On 12 August 1913 nine men shot 2,843 birds on Broomhead Moor, at that time a national record for one day's shooting. The August 1904 issue of *Baily's Magazine of Sports and Pastimes* observed that 'the excellent results obtained at Broomhead are mainly due to skilled, experienced management extending over a long term of years'. The owner, Mr Rimington-Wilson, and his brother took 'the keenest interest in the moors' and the knowledge of the chief keeper for the last forty-five years, Charles Wood, was 'unsurpassed'. Broomhead Moor long had the reputation of carrying more grouse per acre than any moor in Great Britain (Figure 27).

Management of the moors

The report in *Baily's Magazine* claimed that on the best shooting moors the heather was burned solely with a view to the requirements of the grouse. There were no unnecessary sheep to be considered. In the 1870s the Duke of Rutland had stopped sheep grazing on his Longshaw Moors in the summer months. Four years later, the Broomhead Moor keepers claimed that the grouse were adversely affected by the 1,200 sheep and lambs from four local farms and that the dogs, running up the moor after the sheep, frightened the grouse from their nests. At first, Rimington-Wilson listened to the farmers' appeals but in 1879 he accepted the advice of his keepers. David Wood of Old Booth Farm was no longer able to graze 700 sheep on the moor but was reduced to keeping forty sheep on his own land. A telling point for those owners who were not themselves sportsmen was that more income could be obtained from grouse shooting than from renting moorland for sheep or cattle grazing. In 1912 the Duke of Rutland also decided to stop the winter pasturing of thousands of sheep on his Longshaw estate, with the exception of Burbage Moors (Sissons 2002, 142).

On some moors fields were created to grow black oats for the grouse. On Broomhead Moor, for instance, a field known locally as Sod Bank covered 1¾ acres (0.7 ha). The field reverted to heather after the First World War but the banks are still marked on Ordnance Survey maps. Several others can be identified on the Duke of Rutland's Longshaw Moors estate and the Duke of Norfolk's moors in the Upper Derwent valley (Sissons 2002, 84–5).

Another diversion for the 'sportsman' on the moors was the shooting of rabbits. A warren that stretched for nearly a mile under Curbar Edge, covering 70 acres (28 ha), was established in the 1870s by the Duke of Rutland, and the keeper's cottage, known as the Warren Lodge, was built about 1877 (SCR 1942–3, 108–14). Five parts of the Longshaw Moors estate were set aside for rabbit breeding until the 1920s. The lessee from 1914, Charles Markham, and his party once shot 400 rabbits in a day. On Boxing Day 1933 another party of four men shot 712 rabbits on the moors above the River Derwent (SCR 1942–3, 62–4). Meanwhile, mountain hares, whose coats turn white in winter, were imported from Scotland for shooting purposes. They too feed on young heather.

The Wilsons and Stanage Moors

The most enthusiastic 'sportsmen' on the moors to the west of Sheffield were members of the Wilson family, whose chief income came from the Sharrow Snuff Mills which their ancestor had founded in the eighteenth century and which still flourish today. In 1878 William Wilson of Beauchief Hall became Master of the Barlow Hounds and built the kennels at Holmesfield, which are still in use. A spinal injury from a hunting accident forced him to give up foxhunting in 1900, after which he concentrated his energies on grouse shooting. He had bought Stanage Moors from the Duke of Norfolk in 1897 and ten years later he began an extraordinary project that is now of interest to the landscape historian and archaeologist. In the few years after the purchase he ordered the construction of 108 artificial drinking troughs in the natural boulders on his moor, so that his grouse would not fly away and be shot on someone else's moor. As a cranky retirement pastime, my next-door neighbour and I have found and mapped 103 of these. A typical trough is about 45 cm long and 30 cm wide, but some are much larger (Figures 28–30). Rainwater was fed into troughs by long runnels, which were cut to fit the shape of the rock. The troughs were not arranged in a systematic manner, for some are almost adjacent while others are up to a quarter of a mile apart. An account book reveals that a teenage mason, George Broomhead, was paid 7s 3½d per trough. The success of the first half dozen near Stanage Pole encouraged Wilson to undertake a second scheme of seventy-five troughs along Stanage Edge, curving back into the moor, then a third erratic line of twenty-seven near his northern boundary. Five of the troughs seem to have sunk without trace and others were found only after the thick heather was burnt. Some have ingenious designs, including two that were cut into the vertical face of the rock. They are a unique feature, for Wilson's idea was not taken up on any other moor (Hey 2002a, 95–112).

As the moors became more intensively managed for grouse shooting, so the owners and their gamekeepers became more hostile to people who wished to

FIGURE 27.
Boundary stone
separating Richard
Henry Rimington-
Wilson's Broomhead
Moor from grouse
moors belonging to the
Duke of Norfolk.

FIGURE 28.
The first of William
Wilson's grouse
drinking troughs on
Stanage Moor, 1907.

FIGURE 29.
Grouse drinking
trough no. 33 in
Wilson's second
sequence, near Crow
Chin.

FIGURE 30.
Grouse drinking
trough no. 25 in the
third sequence near
Oaking Clough,
revealed by the recent
burning of tall heather.

pick bilberries or to enjoy a walk over rough moorland on their day off work. Bilberry pickers were turned away from Broomhead Moor from 1898 and from elsewhere not long after (SCR 1954–5, 90). Professional men pioneered rambling on the moors during Victoria's reign and tipped gamekeepers in order to gain access. Then the opening of the railway from Sheffield to Manchester via Edale in 1894 provided cheap travel for working-class men and women from the industrial towns. In 1900 the Sheffield Clarion Ramblers, led by the formidable G. H. B. Ward, took their first trip into the heart of the Peak District and soon the battle for 'the right to roam' began in earnest.

The heyday of grouse shooting on the Longshaw Moors estate lasted until the early 1920s. The record annual 'bag' on this 9,270 acres (3,752 ha) of grouse moorland (together with the 'sporting rights' over 2,200 acres (890 ha) of adjacent farm land) was the 3,633 brace of grouse shot in 1893. Even after the First World War annual 'bags' were enormous; for instance, 3,002 brace were shot in 1921 (SCR 1928–9, 104–5). By then, however, the public appetite for grouse on the table was in decline and the cost of rearing grouse was greater than the income from sales. In 1927 the Duke of Rutland sold those parts of his Longshaw estate that lay within Derbyshire to Chesterfield Rural District Council, who let the shooting rights to William Wilson and were even less tolerant of ramblers than the duke had been. In 1935, however, Sheffield City Council unanimously decided to allow certain public access to the moors that they had purchased and to terminate grouse shooting on the 2,407 acres (974 ha) of Burbage and Houndkirk Moors (SCR 1928–9, 166; SCR 1936–7, 49–50).

The Duke of Devonshire and other local landowners continued to manage their moors for grouse shooting. During the year ending 1 February 1935 Thomas Kingsford Wilson of Fulwood House, Sheffield, the cousin of William Wilson, shot 1,004 grouse and 24 other birds on the moors, 643 partridges, 2,112 pheasants, 146 hares, 219 rabbits, 20 woodcock and 29 other birds, a total of 4,197. He was credited, if that is the right word, with shooting about 150,000 birds over half a century. He attributed his prowess 'to drinking Tennants' Bitter Beer when young and Wiley's Black Label Whisky later on'. His nephew continued to shoot grouse, from a chair in a specially lowered butt, after having both legs amputated (Chaytor 1962, 183–7).

Modern developments

Since the 1940s British heather moors have been reduced by 40 per cent to 700,000 acres (283,290 ha) in England and Wales and to 2.5 million acres (1.01 million hectares) in Scotland. In the Peak District the area of heather moor fell by 36 per cent between 1913 and 1980 and the grouse population was reduced substantially. Today, the moors are no longer managed in the old intensive manner, 'bags' are increasingly uncertain, and the sheep have returned with a vengeance. Nevertheless, half a million grouse are still shot in Britain each year and virtually all moor owners rely on the letting of grouse shooting to cover the costs of running their estates.[3]

The Grouse Moors of the Peak District

Grouse are short-lived, whether they are shot or not. They succumb to predators and disease, particularly strongylosis, when their population soars. Even the RSPB and the Ramblers' Association agree that management for grouse shooting is the best regime for the moorlands. Regular burning promotes young heather, keeps down bracken and coarse grass, prevents the spread of silver birch and provides a good habitat for many other birds, such as golden plover, wheatears and curlews. Fortunately, much of the moorland in the northern part of the Peak District is now owned by the National Trust or the Peak Park Planning Board and both these bodies are committed to traditional management systems (Simmons 2003, 244; Hudson 1986; McKelvie 1985).

Grouse moors were once the scene of the fiercest battles for access. Now that 'the right to roam' is on the statute book, it is easier to explore these distinctive landscapes on the ground and to ponder over differences between one local moor and another. Why, for example, are there no shooting butts on the Duke of Rutland's former Big Moor? As the duke does not provide access to his estate records, we cannot find the answer in the archives. But the management of English grouse moors is not a topic that can be studied from an informative set of documents. We have to search widely in local literary sources, draw upon oral memories, and above all tramp over the moors with our boots on, as William Hoskins prescribed.

Notes

1. Regrettably, the Duke of Rutland does not allow access to his estate records.
2. Sheffield Archives, Elmhirst 778/1 and 821; WWM MP102.
3. *The Independent*, 10 August 1993, 17.

CHAPTER SEVEN

Hoskins and Historical Ecology

John Sheail

Generous tribute has been paid to the scholarship and humanity of William Hoskins. Much has been written to explain why his writings and broadcasts found so receptive an audience. This chapter is by way of a modest foot-note, focusing upon his brief association with early developments in historical ecology.

Hoskins laid bare his sympathies in the opening lines of a talk he gave in the Third Programme in December 1964: 'Most English historians are snobs', writing only of 'top people'. They ignored some 97 per cent of the people, except when in brief rebellion – and then only to dismiss them in a line or two as the 'mob'. The theme of his talk was 'Harvest and hunger', and it dealt with the common man and the common place, and the intimate relationship between the two (Hoskins 1964). It was a perspective he had developed to remarkable effect in his *The Making of the English Landscape* (Hoskins 1955). There were, however other pioneers – as Hoskins himself acknowledged. In 1957, Maurice Beresford published *History on the Ground: Six Studies in Maps and Landscapes*, which was, in his words, an 'intellectual journey' through the countryside, equipped with 'an affection for the landscape of town and field', a good pair of boots, and a firm determination to study the documentary evidence and explore the landscape at one and the same time (Beresford 1957, 19, 249). Such writings encouraged historians to get 'mud on their boots'. Crucially for the purposes of this chapter, they also provided a framework of reference for those who, like ecologists, already had muddy boots.

Conservation ecology

Ecology had begun to emerge as a self-conscious natural science only in the 1890s. The early practitioners were mostly plant ecologists. It was not until the 1920s that Charles Elton coined the term 'animal ecology' to describe the other side of their activities. Others terms followed – invertebrate ecology, population ecology, applied ecology – each denoting a particular emphasis in research and teaching. There was nothing particularly remarkable, therefore, about the adoption of 'historical ecology', where the focus was on past habitats and ecosystems. As a focus for investigation, it was everywhere, yet nowhere, within the structures of research and teaching in ecology. It never became so organised as to have, say, a distinctive journal – its findings continue to be scattered through the literature (Rackham 2000).

It was no coincidence that many of the early initiatives in historical ecology were taken by some of the first practitioners in conservation research. As the Nature Conservancy's first regional officers, both Eric Duffey and Norman Moore were acutely aware of pressures on the post-war countryside (Moore 1987). It was their responsibility to respond in the most practical way possible to the unassailable fact that the landscapes of town and country were no museum. Hedgerows were grubbed up and earthworks removed without scruple, as economies and fashions changed. It had always been so. As Beresford remarked of historians, they must avoid the posturing of King Canute, but recognise and keep pace with change (Beresford 1957, 21). The Inspectorate of Ancient Monuments exerted some rudimentary influence, through the Acts of 1910 and 1932, in preserving historic buildings and archaeological sites. The Nature Conservancy, in addition to undertaking the fundamental research required of all research councils, was charged by its Royal Charter of 1949 with providing an 'expert' advisory service, with identifying, establishing and managing a series of national nature reserves, and with carrying out such survey and experiment as was relevant to those executive responsibilities (Sheail 1998). It was unique as a national body in having responsibility for managing tracts of countryside as well as instigating research on their management problems. Such management required both knowledge and understanding as to why species and their respective communities were present and in such numbers as existed. The human impact was recognised as very important: Norman Moore published a paper in the *Journal of Ecology*, illustrating the impact of the loss of Thomas Hardy's Dorset Heath upon its distinctive wildlife species. Some 45 per cent of the heathland recorded by the Land Utilisation Survey of 1934 had been destroyed by 1960, and the remaining heath was now fragmented into over 100 pieces (Moore 1962).

Eric Duffey was a keen naturalist, leaving school in 1938 to work in the natural history department of Leicester Museum. That same year, he attended a course on village church architecture given by Hoskins for the University's Adult Education Department at Vaughan College. He was so fascinated by Hoskins's commentary on the countryside during the numerous excursions that he joined a further course in 1939. Although there were fewer excursions, Duffey was again intrigued by Hoskins's explanations for such features as ridge and furrow and his more general comment on the human influence on the countryside. As a zoology undergraduate at the University in 1946, Duffey attended some of the lectures given by Hoskins, who invited him to contribute to a magazine on town and country. He became so absorbed that he nearly switched to geography in his final year. As the Conservancy's officer in East Anglia, Duffey took part in the research which, in the 1950s, established that the Norfolk Broads were flooded medieval peat workings – a discovery which further emphasised the scale of the human impact even in localities now cherished for their 'naturalness'.

The more difficult task for Duffey and Moore was to persuade even their colleagues in the Conservancy that it was neither appropriate nor enough simply to designate a reserve and 'leave it to nature'. Reserves had to be managed as consciously as any piece of farmland or woodland if the processes which had made the site so distinctive for its wildlife were to be maintained. Nature conservation implied a purposeful and sustained management of the plant and animal communities. There was already embarrassing revelation of how, with the cessation of 'traditional' forms of management, wetland, heath and grassland reserves had begun to revert to scrub and woodland. Multi-disciplinary research teams were established at the Nature Conservancy's new 'applied research station', the Monks Wood Experimental Station, in the early 1960s, close to four national nature reserves in the East Midlands. Duffey was given charge of what became the Lowland Grassland and Grass-Heath Section, and Moore that of the Toxic Chemicals and Wild Life Section, which addressed more explicitly the agricultural habitat (Sheail 1985 and 2000).

The seminal texts in ecology upon natural succession and climax communities, published earlier in the century, were read afresh. Alongside A. G. Tansley's synoptic volume *The British Islands and their Vegetation* (1939), there was the experimental rigour applied to a range of large-scale field studies by E. J. Salisbury and A. S. Watt. The use of palynological evidence had been pioneered by Harry Godwin in the wetlands of East Anglia. An explicitly historical approach was developed by Steven and Carlisle (1959) in their study of the native pinewoods of Scotland. Geoffrey Dimbleby had begun to use both palynological and documentary evidence in reconstructing the history of British heathlands and, working with historians and the Conservancy's officer for the New Forest, in investigating the early agricultural history of the Forest (Tubbs and Dimbleby 1965).

Drawing upon such insights, 'ecological history' began to feature more prominently in scientific discussion. A symposium at Monks Wood in March 1967 reviewed the impacts of a range of human pressures upon the natural environment, ranging from wildfowling and visitor pressures upon national nature reserves to the construction of estuarine barrages. Oliver Rackham, of the Botany School in the University of Cambridge, reviewed the history and effects of coppicing as a woodland practice. Although hardly any of the Cambridgeshire coppiced woods were still actively managed, their present-day structure and species composition gave some ecological insight into the longer-term impacts of the regular removal of underwood, as did the documentation to be found in the College muniments and local authority record offices. The insights gained from such sources helped guide the experimental reintroduction of coppicing into such nature reserves as the Hayley Wood reserve of the Cambridgeshire and Isle of Ely Naturalists' Trust, in terms of assessing the likely impacts upon the microclimate, soils and the incidence and abundance of ground species (Rackham 1967).

As Rackham wrote (1971), the delicate variation and intricate detail of eastern England were well documented and better protected from the changes in silvicultural fashion that had swept so thoroughly through better-wooded areas. The fabric and tradition of medieval woodlands survived. Time, however, was running out. Deciduous woods were being destroyed for arable land or clear-felled and replaced with conifers at an alarming rate. To plan rationally preservation or restoration, there had to be a greater knowledge and understanding of the origins, and particularly the maintenance, of what was now prized so highly. Even if little could actually be protected, a record might at least be made of what was lost. In exciting such interest in what was happening, books such as Rackham's *Trees and Woodland in the British Landscape* (published in Dent's 'Archaeology in the Field' series in 1976) recruited a further body of investigators to the task.

Hedgerow dating

A chapter of Hoskins's book *Fieldwork in Local History* exemplified the emerging interest in vegetation as an historical artefact. As Hoskins (1967, 117–18) wrote, hedges were not only extremely variable in age, but those dating, say, from the early tenth century were likely to show considerable differences in their composition from that of more modern hedges. Those along the woodland edge might still contain evidence of their derivation from ancient woodland. Yet Hoskins confessed to the same inhibition that dissuaded him from writing extensively about industrial archaeology. Engineers and others, with a special technical knowledge, were the best people to write about industrial archaeology, provided they were willing to acquire sufficient knowledge of economic and business history. Hoskins (1967, 11–13) suspected it was easier for them to acquire sufficient history than for historians to attain the requisite knowledge of technology. The same might well have been written of historical ecology, but correspondence with Max D. Hooper since 1965 had pointed to a third way, namely that of collaboration.

Hooper was a member of the Toxic Chemicals and Wild Life Section at Monks Wood, whose research upon the impacts of the new organochlorine pesticides upon wildlife had further emphasised the effects of the wholesale removal of habitats such as the hedgerow. Hooper's interest in landscape history had grown from a wartime visit to the open fields of Laxton in Northamptonshire and the fascination imparted by his classics master, P. H. Reaney, for place-name and archaeological evidence. He had, by 1965, begun to develop a hedge chronology based on the number of shrub species per sample length. Hoskins identified, through correspondence, the location of some twenty-five dated hedges in Devon and, using the botanical detail provided by Hooper, he began to publish such chronological detail, first in the *Western Morning News* and then more generally. Although rarely consulting or forewarning Hooper, there was usually acknowledgement. It was, however, through such an obvious display of active interest in hedgerow history that Hoskins encouraged other local historians to follow. In his *Fieldwork in Local History*, he prescribed how hedgebank maps should be constructed from the documentary evidence, the field evidence either confirming or challenging such sources or, indeed, substituted where the documentation was lacking. A 'wonderful new field of inquiry' was opened up (Hoskins 1967, 124–5, 128–30), in which a true local history demanded both examination of the houses and other buildings of a chosen territory, and a survey, in the countryside at least, of all the hedges. Nevertheless, he both acknowledged and fully appreciated the caveats so strongly emphasised by Hooper and so commonly ignored by later fieldworkers as to the origins of the hedge itself, its original species population, and both the geographical and temporal variations in what might colonise and flourish within the established hedge (Cousins 2004).

Hoskins's eagerness for local historians and 'expert botanists' to join one another in the field was given tangible expression at a one-day conference at Monks Wood in June 1969. The Botanical Society of the British Isles (BSBI) had earlier decided to hold occasional meetings with other bodies. The Meetings Secretary, David E. Allen, had heard of the hedgerow dating method. It was an obvious topic for bringing field botanists and local historians together for what transpired to be the very first time. The Standing Conference for Local History, which acted as co-sponsor, published the main proceedings under the title *Hedges and Local History* (Anon. 1971). Some ninety people attended, almost exactly half being botanists and half local historians. Hooper summarised his findings of a sample of 227 hedges, spread throughout England from Devon through Gloucestershire to Cambridgeshire and Lincolnshire, emphasising how a conjectured recruitment rate of one species per century, as expressed in the broadest terms, was very slow compared with normal grass–scrub–wood succession. Hoskins outlined the range of documents against which such field evidence might be tested. A. D. Bradshaw (Professor of Botany at Liverpool), David Allen and R. H. Richens of the Commonwealth Bureau of Plant Breeding and Genetics suggested in further papers how such dating might be augmented respectively through study of the hybridisation of hawthorn species, the species diversity of bramble, and the detailed distribution of varieties of elm. As intended, the conference recommended that a number of jointly organised local surveys should be carried out in different parts of the country (Anon. 1970; Allen 1971).

Historical Ecology Discussion Group

There was, by the late 1960s, a developing interest in the historical dimension among ecologists generally, but no obvious venue for discussion. An entirely informal committee of Max Hooper, George Peterken, Terry Wells and the present author therefore organised four meetings at Monks Wood in the first three months of 1969 as a way of assessing the value of, and support for, what they called a Historical Ecology Discussion Group. Although it was hoped everyone would derive something of personal value, the overall purpose was to facilitate ecological research. Some fifty-four people, among them historians, geographers, archaeologists and archivists, received a circular, and over forty expressed interest. The first meeting, in January 1969, was led by Collin Bowen (the Principal Investigator at the Salisbury Office of the Royal Commission on Historical Monuments (RCHM)) on field systems and earthworks in the chalk downland. A second meeting, a month later, was introduced by Alan Baker, an historical geographer, on archives and field evidence; a third meeting was led by an archivist from the Northamptonshire Record Office. The meetings were attended by some twenty-five to thirty-five people. The opening of the Monks Wood bar and an informal dinner gave further opportunity for discussion. A further meeting, extending over two days, was led by Oliver Rackham in the autumn of 1969, the indoor sessions on woodland ecology being complemented by the second day spent visiting Hayley Wood. The first meeting to be held away from Monks Wood, in April 1970, was led by the biogeographer Bob Eyre to the uplands and limestone woods of north-east Derbyshire.

There were altogether twenty-seven meetings of the Historical Ecology Discussion Group over a twelve-year period. Colin Tubbs was a regular member. His book *The New Forest*, published by David and Charles in 1968, brought together his uniquely wide, yet detailed, knowledge of the Forest. As he reasoned in the book's introduction, the fact that the processes of change in wildlife habitats are so exceedingly slow means any knowledge of their previous history is especially valuable in discerning what is happening at the present day, and how they might be optimally managed or controlled. Tubbs's purpose was to bring together the archaeological, historical and biological information on the New Forest as an 'Ecological History' – the subtitle given to his book (Tubbs 1968). It was through fieldwork with Tubbs that George Peterken also began to explore the linkage between woodland history and its structure. A paper drawing on their collaborative work since 1963 was published in the *Journal of Applied Ecology*. Three generations of trees were postulated in the unenclosed woodland areas of the New Forest: growth-ring counts of the bases of 141 trees suggested the oldest generation was 200 to 315 years old, and the two younger generations dated from between 1858 and 1915 and from the Second World War respectively. Periodic counts made of the deer, ponies and cattle showed that regeneration seemed to occur only when grazing pressure was below a range of 0.28 to 0.37 feeding units per acre, although that relationship was affected at times by fire and the closure of the canopy (Peterken and Tubbs 1965).

Peterken's appointment to Monks Wood and, more particularly, to the Woodland Management Section, enabled him to undertake a series of studies of the development of vegetation in Staverton Park, Suffolk, the holly wood on Dungeness (Peterken 1969; Peterken and Hubbard 1972) and, more extensively, of Rockingham Forest in Northamptonshire and the Lincolnshire woodlands. From such investigations, at a variety of scales, there emerged the knowledge and understanding with which guidance could be given not only to nature-conservation bodies but also to woodland owners, managers and policy makers generally. A paper published in the *Quarterly Journal of Forestry* laid particular stress on 're-creatability' as the most valuable of the non-marketable attributes of woodland, and made three important points. The first was the significance of continuity· namely, that the site was a primary woodland, as opposed to a secondary woodland where the ground had once been under some alternative land use. Some fifty vascular plant species were found to be more or less confined to such primary woodland in central Lincolnshire. Secondly, such primary woodland contained features, and most obviously the structure and chemical properties of their soils, which could never be re-created once destroyed. And thirdly, there was unique opportunity to study developmental processes, such as those extending over some 200 or 300 years that had enabled the ancient and ornamental woodlands of the New Forest to be formed (Peterken 1974a). The identification of such primary woodlands by their association with species of poor colonising ability (Peterken 1974b) became the basis for an Ancient Woodland Inventory and helped guide nature conservation and forestry policy making (Peterken 1981).

'Old Grassland'

Another regular member of the Historical Ecology Discussion Group was the medieval archaeologist John Hurst. The author's involvement in Hurst's remarkable excavation at Wharram Percy, and the Deserted Medieval Village Research Group, meant that both he and Hurst recognised the immense scope for collaboration between archaeologists and ecologists, both in site protection and research. With the active support of Collin Bowen and Eric Duffey, a two-day symposium was held at Monks Wood in November 1969. It was attended by some 100 archaeologists and ecologists and led by Professor W. F. Grimes and Andrew Saunders of the Inspectorate of Ancient Monuments, and Duncan Poore and Martin Holdgate, respectively Director and Deputy Director (Research) of the Nature Conservancy. Speakers included Ted Smith (secretary of the Society for the Promotion of Nature Reserves), Christopher Taylor of the RCHM and Colin Bonsey, the Land Agent of the Hampshire County Council. The ten papers and discussion were published by the Conservancy as a booklet (Sheail and Wells 1969).

The symposium took as its theme 'Old Grasslands: their archaeological and ecological importance'. Both archaeologists and ecologists reported the heavy loss of sites through ploughing, afforestation and building. A survey in 1964 found that 250 scheduled field monuments in Wiltshire, out of a total of 640, had been destroyed or seriously damaged over the previous ten years. The Conservancy, in the same year, estimated that 90 per cent of the Sites of Special Scientific Interest in Lowland England had been 'liable to a reduction or loss of scientific interest'. Not only might a combined approach help stem such losses, but the report of the official Field Monuments Committee (the Walsh report) reinforced the view of ecologists that the designation of reserves and field monuments could only be justified if appropriate and adequate management was assured (Walsh 1970). Research-wise, both disciplines looked for features which indicated how sites had been used and managed in the past. The use of indicators was fundamental – whether potsherds or the pasque flower, a species intolerant of disturbance (Wells 1968). Both necessarily worked from the evidence as it survived and were, therefore, faced with the dilemma of the representativeness of the earthworks of a deserted medieval village, or the lammas lands of a particular river system. Both kinds of specialist had become increasingly interested in working reconstruction models which tested hypotheses concerning past environments. Thus an experimental earthwork was erected on Overton Down, Wiltshire, to see how archaeological structures were denuded and buried, and alluvial grasslands were grazed and cut in ways thought to have been regularly followed on lammas lands (Sheail 1970; Sheail and Wells 1969).

As Peter Fowler remarked in a note published in *Antiquity*, the symposium was timely, as it illustrated how both archaeology and ecology, albeit self-styled disciplines, were really only specialisms within the environmental field. It was no wonder that they had overlapping research interests and concerns over the continuing destruction of their 'raw material'. Whether dealing with a guardianship site or a nature reserve, there had to be a clarity of purpose – what was good for birds was not necessarily good for the floristic interest. Or, more positively, a primary purpose had to be determined and followed, but with as many secondary roles as possibly could be accommodated. It also implied that archaeologists and ecologists had much to say about the presentation of such sites both to visitors and the media generally, for such perception would not only rebound on those disciplines, but rightly so too. Such sites were being preserved not in the sense of taking them out of use, but rather to promote and display their distinctiveness even more strikingly within the wider landscape (Fowler 1970).

Species indicators

Common to all the initiatives touched upon within this chapter was a striving for such rigour as would win the respect of academic peers and policymakers. It was fitting that the British Ecological Society's annual symposium in European Conservation Year (1970) should be devoted to the scientific management of wildlife communities for conservation, and that historical investigation should be recognised as integral to the technical knowledge required. As Duffey remarked, the classic concepts of ecology had been largely derived from study of situations which had been least subject to human disturbance. There was, however, increasing recognition of the heavy exploitation which the sites of most nature reserves, and indeed the countryside at large, had suffered. As Duffey (1971) illustrated, through a case study of the Woodwalton Fen National Nature Reserve, knowledge of the past was key to understanding the present. Without insights into the history of grazing, cultivation and peat extraction on Woodwalton Fen, and their continued representation in the serial stages of open grassland, scrub and close woodland, there could be no basis for predicting the consequences of different forms of habitat treatment.

For the grassland ecologist, field archaeology offered outstanding opportunities to explore further the notion of species being indicators of long-undisturbed habitats. With Collin Bowen, Terry Wells demonstrated, *via* a survey undertaken in 1970 of the chalk grassland at Parsonage Down in Wiltshire, that the sedge *Carex humilis* might be more abundant in 'old' chalk grasslands but, contrary to previous suggestion, was by no means confined to them (Wells 1985). Further opportunity for such investigation was afforded by survey of the Porton Down ranges of the Chemical Defence Establishment, on the eastern limits of Salisbury Plain. The Nature Conservancy had mounted the most ambitious survey attempted by any country of its conservation resource, namely the Nature Conservation Review (Ratcliffe 1977). Noel King, the Conservancy's officer in Wiltshire, had accordingly alerted Terry Wells to the wildlife significance of the ranges, acquired by the War Office from 1916 onwards and never treated with fertiliser or pesticide. Such documentary evidence as the Tithe Commutation Surveys and the Parish Area Books of the Ordnance Survey, together with the plough marks visible on air photographs suggested that over three-quarters of the 2,750 hectares of the Porton ranges had been ploughed. Six well-defined chalk-grassland types and four scrub communities were frequently separated by linear boundaries, corresponding with grasslands of different conjectured ages. Further evidence of the ages of the communities was provided by the stands of juniper, as surveyed by Lena Ward, and by the size of the ant mounds in what was, in many parts, essentially an 'antscape', using a dating method developed by Tim King (1981).

From such an array of evidence, groups of species, as opposed to individual species, were found to indicate grasslands of different ages, at least within certain time spans. At Porton, grasslands of less than a conjectured fifty years of age were characterised by the presence of *Arrhenatherum elatius, Anthyllis vulneraria, Agrimonia eupatoria, Cerastium arvense, Linaria vulgaris, Pastinaca sativa, Potentilla reptans, Silene vulgaris, Vicia cracca, V. hirsuta* and *V. sativa*. Such species are often found as early colonisers of abandoned arable on chalk soils of moderate fertility. There was a smaller proportion of them at Porton in grasslands of a conjectured fifty to one hundred years of age. Grasslands of over 130 years were characterised by a further and different group, namely *Asperula cynanchica, Carex caryophyllea, Filipendula vulgaris, Helianthemum chamaecistus, Helictotrichon pratense, Pimpinella saxifraga* and *Polygala vulgaris* (Wells *et al.* 1976). Such knowledge of the distinctiveness of the various grassland communities provided a basis for the range-management plans developed and revised from 1973 onwards (Davis and Corbett 2004).

An historical perspective

It is not the purpose of this chapter to lionise what was achieved in historical ecology around the time of European Conservation Year. In a sense, there was little by way of innovation. The leading ecologist, A. G. Tansley, and the Sussex archaeologist, E. Cecil-Curwen, pressed a scheme for the preservation of the South Downs, in evidence to the official National Park Committee in November 1930. They did so on the grounds that the relationship of the 'mixed and attractive assemblage of grasses, mosses and flowering herbs' to the archaeological evidence as to when the ground was last ploughed (say in Celtic or Napoleonic times) was 'of the greatest interest and should yield important contributions to our knowledge' (National Park Committee 1931). In Snowdonia, E. Elfyn Hughes had undertaken detailed field and documentary study since the 1940s of the long-term trends in stocking densities of sheep and cattle in relation to vegetation change and the interpretation of the present-day *Eriophorum* and other communities (Hughes *et al.* 1973).

Neither is it the purpose of the chapter to suggest some kind of whiggish incremental development of those initiatives taken in the late 1960s and early 1970s. The Conservancy's hedgerow research was brought to a close with publication of the volume *Hedges* in the Collins 'New Naturalist' series (Pollard *et al.* 1974). The intention to publish more of the botanical/soils/historical studies of Porton Down and other Defence ranges had to be abandoned as structural changes in the organisation of government research, namely the introduction of the 'customer-contractor' relationship, destroyed such collaborative effort. As to the institutional response, there were clearly bad relations between the Inspectorate and RCHM at a very senior level. The Nature Conservancy was abolished, its conservation and research functions allocated to different government departments. It has remained for later initiatives to alight upon what had been so earnestly advocated and agreed to a generation ago (Grenville 1999).

Any lasting influence of such initiatives as taken at the time of National Nature Weeks, European Conservation Year and beginnings of 'Rescue Archaeology' is to be found rather in individual careers and lives. Out of the entirely unpretentious writings of Hoskins, Beresford, Bowen and Duffey, for example, there developed a much wider appreciation of the scale of human impact and, therefore, of earlier endeavours to manage the natural environment. Where local history and field archaeology provided reference points for the ecologist, articles such as those published by Hooper in the *Birds* magazine of the Royal Society for the Protection of Birds similarly raised awareness among naturalists and conservationists of the relevance and fascination of the historical dimension (Hooper 1970). Further incentive was offered for those wanting to venture out into the countryside, whether through extra-mural classes or less formally by car and on foot (Everson and Williamson 1998). Such inspiration represented something more than a sharing of scholarship. There was a belief that, through a closer understanding of the way landscapes functioned, a saner approach might be found for looking after the countryside and coast of the late twentieth century.

PART TWO

Urban Landscapes

CHAPTER EIGHT

New Markets and Fairs in the Yorkshire Dales, 1550–1750

R. W. Hoyle

In a justly famous essay, W. G. Hoskins wrote of the 'Origin and rise of Market Harborough', a new town established in the Leicestershire manor of Great Bowden in the third quarter of the twelfth century (Hoskins 1963a). At the heart of the town was the space assigned for its market. Indeed, the market was the justification for the town, for a town without a market to draw people to it to buy and sell would have been no more functional than a railway station without trains. The generation following Hoskins elaborated on the formation of new towns in the Middle Ages. There were some memorable single-town studies – Carus-Wilson on Stratford-upon-Avon (Carus-Wilson 1965), for instance – and Beresford wrote on the new towns of Gascony (Beresford 1967). The evidence for the royal grant of market rights was most fully studied by Britnell, who used it to trace the commercialisation of English society in the two centuries before the Black Death (Britnell 1993; 1996).

'Market' has a dual meaning. A market was first a jurisdiction, a local monopoly over buying and selling. It was, second, the space in which the trading took place. A market served to concentrate that trading both spatially and temporally (to one or two days a week) whilst stimulating commercial activity. Markets are themselves spatially differentiated so that vendors of butter are segregated from those of cheese, and certainly from the grain or malt dealers and so on. This space also needs public facilities: paving, a cross (perhaps of symbolic rather than practical value), a tollbooth, possibly a court room. Then there were those elements which private enterprise might provide: shops and pubs (although the public buildings often had shops incorporated into their structure). A market, then, is a distinctive element within the landscape: it also serves to transform the economic society and the wider landscape. An increase in the number of markets implies greater demand, while the rise of new markets may imply a shift in the location of demand. The English understood this transformative aspect in the sixteenth and seventeenth centuries and sought to introduce towns and markets into Ireland precisely because they stimulated the rural economy to operate at a higher level (Proudfoot 2002 and Crawford 2002 summarise much of this literature). Likewise, the establishment of new villages in Scotland after 1730 was part and parcel of policies to increase economic activity (for instance Smout 1970; Philip 2005 is merely the most recent discussion). Fairs served much the same purpose, allowing the exchange of goods – agricultural and manufactured – between town and country. At a later date they were also the locale of the labour market, where hirings were made.

Securing a grant

The result of half a century of writing on new markets in medieval England after Hoskins's pioneering essay is that the processes which resulted in the grant by letters patent of a market or fair in the Middle Ages are now well understood, as is the chronology of grants. Most recently, a valuable gazetteer of medieval grants has appeared (Letters *et al.* 2003; all dates of medieval charters are taken from this without further references). Less attention has been paid to the grant of markets and fairs after this date, although one recent writer suggested that the establishment of new markets (as opposed to new towns) was quite common in seventeenth-century England (Dyer 2002). The process of securing a grant at this late date remained essentially the same as that employed in the Middle Ages. The first step was a petition to the Crown from the promoter of the market or fair for a writ of *ad quod damnum*. This was placed by the sheriff before a jury in the county concerned. The question asked by the writ was whether the grant sought would be to the detriment of the Crown or other existing rights within the county: if the jury found that it was not, then the return initiated the processes leading to the issue of letters patent. This process was used as late as 1791 to establish a new market and fairs at Middleton in Lancashire (now Greater Manchester); from the first enquiry into the procedures to be followed to the issue of the letters patent, the process took eight months.[1]

As we shall see, the process could be much more complicated than this makes it appear, not least because the jurors hearing the writ could hold that the grant of a new market was damaging to existing interests. Moreover, whilst there were always unchartered markets and fairs in existence, there is some evidence to show that 'new' grants may have been made to an existing market seeking authority for its continued conduct after it came under attack from a neighbouring market whose trade was leaching away to the unlicensed inter-loper. Examples from the Yorkshire Dales illustrate this. It was explained in the grant of a market and fairs at Askrigg, of 1587, that there had been a 'crowded gathering' at Askrigg on a Thursday for a long time at which victuals and other wares were sold amongst the countrymen of the district. Other neighbouring towns had tried to suppress the market so that the country people would have to travel to their markets instead. The grant was therefore to answer the need of petitioners from Askrigg and the surrounding countryside not for their own market, but for a legally constituted market (*CPR* 2003, no. 173). Much the same was said when charters for fairs were granted for Adwalton near Bradford in 1577 and Stokesley in Cleveland in 1585 (*CPR* 1982, no. 2208; *CPR* 2002, no. 368.) There are clues that the grant of a charter to Hawes in 1700 followed complaints against the holding of a market there by Askrigg, whose business it progressively took, so that by the end of the century the market for Upper Wensleydale was at Hawes and not Askrigg (*CSPD* 1937, 262, 389). At Settle, the request for additional fair days made in 1708 was justified by the fact that the fairs were happening anyhow, but as they had no legal standing, they brought the landlord no tolls (Brayshaw and Robinson 1932, 126).

These examples should make it plain enough that markets could be a source of contention in the two centuries after 1550. They also offer more or less clear-cut evidence that a charter might formalise a market rather than bring one into existence. And there are good reasons why this should be so. The process of securing a charter was not cheap and the costs might be open-ended if a petition ran into counter-lobbying. A speculative application for a market could therefore chance a sizeable sum of money. Moreover, this was not all that needed to be ventured: a plausible market needed a tollbooth, a paved area, a cross and other street furniture. It might involve laying out a new area as a market place. The best way to guarantee that the investment would earn a return was to develop a site which already had some or all of the functions of a market. This said, there is quite compelling evidence to suggest that at least one and perhaps two of the markets considered in this chapter were developments *ab initio*.

New markets in the Dales

This chapter is concerned with the northern Yorkshire Dales, defined, broadly speaking, as the highlands north of a line starting in Skipton and curving northwards through Ripon, Masham and Richmond. In 1350 the higher Dales were not well supplied with market sites. Swaledale and Wensleydale were both primarily served by Richmond. As late as the 1670s, Richmond said that 'The inhabitants of Wensladaile and Swailedaile are the upholders of Richmond markett for corne'.[2] In Swaledale there was no market centre higher up the dale than Richmond, although Leland notes an unchartered market at Grinton (Fieldhouse and Jennings 1978, 160).[3] Speight, perhaps recording an oral tradition, thought that Grinton market had shifted to Reeth after the latter had secured its charter (Speight 1897, 240–1). In Wensleydale there was Masham and four others in the middle dale: East Witton (granted 1219), Constable Burton (1321), Wensley (1202) and Carperby (1305). Whether all, or indeed any, of the four were still active in the sixteenth century is a moot point: there appears to have been an attempt to revive Carperby in 1534[4] but at a guess there was no market in the dale above Masham in 1550, except perhaps for the unlicensed market at Askrigg. In Wharfedale, a market and fair had been established at Grassington in 1281 and in upper Ribblesdale in Settle in 1249. There is a single early seventeenth-century reference to Kettlewell in upper Wharfedale as a market town: there is no charter (Willan and Crossley 1941, 146).

The only new market established after the climactic of the fourteenth century was at Middleham, which received two grants, one for a Monday market and fairs in 1389, and one for additional fairs in 1479. These grants reflect the political leverage of successive lords of Middleham Castle, and perhaps, too, the need for their household to have a ready supply of victuals. The result is a small town with two market places and two market crosses, a much more elaborate market structure than the town itself required. Richmond doubtless viewed these grants with dismay but may well have thought it prudent to stifle its opposition. In 1440 though, making a plea of poverty, the town noted the Middleham markets amongst those which were depriving it of trade (*CPR* 1907, no. 452). The only other grant of a market in the longeur after 1350 is at Sedbergh in 1516; the town had received an earlier grant in 1251 which had either been forgotten or was so far in abeyance that a new charter was thought necessary to revive the market.

From the mid-sixteenth century we see the establishment of 'new' markets throughout the northern highlands, as well as the award of additional trading concessions to established market centres. Whilst a full account of the elaboration of the upland market network will have to await another occasion, market charters were granted for the first time to upland centres such as Hawkshead (1606) and Ambleside (1650), and villages in peripheral areas such as Workington (1573). Askrigg conforms to this pattern. Established centres sought fortnightly cattle fairs. One of the earliest was at Richmond (1567); Skipton received one in 1597 and Masham in 1632, and Middleham sought grants in the mid-1650s. In the case of the Skipton grant, it was said to be useful to those living within 40 miles (64 km) for the buying, selling and exhibition of horses, cows, bullocks and sheep (Dawson 1882, 268).

The development of new markets and the spread of markets into the upper reaches of the highland valleys can be seen most plainly in Swaledale and Wensleydale. The elaboration of the market network was not welcomed by Richmond, which was forceful in its attempts to protect its local hegemony. When the charter granted to Askrigg in 1587 reports that neighbouring markets had tried to have the informal Askrigg market suppressed, one suspects the hand of Richmond. Forty years later, the town objected to attempts by Darlington to increase the number of fairs it held, and in the mid-1650s it opposed the establishment of a fortnightly fair at Middleham. The first application Middleham made in early 1657 was for a fortnightly fair to be held on alternate Fridays from the first Friday in April to the end of October. The jurors replied that if the grant was made it would be to the hurt and damage to Richmond to the extent of £200 per annum, to Masham of £150, to Bedale of £50 and to Northallerton of £100. Richmond, Bedale and Masham opposed a further application in 1658, citing a potential loss of £200 to Richmond, £110 to Masham and £160 to Bedale, besides the loss to the county (Fieldhouse and Jennings 1978, 169). In all, Middleham secured four writs of *ad quod damnum* in 1657–8.[5] In the early 1670s Richmond was objecting to the idea that fortnightly fairs should be held at Leyburn, arguing that a fortnightly fair would lead in time to a weekly market, and asked, should the grant take place, to be indemnified by £200 a year.[6] Market charters for Leyburn were granted in

1684 and 1686, the first for a fortnightly (cattle) fair, the second, in accordance with Richmond's prediction, for a weekly market. The second of the grants was secured in conditions of secrecy: '… the instructions your honour gives in order to have fairs and a Friday market at Leyburn will be pursued with all secrecy here and if kept in secret in the country I doubt not but that the patent will be obtained without opposition …'.[7] But the secrecy was breached, and the lessee of the tolls at Middleham spent £30 on resisting the grants; however, his efforts were to no avail.[8] By the early nineteenth century the Middleham market was pretty well defunct whilst that at Leyburn flourished (Fothergill 1805, 95).

In Wensleydale, Askrigg market, having been placed on a formal footing in 1587, in turn lost out to Hawes (for much of what follows: Lennie 2001). The development of the town of Hawes is, for the moment, mysterious. A rental of *c.*1560 shows that there were two subdivided vaccaries of East Hawes and West Hawes with nine tenants each.[9] The 1605 survey lists twenty houses (Willan and Crossley 1941, 116–17). The town seems not to have been treated as a separate entity in the Hearth Tax. The relative standing of Askrigg and Hawes in the late seventeenth century is perhaps shown by the return of rooms and stabling commissioned by the army in 1686, which recorded thirty-four beds for hire and stabling for eighty-six horses in Askrigg but only four and seven respectively in Hawes (Richmond, by comparison, had ninety-nine beds and stabling for 228 horses).[10] But Hawes had a chapel to serve the upper Dale by 1483, carved out of the larger parish of Askrigg. By 1680 the inhabitants of the chapelry of Hawes were chaffing at having to pay church rates to Askrigg and, after a series of disputes, the chapelry won its freedom from its mother church in 1687. It seems probable that at the very end of the century the inhabitants of Askrigg challenged the right of the inhabitants of Hawes to hold a market. Hawes countered by securing a charter to confirm their right to hold a weekly market (Hartley and Ingleby 1953, 88–9).[11] At some point over the following quarter century there was further litigation as the Askrigg men tried to have the Hawes market suppressed, but they failed and the centre of economic activity in the upper Dale shifted to Hawes.

Whilst it would be wrong to suppose that every grant of a market was a success – certainly by 1800 a good number of them, including Askrigg, had ceased to be held – it is clear that contemporaries saw the need for more markets in the highlands in the later sixteenth and seventeenth centuries and, in so far as the establishment of a market cost money, they were confident that a new market charter would recover its costs. Why this should be can be explained in several ways. One is that it was an answer to population growth in the Dales: it might not be unreasonable to associate the establishment of a market at Reeth with the development of the Swaledale and Arkengarthdale lead-mining industry in the later seventeenth century. It also seems likely that a good number of the fortnightly markets were intended to serve the cattle trade. Cattle, though, were not the only products sold through these market places for consumption at a distance. Richmond also dealt in butter, which was transshipped through

Yarm, and handknitted goods ('the chief trade of the town from the late six-teenth to the early eighteenth century') and we must suppose that the smaller markets did too (Fieldhouse and Jennings 1978, 153–4).

If cattle were the main export product, then grain was imported through the same markets. In part this reflects the fact that the population now exceeded the capacity of the arable of the district to support it. At Settle, evidence was given in a mill case of 1720–1 that only about a quarter of the inhabitants could be supported by the grain grown within the township. Moreover, Settle innkeepers held that malt made with barley grown in the East Riding was superior to that made from locally grown barley, and a long-distance trade in grain into the manor, through Settle market, had emerged (Brayshaw and Robinson 1932, 125).

The grant of a new market charter is therefore an indirect indication of economic change in the uplands. Who, however, sought these grants? Four categories of grantees can be identified. Firstly, there was the sole corporate town in the district, Richmond. Secondly, a large number of grantees were landlords. Here, *prima facie*, we can see evidence of landowners using markets to improve their estates; we will turn to this in a moment. Thirdly, there are locally prominent individuals who took grants on behalf of their communities or neighbours. This is the case with Hawes, where the petition for the grant explained that the town was not corporate and so incapable of receiving the king's grant. The principal inhabitants and freeholders therefore nominated Mathew Wetherald Esq. to act in trust for them (*CSPD* 1937, 262). Fourthly, it was not unknown for the inhabitants collectively to receive a grant on behalf of their town. The prime case is at Askrigg, but the inhabitants of Middleham sought additional grants in the 1650s and such initiatives can be paralleled elsewhere in the North.

Over the northern highlands as whole, about two-thirds of the known grants were sought by and made to landlords and it is hard not to suppose that their prime objective was to improve their estates along the lines familiar from both Ireland and Scotland. This may not be as clear-cut as it seems, however. When the third Earl of Cumberland sought grants of additional fairs in Skipton (1597) and Kirby Stephen (1606), he was almost certainly acting at the suggestion of his tenants. When his descendant the Earl of Burlington applied for a new charter for Settle in 1708, we may suspect that it was the inhabitants of the town who prompted him to do so, for the manorial inter-est in Settle had begun to atrophy over a century earlier and the relationship between Burlington and north Craven must have been pretty tenuous by the early eighteenth century.

Two landlord initiatives stick out, though, as being especially worthy of consideration. We have already seen – and will explore further – how Charles, Marquis of Winchester, obtained a market charter for a fortnightly market at Leyburn in 1684 and then, having found that the day of the first market was not convenient, secured a weekly market in 1686. (There are reasons to believe that this explanation was highly specious.) In addition, Philip Lord

Wharton certainly comes over as having swallowed the view that markets could improve estates. In early 1687 he had a writ of *ad quod damnum* for a market and fairs at Shap in Westmorland; later the same year he had a writ for fairs at his manor of Healaugh near York; and in 1693 he had a writ for a market at Reeth to serve his estates in Upper Swaledale. He also sought a new market for his estates at Woburn in Buckinghamshire in 1687.[12]

New market places

The cost of establishing a new market began but did not end with the cost of securing the charter. At Askrigg the promoter of the charter, Peter Thornton, received a 21-year lease of the tolls from the Crown, out of which he was to establish the basic infrastructure requirements of the market. By the early eighteenth century the tolls raised by the Askrigg markets and fairs were used for many local purposes, including prizes for the fell race, but the first call on them seems to have been the maintenance of the paving, market buildings and cross (Hartley and Ingleby 1953, 92–6).[13] At Easingwold, where George Hall secured a charter for a weekly market, a fortnightly cattle market and two fairs in 1639 (perhaps acting on the town's behalf), the town came to an agreement with him in 1646 that they would give him a house and the adjacent wasteland on which to build a tollbooth. The new building was to be 10 yards long and 6 yards wide (9 by 5.5 m) with stairs at the west end to an upper storey. It was to be used for the town's court and other meetings. The town also agreed to provide sufficient stone to pave the market place. At Middleham, whose tolls were then owned by the City of London, the costs of maintenance seem to have been passed onto their lessee who, in 1688, expended a little short of £160 on the building of 'toll, shops and shambles'. The following year 6s 6d was spent on paving the shambles and on two new planks, perhaps for seating. This may have all been an attempt to recoup business after the establishment of the market at Leyburn. The tollbooth was a substantial two-storey building, with six open arches facing the market place and external stairs to rooms over. The building probably had a short life, as by 1805 the Middleham market had largely shifted to Leyburn – it was explained that the latter was easier to access as there was no river to ford – and there were discussions about pulling down the tollbooth, which now survives only in an early nineteenth-century print (Fothergill 1805, 95; Brown ?1983, 21).[14]

If this suggests that a village or small town acquiring a market might need to strike a deal with someone to put the market infrastructure in place, then what about the market place itself? The ready assumption – that market places are invariably medieval in their origin – ought to be treated with caution. An example which proves the contrary is Penistone, where a market charter was sought in 1698 and granted the following year in the teeth of opposition from the neighbouring markets of Barnsley and Huddersfield. By 1749 a market square had appeared in front of the parish church and churchyard and at one end of the town street, fringed with inns and shops. But exactly

FIGURE 31.
Reeth in 1971.
Meridian Airmaps 167
71 024, and courtesy
© YDNP

how this came about is uncertain. As Penistone's historian asked, 'Was there, one wonders, a village green on this site before 1699, or were some properties cleared away?', a question which can be posed of all the market places discussed subsequently (Hey 2002b, 98–103). Even where a medieval charter was granted, it may not follow that the market place is of the same date as the charter. Settle has a charter of 1249 and a splendid roughly rectangular market place which had a tollbooth (on the site of the town hall and first mentioned in 1716): but is it medieval? There is no documentary or map material extant which would decide the matter. The Settle historians Brayshaw and Robinson leaned towards the view that Settle had shifted its centre of gravity from Upper Settle (higher up the hill, on the road to Malham, where there is a sizeable green) to the market place, and that that the market place is early modern rather than medieval (Brayshaw and Robinson 1932, 140, 126). This is ultimately speculation: at the moment, the best that one can say is that it is fringed by late seventeenth-century houses and is referred to as a 'very convenient large square' in 1708. It is shown on a recently discovered map of the 1760s in its current form (King 2005). It would be perverse for a town to have a market place without a market: and so where we have a market place but evidence that the market is post-medieval, then the assumption may fairly be made that the market place is itself post-medieval.

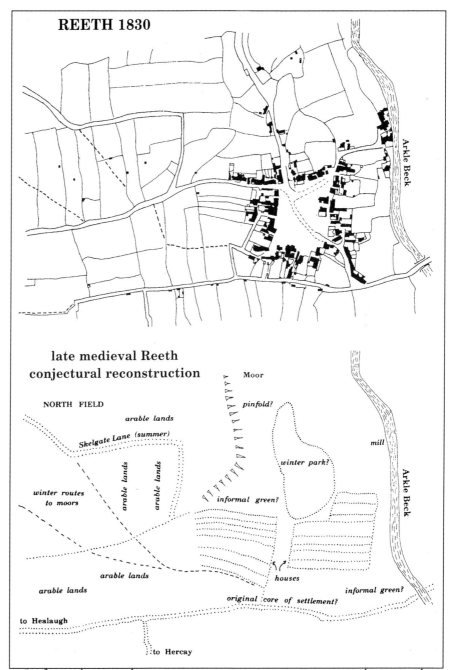

REETH 1830

Arkle Beck

late medieval Reeth
conjectural reconstruction

Moor

NORTH FIELD

arable lands

pinfold?

Skelgate Lane (summer)

mill

arable lands

winter park?

arable lands

Arkle Beck

winter routes
to moors

informal green?

arable lands

houses

informal green?

arable lands

original core of settlement?

to Healaugh

to Hercay

FIGURE 32.
Above: Reeth in 1830;
below: late medieval
Reeth, as conjecturally
reconstructed by
Andrew Fleming (1998,
106).

In fact, where markets came into existence on a customary basis or where charters were secured by the inhabitants or their representatives, there seems to be something of a rule of thumb that the market places are small and meagre. Askrigg provides a good example of this. Here the market place is opposite the churchyard gate, but is little more than a paved triangular green, and any extensive fair must have spread up through the streets of the village. Hawes is no better: the market place is really only a widening of the village street, although from its location one wonders whether it is not a westwards addition to the village on flat and level ground.

However, where markets and fairs were established by landlords as part of the development of their estates, there was a greater chance that the market place might be laid out along rather grander lines. Two examples of this can be offered. Reeth has a substantial market place or fairground today; the northern part of this is flat, but the southern part falls away quite sharply (Figure 31). The indications all point towards the market at Reeth being created after the charter of 1693 and being grafted onto an existing settlement which the documentary evidence shows had both shops and alehouses. Exactly where this settlement was has to be a matter of speculation: there is no early map evidence which helps us and the village as it exists today appears to contain few if any buildings which date to before the second quarter of the eighteenth century. Indeed, some of the oldest buildings in the village appear to be those flanking the green on the west side, where the Kings Arms bears a datestone of 1734, forty years after the establishment of the market. Fleming has offered a conjectural reconstruction of late medieval Reeth, suggesting that the present market place or green incorporates within it the original village green and the rows of tofts which faced onto it, but it is not clear just what the basis of this reconstruction is, or how it was possible to move from the speculative landscape to the evidenced without acquiring the property rights of those who owned the land incorporated in the market place (Figure 32). If this were not puzzle enough, the aerial photograph (Figure 31) and map (Figure 32) both show how what appear at first sight to be straight edges to the western edge of the market place are in fact markedly bowed: that is, there is no building line. Is it a planned market? On the other hand, the island of buildings on the east side of the market place (now the post office and shop) may be a tollbooth; alternatively, they may pre-date the market square. Clinching evidence, one way or another, is for the moment lacking.

The clearest example of a village being remodelled around a new market grant comes from Leyburn, which today possesses a large rectangular market place in which is a detached Victorian town hall after the fashion of Settle (Figure 33). Charters were granted to Leyburn at the request of the Marquis of Winchester in 1684 (for a fortnightly fair) and 1686 (for a weekly market). There may have been a move to secure a market in the previous decade for there survives a protest by Richmond addressed to Winchester using his earlier title of Charles Lord St John and Basing: he succeeded to the Marquisate in 1675.[15] The creation of a market at Leyburn was part of a larger plan which included the development of the house and grounds at Castle Bolton, which lay some 2 miles (3.2 km) to the west and were approached along a drive from Wensley. This estate was intended for Winchester's son, whom he was introducing to North Riding society in the mid-1680s. Writing to him in March 1687, Winchester told him that:

the four new gardens I have built you near the bridge here are finished and planted with the best fruit which I had from London, and I am also building you a fine house of 7 or 8 rooms to answer the gardens and I took such care to get the stones early and led in winter and ye work to begin last week that I hope it will be done by your coming hither. I have also built a bridge over the brook near John Thornton's at Redmire which will be finished this week that we may pass thither for pleasure or business, and ye country to Leyburn market and fairs of which last we have had two very great ones and the market is considerable and I have built a shambles in the market place and paved the market round about and am building a handsome tollbooth begin three weeks since which will cost 'twixt £200 and £300 and a cross for market women to sit on in selling so that I have made Bolton as fine as I can make it and a market to supply you with beast, sheep, corn, fowl, fish and all other manner of things.[16]

The tollbooth or old market hall was replaced by a new town hall in 1856, but a surviving daguerreotype shows a substantial three-storey building with three shops on the ground floor and external stairs to the upper floors. A further building, perhaps the shambles mentioned by Winchester, was demolished in 1799 (Butterworth and Butterworth 2002, 13–14, 56).

Whilst Winchester was certainly the author of the market furniture, was he also the creator of the market place at Leyburn seen in Figure 33 and on a rather crude estate plan of 1730 (Figure 34) which plainly shows his cross, tollbooth and shambles? One point that this plan makes is that there was no unity of ownership in the town, which must have made the creation of a market place difficult to achieve. The surviving title deeds do not suggest that land was bought or exchanges made to clear the way for its laying out.

The difficulty of dealing with freeholds offers a clue to the laying out of the market. In the market place in Figure 34 may be seen two small tenements at the west end of the market (lettercd b and k). These presumably belonged to the larger freehold properties (B and K) to the north. One wonders whether these detached buildings mark a former frontage to the plots B and K, the southern ends of which had been incorporated into Winchester's market. On the other hand, cottages standing further back in plot K and on the plot adjacent to it now mark the frontage of the market place and are plainly visible as early eighteenth-century buildings in Figure 34. Likewise, buildings on the site of k survive in the modern market place. The market place may therefore incorporate within it the property of freeholders.

The 1730 map also shows how there was an alternative centre to Leyburn just to the north, around a triangular green, Grove Square. This may be an earlier focus: significantly, it is labelled 'Leyburn town' on the 1730 map. The surviving rentals certainly show that something was going on, but are opaque as to exactly what. The first extant rental, of 1676, lists twenty-five tenants, of whom eight were sizeable farmers paying more than £10 in rent. By the time of the next rental, in 1683, the composition of the tenants has changed completely, with thirty-six tenants paying a little short of £160, the large tenants

having disappeared. In 1689 forty-four tenants paid £243 annually, but four-teen paid less than a pound (and some of them only 1s a year) for what cannot have been more than cottages.[17] One suspects strongly that some of those creeping into the rental were craftsmen and shopkeepers, and that what the rentals indicate is the normally undocumented process of urbanisation.

Some implications ... and conclusions

The economic development of the highland North, in common with that of Ireland and Scotland, was accompanied by the establishment of new markets and fairs. Some appeared spontaneously and might only be retrospectively accorded formal status by the grant of a royal charter. The reason for seeking the legitimation of markets was, as much as anything, that markets were highly political. Whilst we might see the appearance of new markets as illustrating the development of the rural economy and a growth in trade, the establishment of a new market took trade from those already in existence. Unlicensed markets could therefore be vulnerable to challenges from established (or at least chartered) markets. Attempts to secure additional trading liberties might also be opposed. There is plainly a politics of market rivalry, seen between Richmond and the towns higher in Wensleydale and Swaledale, and then between Middleham and Leyburn and Askrigg and Hawes, which is largely concealed from us.

FIGURE 34.
Leyburn, from an
estate map of *c.*1730.
NYRO, ZBO/M 1/2.

New markets came into existence as the result of both local initiatives and attempts to improve estates by landowners. Who sponsored a new market may have had consequences for the physical form it took and the grandeur of the market's buildings and street furniture. The implication behind the creation of new markets in this period is that some of the familiar market places of the Dales are almost certainly post-medieval in origin. One would like to know, too, whether a longer-established market, such as that at Masham, occupied a space fixed in the Middle Ages or one enlarged in the early modern period. The poverty of the archives, and in particular the lack of early maps, will probably always make it impossible to say for certain: but the possibility should be borne in mind.

There is a further Hoskins connection to this which takes us in a direction which lack of space precludes us from exploring. Hoskins was the great advocate of the notion of the Great Rebuilding. The establishment of additional market centres and additional markets in the established market towns points to economic development. So too does the coincidental rebuilding of the houses of the Dales. Whilst every Dale is different, one is always struck by the way in which they contain an abundance of housing, often of quality, erected in the three-quarters of a century after about 1650. Markets provided the outlet for the products – often cattle – which produced the prosperity which enabled rebuilding to take place. Both testify to deeper currents in the landscape and economy of the highland North.

Acknowledgements

I am grateful to Robert White of the Yorkshire Dales National Park, and the North Yorkshire Record Office, for supplying photographs at very short notice, to Chris Hallas for her interest and to Gill and the boys for enduring an enthusiasm for market places on days out.

Notes

1. Greater Manchester RO, E7/5/1/50/1–19, 50.
2. NYRO, ZBO, NRA, 2298. At the time I used this collection, it was under rearrangement but new numbers had not been assigned to much of the material. References to the NRA list will finally be superseded.
3. The claim that there was a late medieval market at Reeth is based on slight evidence and is almost certainly erroneous. VCH infers the existence of a market from the inclusion of 'tolls' in a feet of fine conveying Healaugh manor of 1513 and from here it has crept into Letters *et al.* 2003, vol. II, 402. But the accounts of Healaugh when in Crown hands in the 1530s do not include tolls, nor is any market mentioned in the estate survey of 1561 or the valor of 1605. *VCH* 1914–23, vol. I, 238; TNA:PRO, E315/288; Ashcroft 1984, 13–22, 46.
4. NYRO, ZBO, NRA 775.
5. TNA:PRO, C202/40/4, 41/4.
6. NYRO, ZBO, NRA list 2298.
7. NYRO, ZBO, NRA 929–30, 933. For the securing of the 1686 charter, see the references in the letters of Thomas Benelowes to Winchester of 16 January, 6 February, 16 February (from which the quote is taken) and 3 July 1686.
8. NYRO, PC/Mid/2/7/6.
9. Corporation of London Archives, CLA/044/03/007/6.
10. TNA:PRO, WO 30/48.
11. *cf.* NYRO, QSB 1699, nos 389–94, 400.
12. TNA:PRO, C202/72/1, 78/1.
13. TNA:PRO, E112/1317/56; E134/7 Geo. II/Mich. 29.
14. NYRO, PC/EAW/3/5; PC/Mid/2/7/10.
15. NYRO, ZBO, NRA 2298.
16. NYRO, ZBO/VIII/2138, 11 March 1686/7.
17. NYRO, ZBO, IV/3/2–8 *passim*.

CHAPTER NINE

Rus et Urbe? The Hinterland and Landscape of Georgian Chester

Jon Stobart

Hoskins viewed the urban landscape as a palimpsest, offering innumerable important clues about the historical development of the town. His own reading emphasised morphology, culture and economy, and was organised under the headings of planned, open-field and market towns (Hoskins 1955). Each of these themes has been developed further in the intervening years: Conzen pioneered systematic analysis of the town plan (see Anon. 2000), whilst Chalklin (1974), Borsay (1989) and Girouard (1990), amongst others, have focused on cultural and economic interpretations. Yet all these readings have shown a reluctance to look much beyond the geographical bounds of the town and consider the influence that rural–urban interaction had on the townscape. The influence of London looms large in some analyses (notably those of Borsay), but the forces for change have been seen as largely urban, even if they lay outside the individual town. In the most recent general surveys of early modern towns, both Chalklin (2001) and Ellis (2001) assess the landscape and built environment in terms of architects and builders; houses, streets and public buildings; degradation and improvement. When the countryside is seen as entering the town, it is often portrayed in terms of the development of fashionable squares in west London and Bath (Girouard 1990, 162–3; Arnold 2004). The first Duke of Buckingham, for example, had *Rus in Urbe* inscribed on the frieze of his London residence, whilst John Wood fronted the Royal Crescent at Bath with a steeply sloping meadow on which grazed sheep and horses. This was an attempt to fuse a romanticised image of the countryside with the elegance and sophistication of the town, and formed a conscious parallel with the landscaped parks which surrounded many English country houses. Of course, this somewhat artificial and abstruse form of rural–urban relationship was shaped very much by the concerns and priorities of urban architects – a result of idealised images of town and country.

A concentration on such developments masks a whole range of more pragmatic and certainly more widespread ways in which the country had an influence on the development and landscape of the town. One important influence which Hoskins himself emphasised was the impact of (rural) land ownership, which could profoundly affect the pace and shape of urban expansion. Thus the common fields around Nottingham effectively strangled physical growth and helped to produce the squalid courts and yards that characterised the town in the mid-nineteenth century. In Stamford, it was the power of Lord Exeter which prevented land from becoming available for development and ossified the town in its early modern form (Hoskins 1955). Here, the rural is seen as a constraining, even negative influence. Everitt (1979) and Borsay (2003), however, highlight a range of dynamic and positive links between towns and their hinterlands. Towns were administrative centres, nurseries of skill, social and political centres, and mediators of new cultural activities and attitudes. In all these roles, the links between the county town and its hinterland – not least in the form of the rural gentry – were close and mutual. The nature of the hinterland would thus influence the economy, society, culture and built environment of the town.

The aim of this chapter is to build on these ideas by exploring how the geography and nature of the hinterland helped to shape a town's character and landscape. I take Chester as the object of study, in part because, as Everitt (1979) argued, county towns had especially close links with their hinterlands. However, Chester's position at the western edge of Cheshire and its role as a wider regional centre meant that its relationships with its county and the geography of its wider hinterland were more complex, and the consequent influences that these had on the townscape were more nuanced, than Everitt would allow. Crucial for my argument here, though, is Everitt's more general assertion of a causal link – a mutually constitutive relationship – between town and hinterland. Thus, the analysis is divided into two halves. I begin by reconstructing something of the geographical bounds of the hinterland and the nature of the links which tied together town and country. I then build on this by offering an assessment of the ways in which these links helped to shape the landscape of Chester in the eighteenth and early nineteenth centuries, highlighting especially the influence of the rural gentry (see Borsay 2003).

Defining the hinterland: boundaries and links

Establishing the geographical bounds of any region is a conceptual as well as an empirical exercise. Without becoming bogged down in a lengthy discussion of how regions might be defined, it is useful to make some reference here to the work of the Finnish geographer Ansi Paasi (1986). He emphasises, amongst other things, the importance of spatial and functional cohesion (what he terms 'territorial shape'), and group identity with and within the region (so-called 'conceptual shape'). For our purposes, the first of these involves tracing the activities and material linkages which tied Chester to its hinterland, whilst the second requires us to uncover something of the identity of and people's identity with the region defined.

In terms of political and administrative activity, Chester was the location of the county assizes and quarter sessions. Naturally, the jurisdiction of these courts was defined by the county boundaries, as were the linkages they engendered. The ninety or so Justices of the Peace who served in the mid-eighteenth century were mostly drawn from Cheshire's rural gentry and clergy (*VCH* 2003, 61–2). The interests of county and town were thus tied together, not least because these legal and administrative links were overlain by the social seasons which developed around the sittings of the courts. The grand processions which marked the start of the Assizes brought together the city and county authorities, whilst Chester formed the natural social centre, more generally, for many of Cheshire's rural gentry. It thus served to integrate the middling sorts of town and country in an atmosphere of fashionable sociability (Stobart 1998, 2002). This town–county link was strengthened by Chester's role as the centre of polling and electioneering activity in the elections of Cheshire's two MPs. Again, this periodically drew the county's elite and freeholders into Chester. Conversely, about one-third of the freemen who made up Chester's electorate were resident outside the town, mostly in Cheshire, but with small numbers spread across seven other counties (Kennett 1987, 20–1). Thus whilst the core relationship was between city and county, a much larger region could also be drawn. Such a situation was by no means unusual and gave rural interests considerable importance in the political affairs of many towns (Ellis 2001, 114–20; Borsay 2003, 285–8). In Chester such groups, and especially the increasingly influential Grosvenors, helped to maintain the town as a Tory stronghold through much of the eighteenth century, but the interests of county and town did not always coincide. For example, attempts to improve the Dee navigation in the 1730s generated real conflict between the rural squires who farmed the land through which the channel would be cut and Chester merchants. Secret opposition from Sir Richard Grosvenor, the city's MP, led to a number of violently contested elections in which the issue of the navigation scheme, and the apposition of town and country more generally, became central issues (Baskerville 1980).

A wider hinterland was also defined by Chester's role as a diocesan centre. The see, created in 1543, encompassed parts of Westmorland, Cumberland, Yorkshire and north Wales, as well as the whole of Lancashire and Cheshire. Whilst the northern section of this area was under the semi-autonomous authority of the Archdeacon of Richmond, the Consistory Court at Chester formed an important legal centre for Cheshire, Lancashire south of the Ribble and certain parts of Denbighshire and Flintshire. This led many clergy to reside in the city, adding another layer to its social composition, and drew many more into the orbit of the city. A typical example is Peter Lancaster, the rector of Tarporley, a village some 16 km from Chester. His probate inventory shows that, when he died in 1709, the vast majority of his property (including over £40 of books) were in the prebendary house in Chester rather than the rectory in Tarporley.[1] Yet his presence in both places linked them at a personal and institutional level. Furthermore, the role of the Consistory Court in granting probate made Chester an important location in the distribution and redistribution of property and wealth in north-west England, and linked the city to commercial developments elsewhere in the region (Stobart 2002, 178–80).

The social sphere of Chester was also extensive. As a cultural centre, the town drew visitors from across north-west England and north Wales, both to its established winter season and its summer races, which were timed to coincide with the assizes. As with the established resort towns, aristocratic support was important, and the Grosvenors helped to make Chester's gatherings the most fashionable in the region (Kennett 1987, 36–7). This provided an important boost to the city's economy at a time when many traditional activities (such as leatherworking, textile production and overseas trade) were in relative or absolute decline. It also served to further integrate the gentry and middling sorts of town and country in an atmosphere of fashionable sociability. A measure of the geography of these social links can be gained by mapping the distribution of the executors and administrators named in the probate records of Chester residents (see Stobart 2002, 180–1). These people included friends and family, business associates and fellow professionals. Their distribution suggests strong interaction between the city and its immediate surroundings, and a wider hinterland stretching across Cheshire and into Lancashire, Shropshire and northeast Wales. Naturally, no single individual enjoyed such extensive links; but, taken together, wide-ranging social networks were centred on the town, and tied its fortunes to those of the villages and towns of the surrounding region.

Finally, and perhaps most essentially, economic activities served to draw together town and country. At a basic level, this involved the buying and selling of goods: the market area thus defined a town's economic hinterland. The problem here is that the size of this market area depended upon the nature of the goods and the presence of competing centres, as well as the character of the town itself. To exemplify: records from the city's horse markets show that most individuals travelling to Chester to purchase horses in the late seventeenth and early eighteenth centuries came from within 19 km.[2] This reflected strong local demand, but also the presence of horse markets in both Nantwich and Wrexham. In this way, it was probably typical of the market area for many everyday items offered by Chester traders. Where the quality of the goods or services was high, the market area could be much larger. The upholsterer Abner Scholes, for instance, had book debts owing from a range of wealthy customers – including two baronets, five ladies and thirteen esquires – across Cheshire and much of north Wales.[3] Such people were evidently willing to overlook the services available at smaller towns to acquire high-quality furniture from a craftsman. Chester's economic region was clearly extensive, particularly in the under-urbanised areas of north Wales, and demonstrates the mutual dependence of urban tradesmen and their rural customers. But such economic interaction was itself reliant upon other forms of linkage for its successful articulation, most notably transport. The network of coach and carrier services listed in early trade directories reflects closely the economic linkages sketched above. The *Universal British Directory* (Barfoot and Wilkes 1794, 2, 722–5) lists fifteen coaches and wagons a week to Nantwich, nine to Frodsham, fourteen to Liverpool, seven to Wrexham and twelve to Whitchurch. These services define Chester's immediate hinterland, but the geography of its wider carrier and coach network is perhaps more telling. Direct services to east Cheshire and Lancashire were relatively limited (although connections could, of course, be made), whereas there were thirty-three coaches and twenty-six wagons each week connecting Chester to at least twenty-three towns and villages in north Wales, including places as far away as Bala, Pwllheli, Beaumaris and Holyhead.

It is significant that, over and again, the linkages which drew together town and country – and the 'territorial shape' that they delineate for Chester's hinterland – had scant regard for county boundaries and the communities that they supposedly defined. In a way, this is hardly surprising: given Chester's location and the under-urbanisation of north Wales, it is little wonder that the inhabitants of Denbighshire and Flintshire, in particular, looked to Chester for social, cultural and economic services. To what extent, though, did these same people identify with Chester and Chester with them? Did north Wales form part of the self-conscious society which Everitt (1979) identified as central to the definition of early modern regions? To answer this question, we must try to identify and delimit the 'conceptual shape' for Chester's hinterland – a task which is methodologically far more difficult than reconstructing a set of material-based interactions and networks. However, there are three sources which can be used to gain some insight into this aspect of urban–rural relationships.

Firstly, there are newspapers and the advertisements that they contained. These were read most widely by the middling sorts – the group at the heart of Everitt's county community and the prime consumers of the goods and services being advertised. Whilst it is very difficult to establish with any certainty the distribution of readers, it is possible to map the distribution of advertisers. This reveals the sphere of influence in which advertisers felt themselves to lie and thus defines a perceived region as well as an area of supply for higher order goods and services. Moreover, if we assume that the geography of readership corresponded broadly with that of advertising, then this pattern tells us much about the distribution of those wanting to keep in touch with, and be part of, Chester's social, economic and cultural activities. Figure 35 can thus be seen as a broad proxy for Chester's conceptual region: it spread considerably beyond the county boundary and had perhaps its strongest expression in north-east Wales. Secondly, there are the county histories, and the histories and guides to Chester which were published in increasing numbers from the late eighteenth century (see Sweet 1997). The former, most notably Ormerod (1819), clearly emphasised the coherence and identity of the county and often stressed the links between Cheshire and Chester. There was little attempt to look beyond the county or to define a 'natural' region, as we see, for example, with Aikin's (1795) *Description of the Country round Manchester*. Whether this county focus reflected a functioning region is, in many ways, immaterial. As a projection of the mind-set of author and subscribers, it joined county and town in a single coherent identity. However, the histories and guidebooks of Chester tell a rather different story. Perhaps recognising the reality of the market for their volumes, they noted the links with north Wales as well as Cheshire, echoing

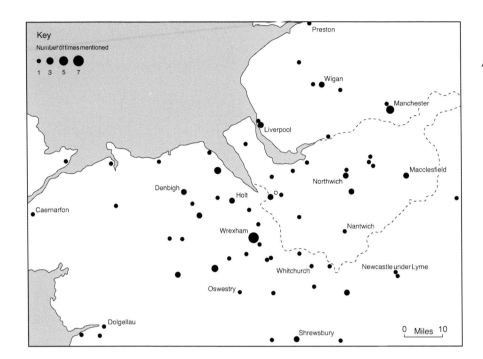

FIGURE 35.
Places mentioned in
Chester newspaper
advertisements,
1739–49

Aikin's (1795, 388) observation that Chester was 'a sort of provincial metropolis, not only for its own county but to neighbouring counties of North Wales'. Some went further and included specific information which drew north Wales into Chester's conceived region: Cowdroy's (1789) guide and directory, for instance, included entries for a number of Cheshire towns and for Wrexham alongside its listings of Chester tradesmen. This impression is graphically reinforced by the third source: maps of Chester, particularly that produced by Hollar in 1653 and republished by William Batenham in 1831.[4] As well as a ground plan and prospect of the city, the map includes the coats of arms of the Barons of the County Palatine. There were eight in all: seven from Cheshire (Kinderton, Malpas, Dunham Massey, Nantwich, Halton, Shipbrook and Stockport) and one in north Wales (Hawarden). In addition, an inset 'Mapp of Cheshire' is, in fact, centred on Chester and includes large parts of north Wales, marking Chirk Castle, Holt Castle, Denbigh and St Asaph. Chester is thus set firmly in a conceived region that encompassed much more than the county of Cheshire.

Impacts on the landscape

If Bristol was, as Estabrook (1998) argues, culturally and socially isolated from its rural environs, then this was not the case elsewhere. Chester, along with many county towns, looked outwards, and the links which existed between the town and its hinterland involved considerable interchange of goods, people, capital and information. Significantly, these flows came from the west as well the east, a point not lost on contemporary commentators; Fiennes

(1685–1712, 178) noted that 'the trade and concourse of people to it is chiefly from the intercourse it has with Ireland [and] with Wales'. These links had an important impact on the character and built environment of the town, both in terms of its general development and some specific aspects of the landscape.

As with other county towns, Chester experienced a cultural flowering and an economic reorientation during the decades following the Restoration (see Borsay 1989). In the place of declining traditional industries grew a burgeoning range of consumer and leisure services and a high-class retail sector. Metalworking, textile manufacturing and leather trades had accounted for every second admission to the freedom of the town between 1650 and 1675, but they made up just one-fifth of admissions by 1750–75. Conversely, luxury trades and retailing grew from one-quarter to two-fifths of admissions (Stobart 1998, 10–12). This economic transformation was matched by significant changes in the built environment of the town. There was a move away from the vernacular architecture which attracted negative comments from metropolitan visitors: Defoe, for example, thought that the Rows 'make the city look both old and ugly' (Defoe 1724–6, 392). New buildings were constructed along fashionable neo-classical lines and the Rows experienced an extensive make-over, being refaced with plaster or brick, and often realigned to produce an image of modernity in keeping with Chester's status as a social and cultural centre. At the same time, a growing infrastructure of polite leisure was established: there were assembly rooms, cock-pits, bowling greens and promenades; a theatre, race course and music festival (Stobart 1998, 6–10; *VCH* 2003, 143–5). As elsewhere, it is possible to see Chester's renaissance as being at least partly to do with urban–rural interaction, since many of these facilities were built in response to demand from the rural as much as the urban elite (see Borsay 2003). Assemblies took place during the winter season, when many rural gentry visited or took up residence in the town, and prizes at the summer horse races were often put up by the landed elite (Stobart 2000; Kennett 1987, 36–41; Borsay 1989, 199–212). Specific links between the rural gentry and the establishment of urban infrastructure were also apparent in Chester. The earls of Shrewsbury were instrumental in making the Talbot Inn on Eastgate Street one of the principal social centres of the town, whilst one of the patentees of the Theatre Royal came from a well-to-do family based in Gresford and later Rossett, just across the Welsh border (Edmonds 2001–2, 70–2; *VCH* 2003, 144). Links with a wider hinterland were also important in shaping the urban economy, culture and landscape: the funds to restore and maintain the walls as a fashionable promenade, for example, came from a so-called murage duty levied on imports of Irish linen (Broster 1782, 14).

Chester's role as an ecclesiastical and secular administrative centre also had a major impact on the landscape of the town, principally, but not exclusively, in terms of two key buildings: the castle and the cathedral. Quite apart from their sheer size, they dominated prospects of the town. The castle was the physical manifestation of a complex series of links between Chester and its hinterland. In one capacity, it housed the garrison and thus embodied the town's role as a strategic political and military location within the region and its links to national policies and events, most notably the periodic embarkation of troops for campaigns in Ireland (see Stobart 2002, 191–2). More mundanely, but perhaps more profoundly too, it was the seat of county government: it housed the court rooms for the assizes, the shire hall, the prison and the county militia. Its extensive remodelling between 1788 and 1813 by Thomas Harrison produced 'the grandest ensemble of neo-classical public buildings in Britain' and transformed the south-west corner of the intramural area. Significantly, this took place under the auspices of the county authorities, as did subsequent extensions to the site (in 1830) which required a diversion of the city walls (*VCH* 2003, 225–6). The cathedral, too, embodied a web of links to a broadly defined hinterland. It was the spiritual and administrative centre for a huge diocese which, by the early nineteenth century, contained nearly 2 million people spread over 10,620 km^2 (Beckett 2005, 22). As well as the bulk of the cathedral itself, there were the houses of the bishop, prebendaries and other members of the cathedral establishment, mostly ranged around Abbey Square, which was gradually built up through the 1750s to the north-west of the cathedral itself. These set the tone for later residential developments on Northgate Street, King Street and White Friars, and later on Nicholas Street and in what became Stanley Place, and thus did much to shape the residential landscape of intramural Chester (*VCH* 2003, 225–7).

The impact of hinterland links on the style and scale of residential buildings went further than this. As with towns across the country, Chester experienced widespread redevelopment of its middle-class housing stock during the eighteenth century. And, as elsewhere, this was built for the rural gentry as well as an increasingly prosperous urban elite (Borsay 1989, 41–59; Girouard 1990, 101–26; Borsay 2003, 282–4). In fact, there was something of a distinction in terms of the size and nature of the housing built for these different groups. Townspeople, especially professionals and prosperous tradesmen, generally occupied the three-storey terraces lining Nicholas Street, Stanley Place and the like; the rural gentry had altogether grander houses, usually individually built and sometimes detached. Amongst the earliest of these were the half-timbered town houses of the Grosvenors and the earls of Shrewsbury on Lower Bridge Street, but the trend towards the neo-classical was clearly marked with the construction in 1676 of the five-bay Bridge House for Lady Mary Calveley and the remodelling in 1700 of nos 28–34 Watergate Street as an eight-bay mansion for George Booth of Dunham Massey (Brown 1999, 167, 183; *VCH* 2003, 223–4). By the mid-eighteenth century, de Lavaux could mark on his town plan twenty-four substantial houses spread across the town, and there were at least five more besides.[5] Over half of these were owned by rural gentry, including leading Cheshire families such as the Grosvenors, Cholmondleys and Egertons, and several Welsh landowners (Aikin 1795, 388).

These houses helped to shape the character and landscape of Chester both inside the walls and in the expanding suburbs to the east of the town. They brought the country into the town in the person of their occupants (with whom, of course, came a certain set of tastes, desires and demands); in their architectural pretensions; and in the shape of their sometimes extensive gardens and orchards. As with grand town houses being built across the country during the eighteenth century, there were strong echoes of the country mansion in the neo-classical style and in the attempt to position the house in its own space (Girouard 1990, 101–26). This sometimes involved setting it back from the road or fronting the property with railings, both of which appear to have been done with Bridge House. The effect was grandest, at least in Chester, at Forest House. This stood behind a forecourt about 30 m deep, flanked by low service buildings and guarded by an imposing gateway (*VCH* 2003, 226). Behind the house, a garden some 70 m by 45 m ran back to paddocks. Such extensive grounds were typical of the substantial houses ranged along Foregate Street, and might be seen in terms of Bath-inspired notions of *rus in urbe*. More pragmatic explanations are probably nearer reality: grazing was needed for horses and even the smaller gardens found tucked behind town houses within the city walls would have provided space for fruit trees, herbs, chickens and perhaps pigs.

The impact of the rural gentry on Chester was felt most strongly through the town's connection with the Grosvenors. From their seat at Eaton, just 4.8 km south of the town, they were intimately involved in Chester politics, culture and society, and had a growing influence on its landscape and architecture. Initially, their impact was fairly modest. Their town house on Lower Bridge Street was large, but in keeping with those of other gentry families. However, when he successfully petitioned the Corporation to enclose the Row in 1643, Sir Richard Grosvenor set a precedent that was quickly followed by other gentry householders so that, by the early eighteenth century, the Rows and their attendant shops and workshops had largely gone from what was increasingly a respectable residential street (Brown 1999, 166–7). The family's influence spread after the election of Sir Thomas as one of the town's two MPs in 1678, an event which heralded the Grosvenor's largely uninterrupted assurance of one seat (and sometimes both) through to the reforms of 1835 (*VCH* 2003, 131–2, 156–60). This helped to cement the Grosvenors' position at the heart of local society, but also brought conflict into the social and cultural sphere. Rival assemblies were organised along political lines after 1808 and near riots occurred in the theatre during 1810. Notwithstanding this, with their purchase of the Royal Hotel (formerly the Talbot) in 1815, they controlled the town's principal centre for polite leisure and subsequently formed the central attraction at many assemblies and balls. They were also patrons of Chester races and major benefactors of the infirmary and the museum (Hemingway 1831, vol. 2, 408–9; Kennett 1987, 37; Edmonds 1998–9).

All this, of course, had a bearing on the landscape of the urban renaissance (see Stobart 1998), but it was in the nineteenth century that the imprint of the Grosvenors' architectural and aesthetic ambitions were most clearly set onto the town. They paid for two parks (most famously the eponymous Grosvenor

Park overlooking the river to the south-east of the town), and built schools, a nurses' home and a new parish church. Their importance was signalled in the naming of Grosvenor Bridge and Grosvenor Street: respectively the first new crossing of the river Dee (and for thirty years the longest single span stone arch in the world) and the first major departure from the town's medieval street plan. Significantly for the current argument, the bridge was built of limestone from Anglesey and sandstone from Peckforton (in central Cheshire) and thus embodied the geography of Chester's hinterland. Most important in terms of the townscape, however, was the pivotal role of the Grosvenors in Chester's vernacular revival. This was pioneered by Thomas Penson in his work on Eastgate Street for Richard Grosvenor, the second Marquis of Westminster, and the mercers Charles and William Brown. It was later developed by Thomas Lockwood and John Douglas, both of whom undertook several commissions from the Grosvenors for rebuilding premises on Eastgate Street and especially Bridge Street, where the family had become major landowners. In many ways, then, the Grosvenors can be seen as substantially responsible for the way that Chester looks today. They were not, however, immune from the check of popular local opinion, for, as Borsay (2003, 284) notes, even major landowners had to be mindful of the importance of the town in underpinning their political power. Thus, when the Duke of Westminster commissioned W.T. Lockwood in 1910 to rebuild St Michael's Row on Bridge Street he produced a dramatic four-storey frontage faced with white and gold faience tiling. A storm of protest forced the Duke to have the building demolished and rebuilt in the half-timbered style which was, by this time, Chester's hallmark (Brown 1999, 125–30).

One final way in which Chester's links to its rural hinterland shaped the landscape of the town was in terms of absence, rather than presence. Hemingway (1831, vol. 2, 341) noted the cultural and social attractions of the town, but then added that 'the absence of manufactories, and the crowds of the lowest rabble they engender, render it a desirable residence for the higher classes'. Leaving aside the hyperbole, Hemingway was astute both in identifying this enduring aspect of Chester's economic and environmental character, and in presaging a fierce debate which took place among Chester's political elite in the 1840s (Herson 1996). Taking these in turn, it is apparent from trade directories and maps that the declining industries of the eighteenth century were not replaced by large-scale industrial development in the early nineteenth century, despite developments elsewhere in the region. Stockdale's 1795 map shows the established cluster of mills along the river Dee immediately south of the town; a second concentration of activity to the north of the Roodee (an area of open land used as a racecourse); and a new steam mill on the canal to the east of the town. Over the next fifty years activity in the first two slowly declined, whilst the canal corridor witnessed some development in the shape of a lead works and further corn mills.[6] Some development also took place immediately to the north-east of the old town, with a cluster of small engineering works being established around the railway; but the real area of growth was at Saltney, around 2.4 km from the town. Here, a cluster of engineering works, oil refineries (which used crude oil extracted from local Flintshire coal) and bone manure works grew up on either side of the Welsh border, earning the sobriquet of Chester's own 'miniature Black Country' (*Chester Chronicle*, 5 July 1884; Herson 1996, 26; *VCH* 2003, 233–4).

The reasons for the lack of large-scale industrial development were complex, but the attitude of the town elite (including the corporation) and the policies of local rural landowners were both significant. Herson suggests that there was a 'struggle … for the soul of Chester' between those who urged that 'Chester must henceforth depend on the introduction of manufactories and not on her attractions as a place of genteel residence' and a more conservative faction who argued that industrialisation would cause environmental and social degradation, driving out the gentry already in the town (Herson 1996, 19, 22–3). This struggle was played out in the council chamber, in the local press and in the process of dealing with applications for industrial development within the town. Ultimately, the conservatives largely prevailed, not least because of the increased if temporary prosperity brought by the railways, which strengthened and extended Chester's ties with its hinterland. Significantly, then, it was concern for the town's external image and links which appears to have driven political decisions about industrial investment. It was no accident that large-scale development took place at Saltney, well away from elite residential areas in the old town. Moreover, external forces came to bear directly on the nature of development, and hence on Chester's landscape and identity. The Grosvenors encouraged the industrialisation of their land at Saltney in the mid-nineteenth century, but prevented any form of development on the approaches to the Eaton Hall. Similarly, Lord Howe's estate across the river from the Roodee was developed as an exclusive suburb, whilst land to the north-east (in Hoole and Newton) belonging to the Earl of Shrewsbury, Rev. Peploe Williams Hamilton and the Earl of Kilmorey was developed with restrictive covenants that prevented industrial use (Herson 1996, 27). Thus the lack of industrialisation seen in Georgian and early Victorian Chester, and hence the essentially residential and commercial nature of the town and its landscape, can be attributed, in part at least, to a concern for and the policies of the rural gentry.

Conclusions

In this chapter I have attempted to reconnect town and country in the long eighteenth century. Whilst contemporary commentators made much of the cultural divide between the two – urban sophistication and modernity being contrasted with rural backwardness (Sweet 2002) – it is apparent that links remained strong and wide-ranging. Chester was intimately bound to a hinterland which was most strongly defined in west Cheshire and north-east Wales, but which stretched to encompass the whole county, parts of Lancashire and Shropshire and much of north Wales. Its territorial shape was defined through tangible economic, social and political interaction, and its conceptual shape by its shared culture and the mutuality of its relationship with Chester. More importantly for the themes of this volume, it is clear that the links between town and country were instrumental in shaping the identity and landscape of Chester. As Herson (1996) argues, an orientation towards the rural gentry loomed large in the mind-set of Chester's elite well into the nineteenth century, reflecting generations of economic and social interdependence between the town and its hinterland. Unsurprisingly, then, the landscape of the town owed a great deal to this urban–rural axis, which brought the country into the town in very tangible and pragmatic ways (see Borsay 2003). The castle and cathedral epitomised its links to a wider hinterland and, through remodelling, expansion and associated residential development, gradually spread their influence across ever larger parts of the town through the eighteenth and early nineteenth centuries. More fundamentally, Chester's economic and cultural renaissance owed much to the patronage of rural gentry. Their houses and the infrastructure of polite leisure peppered the townscape, helping to remodel and modernise the built environment. Such influence was most apparent with the Grosvenors, who played a key role in Chester's reinvention of its 'lost' vernacular architecture in the mid-nineteenth century. This is arguably the greatest legacy of rural elite influence on Georgian Chester. A further significant aspect of the development of Georgian Chester was the unwillingness of the rural gentry to embrace industrialisation, a stance which brought serious economic and social problems in the early and the late nineteenth century. However, this economic conservatism, combined with the aesthetic and architectural conservatism of the black and white revival, effectively made modern Chester, laying the foundations for its tourism and service-sector revival in the late twentieth century. The key to both the present and the past of the town is thus to be found in its external relationships as well as its internal workings.

Notes

1. CCA, WS 1709, probate inventory of Peter Lancaster of Tarporley.
2. CCA, SBT/2, Sales and purchases at Chester Horse Market, 1660–1723.
3. CCA, WS 1756, probate inventory of Abner Scholes of Chester.
4. Chester City Library (CCL) MF 1/5, The Ground Plan of Chester: W. Hollar, 1653.
5. CCL, MF 5/3, Plan of the City and Castle of Chester: A. de Lavaux, 1745.
6. CCL, MF 1/12, Plan of Chester: I. Stockdale, 1796. See also CCL, MF 5/5, Plan of the City of Chester: J. Wood, 1833; MF 2/17, Plan of the City and Liberties of Chester: T. Thomas, *c.*1853.

CHAPTER TEN

The Suburbanisation
of the English Landscape:
Environmental Conflict
in Victorian Croydon

Nicholas Goddard

The town of Croydon, situated about 16 km south of London, was a Victorian pioneer of public water supply and sewage disposal (Goddard and Sheail 2001; Lancaster 2001; Goddard 2005b). The focus of this chapter is an exploration of issues of environmental conflict which were integral to Croydon's urban growth and have been relatively neglected in studies of early suburbanisation, which emphasise the spread of the built environment or development strategies of speculators linked to transport or building styles (Jackson 1973; Thompson 1982; English Heritage 1999). Here, three particular areas will be concentrated on: the supply of water, the disposal of sewage and the preservation of open space. All these brought into sharp relief the delicate balance between an urbanising society and the natural environment in which it was situated, and between individual rights and collective progress. The provision of a universal and continuous water supply, for example, raised important issues regarding the ownership of groundwater rights and their exploitation; sewage disposal opened up the question of river pollution and its prevention; and the preservation of open space generated intense discussion of the purpose and appropriate regulation of amenity areas. The suburban landscape which was formed included elements relating to the sanitary improvement which enabled its growth, such as an elaborate water tower and extensive sewage irrigation grounds. Landscape form related to preserved open spaces, and recreation grounds included sports pitches, gravel paths, seats, flower and shrub beds, and accoutrements such as pavilions, bandstands, drinking fountains and urinals. All of these elements were contested in various ways between different class and interest groups, while the indirect effects of suburban growth – such as the abstraction of underground water and the pollution of watercourses – extended well beyond the local area. While the emphasis in this chapter is on landscape and ecology in Victorian Croydon, the wider significance of the 'environmental conflicts' identified are stressed, and a plea is made for an environmental history perspective to be recognised more explicitly than has hitherto been the case in studies of 'suburbanisation'.

The Water Question

Croydon was the first of fifteen towns to establish a Local Board of Health under the provisions of the Public Health Act of 1848 (Goddard and Sheail 2001).[1] The Local Board quickly embarked upon a vigorous programme of environmental improvements, including the draining of contaminated ponds in the central area and the culverting of the course of the Wandle through the town (Blackmore 1952; Lancaster 2001, 148–58). Under the direction of the General Board of Health a comprehensive water supply system and sewage disposal system were installed; the water supply was formally inaugurated by the Archbishop of Canterbury in 1851. The water was sourced from wells sunk into the underlying chalk aquifer in the central part of the town; from there it was pumped to a covered reservoir built on a nearby elevation (Park Hill) for gravity distribution to the town's residences. In 1867 this was augmented by means of an additional water tower to meet the need of consumers rapidly colonising the more elevated – and favoured – areas of the parish, away from the town centre. The elaborate construction, executed by the Board's then engineer, Baldwin Latham, dominated the landscape to the south of the town and, as a distinctive feature representing one aspect of Croydon's much vaunted sanitary progress, quickly assumed something of an iconic status.

But the town's water supply quickly engendered controversy and conflict. The river Wandle was intensively utilised for industrial purposes and also had a high amenity value; the Local Board soon faced concerted legal action from mill owners, who claimed that the abstraction of groundwater had diminished the flow of the river to the detriment of their businesses. An action was launched against the Board in 1854 in the name of a prominent mill lessee, the purpose of which was to restrain the Board from continuing its abstraction and which centred on the disputed rights to groundwater. The 'Great Water Case' began at the Kingston Assizes in 1854 and was finally resolved in favour of the Local Board by the Lords of Appeal in 1859 (Lancaster 2001, 190–2). Apart from its profound local importance, in that if the Board had lost the case there was the danger that the whole of its investment in water supply would have had to be written off, *Chasemore v. Richards*[2] had a far-ranging significance for the wider exploitation of underground water. In upholding the right of a landowner to draw upon water lying beneath the soil, and in deciding that mill owners (and others) had no claim to groundwater in undefined channels or fissures (Will 1899, 255–6; Gale 1916, 264–9), the judgement opened the way for extensive and often uncontrolled exploitation of underground water around London and elsewhere until the 1947 Water Resources Act. This 'indirect effect of industrialisation' led to what has been termed an 'ecological crisis' in early twentieth-century Hertfordshire (Sheail 1982), and the excessive abstraction of groundwater in south-east England, despite licensing and controls, remains a matter of acute concern.

From the outset, the Local Board grossly underestimated the increase in demand that its provision would generate. For example, the extent to which the prized 'pure' water would be utilised for gardening purposes was not anticipated; nor was the rate of population growth, which the town's reputation for water itself encouraged, initially planned for. Control measures considered by the Local Board in the 1850s included the imposition of 'hosepipe bans' and the possible substitution of metered supply for charges based on rateable value (Goddard 2005b, 143). Although savings were achieved by stringent policing of water waste and the identification of leaks, the remorseless growth of population, which rose from *c.*20,000 in 1851 to *c.*80,000 by 1881, stimulated a search for new sources of water which was started in the 1880s and has continued to the present.

An early response to the supply problem was the increase of the capacity of the pumping engines. This was done in 1867 and 1876; the following year the prominent water engineer J. F. Bateman was commissioned by the Local Board to investigate not only the quality and purity of the Croydon water (which had been severely compromised by a typhoid outbreak) but also to investigate the adequacy of future capacity in relation to expected population increase; he concluded that the supply was then sufficient to meet the needs of a population of 80,000 (Bateman 1877). A further report by Robert Rawlinson in 1882 drew attention to the 'prospecting' by existing Metropolitan and new waterworks companies for water sources not far from Croydon, concluded that the prime question as to the future of the Croydon water would 'not brook much further delay', and suggested that the Board should be planning for a future population of 150,000–200,000 (Rawlinson 1882, 18–19). He directed attention to the potential of the chalk to the south of the town for supplying additional water. In 1884 a new borehole was sunk on land at Addington Hills (earlier acquired by the former Local Board for recreational purposes) which supplied an additional high-level reservoir; this was landscaped to safeguard against visual intrusion in a highly valued amenity area.

At the end of the nineteenth century the supply of water for the metropolis became a highly charged issue (Sheail 1982). The corporation extended its supply by sinking further wells in 1897, but in 1908 a group of riparian owners on the lower Wandle succeeded in gaining a private Wandle Protection Act which placed restraints on further abstraction from existing boreholes. The security of the water supply, and the ability to utilise sources to support expansion, remained problematic throughout the twentieth century; in 1904 part of the supply to the northern part of the borough was provided by the recently established Metropolitan Water Board.

In 1950 a High Court action (19 June) was launched by two of the remaining Wandle commercial concerns against the County Borough of Croydon and the British Electrical Authority in opposition to a proposal to divert effluent to the cooling system of the new Croydon 'B' generating station. Part of the action surrounded the extent to which the riparian owners were entitled to 'enjoy' the effluent in compensation for the water which was abstracted for public supply.[3] Although unsuccessful, the action demonstrated the continued complexities of the 'water question' in Croydon since the first pioneering works of the original Local Board of Health.

A further area of controversy surrounded the quality of the water supply. Contrary to expectations, there was a serious outbreak of typhoid soon after the inauguration of the public supply, which was repeated in 1875. On both occasions the Local Board was concerned to deflect any claim that there was a causal link with the water supply, although the epidemiology of the events was such that the water was highly implicated (Goddard 2005b, 139–40). Although in the late nineteenth century Croydon 'traded' on its somewhat dubious reputation as the 'healthiest' of the large towns in Britain (Martin 1900, 5) – the mortality statistics were skewed by the immigration of a relatively young and affluent population – paradoxically there was a further significant typhoid outbreak as late as 1937 (Frazer 1950, 461).

'The greatest difficulty'

The first Croydon sewers discharged into the Wandle downstream from the town after passing through a filter house where some of the solid material was removed. Not long after they began operation, a number of injunctions were served upon the Board by riparian owners who claimed that the sewage had polluted the river and occasioned fish mortalities. During the 1850s the Board experimented with a number of treatments involving various chemicals in the hope of purifying the sewage, but to no avail. Whereas the millers were less concerned about the quality than the quantity of the water, and recognised that effluent could advantageously supplement the flow of the river so long as suspended matter did not silt the millponds, those who valued the river for its amenity value were much less easy to placate.

It was not that the Board did not recognise its responsibilities; it was admitted that 'we have no right to do injury to others that good may come to ourselves' (Carpenter 1859, 20), but while under instructions from Chancery to do 'all that science would permit' to remedy the nuisance, science was unable to provide a ready solution. This brought into stark relief the conflict between individual interests and the collective good of an urbanising society. Although the Wandle was intensively utilised for milling operations, the river was also strictly preserved for angling purposes, trout being the species sought after by the fly-fishing method, which was growing in vogue and was increasingly recognised as an upper-class sport. It was a style of fishing that was particularly suited to the clear alkaline water of the river. The Local Board's discharge of sewage into the river occasioned the death of fish; the injunctions served on its members required them to either purify the sewage or desist from ejecting it into the watercourse.

A leading complainant was Alfred Smee, who rented fishing on the river in the parish of Wallington from 1858 onwards and developed a famous 8-acre (3.25 ha) garden (Figure 36) adjacent to the river, which housed one of the most extensive private collections of plants and trees in Europe. It was a privileged area – Smee (1872, 19) recognised that the village was 'rather a residence for the rich than for the poor' – but the rural tranquillity was rudely disturbed by the Local Board's upstream operations:

> The effluvium was noxious; the fish died; and foul mud was deposited at the bottom of the river. It became a question whether I should abandon my garden, but I determined otherwise, and commenced an agitation to stop pollution of rivers. (Smee 1872, 32)

Two circumstances saved the Board members from the serious penalties, including imprisonment, which were threatened; the Local Government Act of 1858 allowed local authorities for the first time to acquire land outside of their immediate jurisdiction for the purpose of sewage treatment, and land became available for the Board to set out sewage irrigation grounds. The Beddington works, which were established in 1860, represent an early indirect effect of suburbanisation on the surrounding landscape, and the amount of ground given over to the cleansing of sewage by running it over the ground in the mode of early water-meadow techniques was itself a significant new form of land use – 560 acres (228 ha) were devoted to this purpose in Beddington by the 1880s. The map reproduced from Smee's memoir of his garden clearly portrays Croydon's urban encroachment into the then undeveloped Surrey countryside (Figure 36).

The Beddington grounds appear to have produced a tolerable effluent and game fishing continued through the 1860s and 1870s. Adverse ecological changes in the river continued: there were complaints of the nuisance caused by an alien invasive plant species, *elodea candensis*, which was then colonising waterways throughout England (Goddard 2005b, 147), and it is reasonable to suggest that its rapid growth in the Wandle was encouraged by the higher nitrate content brought in by the treated sewage effluent. The Beddington sewage grounds themselves also created a certain amount of complaint, as in the hot summer of 1868, when the grounds certainly appear to have intruded on the 'smellscape'[4] of Croydon, and there were also reports of illness in the area adjacent to Beddington – the Board's engineer had to make considerable efforts to refute any causal link to the sewage irrigation (Latham 1870). Actual conditions on the Beddington sewage farm varied, and wet or cold winters posed a problem, as the capacity of the land to absorb the sewage was inhibited by frozen or saturated ground. Visitors could find the ground to be in a 'pestilential and sodden condition' (Letheby 1872, 22), and Smee bitterly denounced the Beddington operation, having complained that the irrigation scheme was so badly carried out that a 'pestilential marsh' was created (Smee 1872, 32; 1875–6). He drew attention for the first time to the danger of the accumulation of inorganic poisonous substances, which has

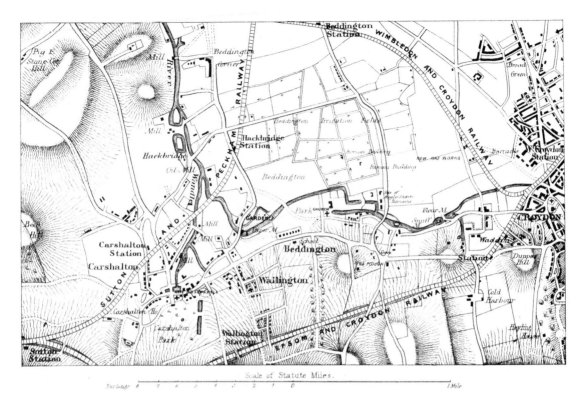

been one of the more recent objections to recycling sewage onto the land (Goddard 1996, 284).

A second irrigation area was created by the Local Board in 1865 for the expanding district of Norwood, to the north-east of the town centre (Walker 1890, 2). As at Beddington the problem was to keep treatment capacity maintained to meet the requirements of the rapidly expanding population, and by the 1880s it was clear that the original area of 65 acres (26 ha) at Norwood was no longer fit for purpose. The enquiry into the then corporation's plan to acquire land by compulsory purchase to extend the ground revealed an interesting array of public attitudes to the provision of sanitary services. The alternative to expansion was for the borough to link into the new West Kent Drainage Scheme, but that was perceived to be a more expensive option and one which could not deal with storm water flow. It was additionally held that the scheme would contribute to the then deteriorating condition of the lower Thames. Objectors pointed to the alleged nuisance of the existing Norwood works, but the extent of this proved very difficult to establish. The essential point was the fear that property values would be adversely affected if the extension was carried out, and that the existence of the Norwood farm itself inhibited further development on adjacent land. Indicative of the motive for opposition was the representation at the enquiry of a number of building societies and the South Eastern Railway, yet the paradox was that those who gained most from the borough's reputation for superior sanitary arrangements

FIGURE 36.
Alfred Smee's garden in relation to Croydon, *c.*1872. Irrigation grounds to the north, Duppas Hill to the south-east. From Smee 1872, by permission of the Syndics of Cambridge University Library

were the most vocal in opposing the extension of the very means by which their new suburban lifestyles had been enabled (*Norwood News* 6 and 13 February, 24 April, 8 May 1886). Their opposition was in stark contrast to the attitudes expressed in the campaign of the early 1860s to have the Norwood works established, when it was held that the district must be drained or it would 'stink all its inhabitants into fever and the coffin' (*Croydon Chronicle* 25 October 1864).

However, complaints about smells, water pollution and alleged ill-health continued into the twentieth century and were the subject of continuous investigation (Strachan 1904). Alfred Carpenter (1859, 20) had correctly identified the sewage outfall as the 'most difficult problem' nearly fifty years earlier, and formal bacteriological treatment, initially trialled by Croydon's near-neighbour Sutton (Pidgeon 1899, 261–2) and first begun at Beddington in 1902, eventually allowed a more space-intensive treatment of sewage. While the works were only begun in 1860 because of intense legal pressure, it was through the Local Board's pioneering efforts that the sewage farm became a familiar component of the late nineteenth-century suburban landscape. Trout fishing on the river did not survive the First World War, and later attempts to restock were unsuccessful, due in part to pollution from surface run-off (the increase of which was also a result of urbanisation of the catchment); by the 1920s much of the middle and lower reaches of the river were reported as being in a neglected and foul condition (Surrey County Council 1923).

FIGURE 37. View of Beddington Church from Alfred Smee's garden, *c.*1872. An air of rural tranquillity prevails. From Smee 1872, by permission of the Syndics of Cambridge University Library

From open spaces to 'pleasure grounds'

Croydon's Victorian residents valued the local landscape of the Wandle valley; it was famously praised by Ruskin, who had early associations with the town (Ruskin 1873, 1; 1885, 40) and the downlands to the south of the central area. An early historian of the town extolled the 'sylvan charm of Croham Hurst, the wolds of Duppas Hill or still wilder, the heather-clad mountain range on Addington Hills (Anderson 1882, 244), where the North Downs attain an elevation of around 460 ft (140 m) and are covered with gravels which support an acidic-loving vegetation. These landscape features added to the attractiveness of the town but there was an early awareness that the development upon which local prosperity depended threatened the very existence of the open space and amenity areas which brought so many incomers to Croydon. The provision of open spaces and recreation areas became a key issue for the Local Board and its successor in the 1880s and 1890s as the population continued to increase at a prodigious rate.

Under the terms of the 1796 Enclosure Award, 237 acres (96 ha) had been allotted to the inhabitants of Croydon in various parcels distributed throughout the parish. This land was overseen by the town's Wastelands Trustees and during the first half of the nineteenth century had been utilised for a variety of purposes, including the extension of graveyards, the construction of the Town Hall and Butter Market, and the extraction of gravel for road maintenance; by the time that the Local Board began an application to acquire the powers of the Trustees in the late 1860s, very little 'wasteland' remained. Open space under private ownership within the parish was used permissively, and rights of way were jealously guarded; however, with an expanding population and the associated commercial potential for development, permissive use came under increasing strain in the 1860s and 1870s as community access to some of the most valued local amenity areas became threatened.

The first open space acquired by the Board was an elevated area of 6 acres (2.5 ha) known as Duppas Hill, which it obtained from the Ecclesiastical Commissioners for the sum of £2,800 in 1863. Negotiations had begun with the former Archbishop of Canterbury in the late 1850s, but expenses associated with the 'water question' had then disinclined the Board to commit to additional expenditure (Lancaster 2001, 192). As Duppas Hill (Figure 38; *cf.* Figure 39) was close to the town centre it was perceived as a particularly valuable amenity, especially given the recognition that it 'would soon have town all around it'. In the same year members of the Board expressed concern about the threat to unrestricted access over Croham Hurst, 'the most picturesque and healthy spot in the neighbourhood'; the tenant had found the seats provided by the Board along footpaths to be prejudicial to the enjoyment of individual privacy, and there were also allegations of damage and trespass (*Croydon Chronicle* 17 and 24 January, 11 July 1863). Later, the owners of the Hurst (The Whitgift Trustees, acting for the leading Croydon charity) let the area as a keepered game preserve. The fashion for 'battue shooting' was clearly incompatible with unrestricted use of public rights of way and was the subject of a forthright leader in the *Croydon Chronicle* which attracted sympathetic public response; children, it was alleged in a Board of Health discussion, were insulted by gamekeepers 'for picking primroses and violets'. The Board attempted to acquire the shooting rights but its offer was refused by the Trustees who, answering to the Charity Commissioners, had an obligation to maximise the income of the trust even if this objective appeared to conflict with the interests of the Croydon inhabitants as a whole (*Croydon Chronicle* 10, 17 and 24 May, 7 June 1874).

Still more concern was evident in 1875 when the owner of the Addington Hills attempted to enclose an area of open common by the erection of a wire fence. The suspicion was voiced that the hills would only be left open to the public so long as the leading front of building development remained some distance away. Local agitation[5] on this issue was orchestrated by a hastily formed local branch of the national Commons, Open Spaces and Footpath Preservation Society, which had been founded ten years previously (Williams 1965) and which was instrumental in allowing the Board to acquire 80 acres of the Addington summit for £5,000 in 1876 (*Croydon Chronicle* 8 May, 11 and 18 June 1875).

The ownership of two substantial tracts of open space presented the Board with unanticipated questions of management, particularly regarding the extent to which it was desirable to develop the sites and provide additional amenities. The Board's view was that Duppas Hill was essentially provided for 'quiet recreation'; they were disturbed to receive reports of uncontrolled gatherings of young people, with their tendency to 'romp', on Duppas Hill at holiday times. Complaints were received about damage to fences and seats, and such were the 'vile oaths' heard on the Hill that the area was said to be useless for the enjoyment of persons of respectability. In June 1873 a Drum and Fife Band had led to complaints from the local residents, who also vigorously opposed the use of the land as a proposed venue for the Bath and West Show, scheduled for 1875, on the grounds that the scale of the event posed a threat to their privacy. This led to the suggestion that the Board should appoint a guardian to keep children under control, and should provide some shelter, gravel paths, and even the sale of refreshments on the model to be seen at Battersea Park (*Croydon Chronicle* 7 June, 11 October 1873).

The desirability or otherwise of such developments initially sharply divided public opinion; a particularly significant issue was the degree to which preserved space should be allowed to retain its 'natural' characteristics or be organised and controlled with increased amenity provision. A leader in the *Croydon Chronicle* (10 August 1876) held that visitors to Duppas Hill did not wish to be watched over by a man in the uniform of the Board of Health, while the erection of a lodge would disfigure the place and generate 'a kind of aesthetic fever that will drive people away like a bad odour'. An objection was lodged against the 'unromantic' gravel paths which had been laid down at Duppas Hill, although, in response, a letter to the *Croydon Chronicle*

(15 and 22 April 1876) from 'two ladies' held that the paths, if 'unromantic', were certainly 'most useful' in permitting access. There was a significant class dimension to debate on these issues. In discussion at the Board of Health (7 September 1876) of a letter from a prominent magistrate which opined that Duppas Hill ought to be kept in as natural a condition as possible and that no alterations or additions to these were required, it was pointed out that the objector was someone who had a large private garden for walking, no children, and was in a position to retreat to his home where refreshment would be on hand if the weather turned inclement.

Similar considerations applied at Addington Hills. Soon after the Board's acquisition it was reported that a swing had been erected (which was immediately ordered to be pulled down), that donkeys had been tethered on the land, and that heather had been burnt. This led to the appointment of a warden to prevent further 'depredations'. An application to erect a tent posed a particular dilemma; this, it was thought, might be in order for a school or respectable employer but members of the Board were extremely wary of the intrusion of East End 'excursionists' with 'aunt sallies and all forms of objectionable amusements'. It had been found that posters advertising trips to Addington Hills had been displayed in London, and the Board held that the Hills had been acquired for the people of Croydon, not 'Whitechapel excursionists' down for 'bean feasts' given that the 'habits of the English race, when out for a holiday, are neither conducive to happiness or propriety' (*Croydon Chronicle* 27 June, 15 July 1876).

Having secured Duppas Hill and Addington Hills, the Board established an Open Space Committee to pursue the acquisition of public space in a

FIGURE 38.
Duppas Hill, *c.*1900.
The fountain was
donated to the
borough in 1886.
Croydon Local
Studies and Archives
collection, by
permission

Environmental Conflict in Victorian Croydon

FIGURE 39.
Park Hill recreation grounds, *c.*1900. Note Latham's water tower in background. Croydon Local Studies and Archives collection, by permission

more systematic way. It was particularly recognised that land provided near to poorer areas could have sanitary benefits, but the costs were prohibitive as this land was also favoured for building purposes. Following the offer by the Ecclesiastical Commissioners of 14 acres (5.5 ha) of land at £800 per acre, there was discussion as to whether spaces in the more central areas of the town, where they would have most benefit for recreation, should be acquired, or whether cheaper but more distant land should be selected.

As population increased, the acquisition of recreation grounds became a pressing issue during the last two decades of the nineteenth century, and during the 1880s there was a significant shift in attitudes towards such provision. There were few supporters of the Local Board's application to the Local Government Board to borrow £18,000 for the purchase of land for recreational purposes in 1882. Apart from the expenditure and its implications for the local rate, objections came from residents who lived close by the proposed new areas, while others held that money would be better spent on improving the 'dens' of the poor. Alfred Carpenter held that the proposed sites would be largely used by nursemaids and the well-to-do who already had large gardens for their children and were able to take regular holidays for a change of air (*Croydon Review* 3 November 1882).

After the town's incorporation in 1883, responsibility for open spaces was delegated to the new borough's Roads Committee, which soon came under pressure from residents to acquire the remains of the undeveloped open space in the more central areas of the parish. In 1887 memorials were presented on the matter from residents in the expanding Upper Norwood ward and from the West and Central wards (Borough of Croydon Roads Committee minutes 17 May, 27 September 1887). In both cases the petitions were prompted by the realisation that if action was not taken immediately, there would be no opportunities to acquire land in the future. Recreational land was considered vital to keep 'idle and listless' youths off the streets, while in the central districts preserved areas could include the provision of cricket and tennis grounds, a drill area for the Volunteers, assembly places for festive gatherings and other uses as the population increased. Given that the Roads Committee had a range of proposals to consider, it proposed that the whole question of the acquisition of recreational grounds was put on a systematic footing and that 1d in the pound of the borough's rateable value, equivalent to a capital sum of £25,000, be allocated for the purpose (Roads Committee 27 September 1887). 'Recreation Grounds' first appear as a distinct topic in the Croydon Council minute book for 1887 (Figure 39).

After visits and inspections, the Roads Committee recommended a number of additions to its recreational portfolio and the borough council's proactive stance appears to have been genuinely popular. At the opening of Wandle Park (where the Wandle emerged from a culvert installed by the old Local Board) a gathering estimated at 25,000 people assembled for a procession, opening ceremony and fireworks. The work done by the corporation to reclaim an unpromising swampy marsh was held to result in a 'miniature Hyde Park':

> The time had gone by ... for arguing to as the necessity and importance of these breathing spaces in the midst of large populations, for the health and well-being of the community generally. Their existence is universally looked upon as absolutely requisite both from a moral and physical point of view. (*Croydon Chronicle* 17 May 1890)

In the 1890s the recreation grounds became much more regulated and there was a steady increase in the range of facilities provided. Boating had been available on the lake created in Wandle Park from the outset; here and elsewhere additional facilities for public enjoyment included the provision of seats, flowerbeds and bandstands and a wider range of refreshments; indeed, the term 'pleasure grounds' was sometimes used in the Roads Committee minutes. Football was added to the list of acceptable sports, and the byelaws consolidated and rigorously enforced by uniformed park-keepers; prosecutions for vandalism and theft perpetuated by children increased, reflecting the wider late nineteenth-century 'cycle of anxiety over juvenile delinquency' (Gillis 1975). Whereas in the 1870s open space had sometimes seemed to pose a threat to Croydon residences, by the 1890s an 'increasingly assertive middle class elite' (Morris 1989, 108) – the very interests that had opposed the Norwood irrigation area – saw recreation areas as a way of controlling 'the crowd'. In the 1890s Croydon's nine recreation grounds, local walks and ready access to countryside featured heavily in guide books and helped to attract still more incomers – an early example of what is now termed 'boosterism' – which enabled Croydon to receive the accolade of 'London's most important suburb' (*Gentleman's Magazine* 10 July 1907).

'The Hurst, the whole Hurst and nothing but the Hurst'

Despite this generous provision of recreation grounds in the Borough, Croydon residents were highly sensitive to the threats posed to the remaining 'natural' scenery from further speculative building, which was itself a reflection of the prosperity for which the town was noted. As a correspondent to the *Croydon Chronicle* (4 February 1899) pointed out, it was only Shirley (Addington) Hills where it was possible to escape from the sight of London, and landscape was never more appreciated than when threatened with bricks and mortar. When the owners of Croham Hurst (the Whitgift Foundation) proposed to engage in development, a popular movement was quickly established to secure it for the town. Although Whitgift Governors had an obligation to realise the area's development potential, as they had successfully done elsewhere, given the sensitivity of the issue they offered the corporation an opportunity to lease for recreational purposes an upper portion of some 35 acres (14 ha) on favourable terms. The corporation resolved to accept this offer, but the public reaction was that this was insufficient; memorials and deputations were received urging that the Council acquire the whole of the area 'to be preserved for the use of the people for ever'. Under the rallying call of 'The Hurst, the whole Hurst, and nothing but the Hurst', the Croham Hurst Preservation Society was able to demonstrate an impressive array of public support, which appears to have come from all parts of the borough and included the Croydon Chamber of Commerce, the Trades and Labour Council, the National Trust Society, the Croydon Labour Church and additional supporters from London, emphasising the Hurst's wider amenity and educational value; it was even said that schoolchildren were to get up a petition with the cry of 'what is the use of a half-holiday if there's no place to go?' (*Croydon Chronicle* 18 March 1899).

Yet to others the case was not so clear-cut. The *Croydon Chronicle* (20 January 1899) made the point that the additional burden on the ratepayers might damage local prosperity, and was particularly sensitive to the notion that the Croydon ratepayers should acquire the amenity to benefit 'Sunday trippers and holiday rowdies'; further, it was wasteful to allow the land to remain idle when income derived from it would be ploughed back into local education. Croydon, it held, was already well provided for with recreation grounds and the Addington Hills, while the present view from the summit of the Hurst would inevitably become more circumscribed by development in the future. However, under remarkably sustained pressure from resolutions and deputations the Council resolved to enter into negotiations to purchase the whole of the Hurst in 1900 and the extended area was acquired the following year.

During the preceding thirty years much attention had focused on the acquisition of definable open areas for broadly recreational purposes. The upland areas of the parish had received most attention, although turn-of-the-century guidebooks also featured walks along the Wandle as part of the town's attraction. Although the areas downstream of Wandle Park to the parish of Beddington appear to have kept some of their pre-suburban character, much of the Wandle valley was by this time under threat from urbanisation and industrialisation. Ruskin had earlier deplored the neglect and pollution of the western source of the river at Carshalton:

> I have never seen anything so ghastly in its inner tragic meaning … as the slow stealing of aspects of reckless, indolent, animal neglect, over the definite sweetness of that English scene … the human wretches of the place cast their street and house foulness; heaps of dust and slime, and broken sherds of old metal, and rags of putrid clothes. (Ruskin 1873, 2–3)

In 1908 the River Wandle Open Spaces Committee was formed. It consisted of delegates from the Common and Footpaths Preservation Society, the Kyrle Society and the National Trust, and counted Octavia Hill amongst its members. Some councils along the lower course of the river had already acquired parts of the river bank, and the new committee launched a public appeal for funds to acquire further tracts upstream, with the objective of making the river environs the 'lungs of the neighbourhood'.[6] Although limited progress was reported by 1914 and the committee continued in existence until 1929, the land acquired was later transferred to the National Trust. It is only comparatively recently that a concerted effort has been made to restore the amenity value of the lower Wandle valley (Figure 40).

FIGURE 40.
The Wandle, *c.*1925. Note the shallowness of the water. Museum of English Rural Life, Rural History Centre, University of Reading, by permission

Concluding comments – and an environmental renaissance?

Because Croydon was a Victorian pioneer, the environmental conflict had a much wider significance; the early partial failure of the sewage system provided ammunition for those who were opposed to the Chadwickian project, while the pollution of the Wandle encouraged a number of legal actions against local Boards of Health and other responsible authorities and was used as an environmental justification by large towns for not investing in often much-needed sanitary infrastructure (Goddard 2005a). Within Croydon, a significant shift in environmental attitudes has been demonstrated in, for example, the transition of sewage irrigation treatment in public perception from a health necessity to nuisance or the preservation of open space from threat to amenity. Early suburban environmental attitudes are a theme which I hope will be taken up in future studies.

Irrigation continued at Beddington until the works were updated in 1966; since then the area has seen comprehensive redevelopment of much of the grounds formerly given over to sewage treatment. At the same time the Norwood farm ceased to function and after a local campaign to save the area from development, Norwood Country Park was opened in 1990 – another example of continuity in suburban landscape.

Walking from Croydon and Carshalton through Beddington in August of 2005, I observed that the Wandle, although clean and clear, was seriously depleted in its flow, admittedly after a very dry winter and spring. Yet further down stream I found anglers fishing for a variety of coarse fish, and fine specimens can now be found in the middle reaches of the river – particularly near to the outfall of the Beddington works, which significantly augments the flow of the river. The Wandle valley has a nature trail and wildlife preserves (although the same casual vandalism which so exasperated the Victorian pioneers is still apparent). Within recent memory the lower river has been transformed from an open sewer to a living stream, with trout even being caught on the fly in the reaches near to Wandsworth![7] The opening of the old Local Board of Health's conduit through Croydon has been mooted, and under the auspices of a highly proactive local action group perhaps it is not too optimistic to look to a twenty-first-century 'Environmental Renaissance', not only in the local area but also in other suburban districts where the landscape has been despoiled and the environment neglected.

Acknowledgements

I am grateful for anonymous suggestions for the improvement of this chapter and for use of the resources in the Croydon Library Local Studies and Archives section. I have also valued conversations with Dr Rohan McWilliam of the Anglia Ruskin University History Department. Thanks are also due to Cambridge University Library and Croydon Library for assistance in the production of the illustrations.

Notes

1. The proceedings of the Croydon Local Board of Health were reported in the *Croydon Advertiser* (and other local newspapers). The Local Board normally sat on Tuesdays fortnightly and the reports appeared in the following Saturday's weekly edition of the *Advertiser*.
2. Chasemore was the tenant and Richards the Board's secretary.
3. The papers relating to this case are available at the Croydon Library Local Studies and Archives Section.
4. A term first used by the geographer J. Douglas Pourteous.
5. Leaders were F. H. Coldwells, a nurseryman and 'working man's representative' on the Croydon School Board, and J. Spencer Balfour, first mayor of Croydon but best remembered for the 1892 *Liberator* scandal. See McKie 2004. Coldwells was later a Liberal MP and implicated in the scandal as a business associate of Balfour.
6. Reports of the Wandle Open Spaces Committee are available at the Croydon Library Local Studies and Archives Department.
7. See, for example, 'Wandle catch is the "best for 100 years"', *Fly Fishing and Fly Tying* May 2006.

PART THREE

Landscapes Perceived

CHAPTER ELEVEN

Wilderness and Waste – 'The Weird and Wonderful': Views of the Midland Region

Della Hooke

Views of the wilderness

Early views of the wilderness

Removed from the familiar world of everyday life, wilderness areas throughout history have been regarded with awe – as places close to the supernatural. Moses is said to have received the word of God while on Mount Sinai, travelling with the children of Israel through the wilderness of Horeb (Exodus 20), and it was upon a 'high mountain' that Jesus showed himself to three of his disciples as the son of God before his crucifixion (Matthew 17; Mark 9; Luke 9). Hills figure again in the well-known psalm: 'I will lift up mine eyes unto the hills, From whence cometh my help' (Psalm 121). The Greek gods, too, were thought to live upon Mount Olympus and, as we shall see, uplands continued to play a role in later folklore and mythology. But while wilderness areas might be seen as a source of inspiration they also had a darker side. After his baptism, Jesus wandered for forty days and forty nights in the wilderness, where he was tempted by the Devil (Matthew 4; Luke 4), and in folklore the Devil and other supernatural beings remained a force to contend with in the mountains. Forests were involved in the elaborate courtly ritual of the hunt and served as a training ground for those knightly pursuits necessary for the defence of the realm, but they were also the abodes of those who rebelled against the rules of society – of outlaws and poachers. As late as the eighteenth century, travellers like Celia Fiennes and Daniel Defoe were terrified to travel across the Peak District moorlands without a guide.

The Old English term *wēste*, derived from old Germanic sources and akin to the Latin adjective *vāstus*, 'empty, desert', always conveyed a sense of open uncultivated or uninhabited country, often regarded as unproductive and desolate, and this, in turn, gave rise to the term *wēstengryre*, 'terror of the waste', in the Exodus poem, here meaning 'terror of the desert'. In imitation of Christ's wandering in the wilderness, Christian hermits in early medieval England continued to seek out lonely places in which to test their faith: many monastic foundations claimed an origin as hermitages in this way, among them both Great Malvern and Little Malvern priories on the Malvern Hills (Worcs.).

Changing attitudes to wilderness

Throughout early history, wildernesses seem generally to have been regarded as, if not places engendering fear, at least ones which were less desirable than tamed landscapes. Even when kings and lords were extending their forests, chases and deer parks, these were still places to hunt for sport rather than enjoy for their own sakes. When Henry V built a 'Pleasaunce', a moated pleasure-house, in the grounds of his castle at Kenilworth (Warwicks.), the poet Thomas Elmham tells us:

> There was a fox-ridden place overgrown with briars and thorns. He removes these and cleanses the site so that wild creatures are driven off. Where it had been nasty now becomes peaceful marshland; the coarse ground is sweetened with running water and the site made nice. (Thompson 1964, 223, translating Thomas of Elmham)

Much later travellers, like Celia Fiennes (in 1698), also preferred the pastoral lowland scenes: Blackstone Edge in Derbyshire was 'a dismal high precipice' from which she was glad to descend to 'a fruitfull valley full of inclosures and cut hedges and trees' (Fiennes 1685–1712, 221–2). It was only with restrictions on travel brought about by war and troubled conditions on the Continent that travellers began to appreciate the wilder landscapes of Britain. In the late eighteenth century (1770) Thomas Pennant had described the view from Snowdon as 'horrible. It gave an idea of numbers of abysses, concealed by a thick smoke, furiously circulating around use' (Pennant 1778–81, vol. 2, 172) and William Gilpin, too, very much a lover of the newly favoured 'Picturesque' style, found the Pass of Llanberis 'a bleak, dreary waste' (Andrews 1989, 135), but in 1791 Wordsworth appears to have been less disagreeably moved by the drama of the place (Andrews 1989, 138). In the Midland region it was the valley of the river Wye that attracted Gilpin, its river scenery less forbidding than that of mountainous districts, despite the fact that its banks were 'sublimely steep and wild' (Andrews 1989, 94; Gilpin 1782) – Tintern Abbey was among the features that supplied the requisite atmospheric ingredients to the scene and rescued it from being a 'true' wilderness. To the agriculturalists of the later eighteenth century, 'wilderness' was literally land that was going to waste: although the Forest of Needwood (Staffs.) might be 'wild and romantic', William Pitt argued in his report of 1796 that 'its continuance in its present state is certainly indefensible' (Pitt 1796, 102–4). Few of the more extensive wastes of Worcestershire, on the other hand, such as the Malvern Hills or the Wyre Forest, merited the attention of the agriculturalists because of their poor soils – in this county only some of the smaller commons were considered capable of improvement. In the early nineteenth century John Duncumb (1805, 94–5) found the view over the Herefordshire woods and commons looking from Mordiford towards the east 'cheerless' when compared with the fertile meadows or beautified pastoral parkland to the west. However, nineteenth-century 'Romantics' found a new admiration for the wilderness, which has been expressed in countless poems and writings through to the twentieth century. Many, like the Brontë sisters, Thomas Hardy or, later, Francis Brett Young and Mary Webb, set their characters within turbulent wild landscapes; others, like Richard Jefferies or Margaret Fairless, described the landscape in minute detail. From landscapes of horror or unease through to ones arousing, at best, awe, or, at worst, disappointment, the wilderness was throughout history always a place that was 'different'. It enjoyed a special position in people's minds that can be investigated through archaeology, folklore and legend.

Marginal areas in archaeology, folklore and legend

Liminal and mythological landscapes

A liminal place is one on a threshold – often one leading to a different world. Partly because 'wilderness' regions such as mountains, forests or marshes were usually sparsely populated, and were often to be feared, they acquired a special spirituality as the boundary between the living and the spirit world. Undeveloped regions were also often those that served as frontier and boundary regions between kingdoms or, in early days, the meeting places of neighbouring tribes: prehistoric barrows were often sited along boundaries as if to establish claims to land strengthened by the presence of the ancestors; stone circles might be found in similar locations in the borderland and eastern uplands of the Peak District. Prehistoric man made votive offerings to the gods in marshes and lakes and, in Shropshire, there is also evidence of this in an upland region (A.Wigley pers. comm.). In Herefordshire, items of Bronze Age metalwork have been found in watery locations along the Severn gorge and in the Arrow valley, the most recent a fine but unfinished dirk from Admarsh near Eardisland (White 2003, 35–7). Tales of buried treasure in ponds may thus have some archaeological basis. Related to the concept of ponds and pits offering access to the underworld of the gods and supernatural beings might be the legendary association of mythical creatures like Beowulf's adversary Grendel occasionally also alluded to in Anglo-Saxon charters. A pond which looks today like little more than a water-filled marlpit was apparently the 'Grendel's pit' that served as a boundary landmark on the boundary of Abbots Morton (Worcs). Near the northern border of the Hwiccan kingdom lay Tyesmere, associated with the Anglo-Saxon god Tíw (Hooke 1990, 43–6, 135–42), once a mere on the southern flanks of the Lickey Hills (Worcs.). There are legends, too, of rivers being 'greedy' for lives – the river Wye is said to have required an annual victim (Palmer 2002, 16).[1]

Christianity often subsumed the gods and monsters of the pagan world into the Devil, who also became associated with wilderness locations, whether mountain, forest or fen (Hooke 2006, ch. 8). Hills were obviously seen as places of spiritual vulnerability. The rough topography of the summit of the Stiperstones

(Salop) was, for instance, thought to be the work of the Devil (Figure 41). It was said that if the Stiperstones should sink into the ground then all England would be ruined. Failing to stamp them into the ground and angry because he was not able to destroy the people of the fair county of Shropshire, the Devil is said to have sat in a niche in the rocks and hurled stones periodically from the summit ridge. Another story tells how when he discovered a vent letting air into Hell he tried to block the crack with rocks; when he was unable to do this he resorted to his chair and in his impatient rage his apron strings broke, scattering the rocks over the hillside (Douglas 2001). The 'Devil's Chair' and the surrounding scree are features of the ridge. Mary Webb, in her novel *The Golden Arrow*, notes how local superstition claimed that around 22 December all the ghosts of the county would congregate there and if a storm broke out it was a sign that the Devil was 'in his chair'.

Hills allegedly created by the Devil are common in regional folklore: others formed by his dropping sacks of earth after the intervention of humans include two conical hills known as Pyon Hill and Butthouse Knapp, near King's and Canon Pyon (Hereford) (Palmer 2002, 10). Several reflect a clash with Christianity: Meon Hill, an outlier of the Cotswolds in southern Warwickshire, is said to have been created by a great mass of earth flung by the Devil to overwhelm the newly built abbey of Evesham (Worcs.) that was deflected by the prayers of Ecgwine, its abbot; a conical hill near Stratford-upon-Avon became known as the Devil's Bag of Nuts as it was allegedly caused by the Devil, out

FIGURE 41.
A view of the Stiperstones in Shropshire, from the west.

gathering nuts in September, dropping his bagful of nuts when confronted by the Virgin Mary (Palmer 1976, 71).[2] However, it was not always the Devil that caused hills to rise up. The Wrekin (Salop), a massif of hard old rock that dominates the skyline for miles around, has two origin myths, both involving giants. In the first, two giants set out to build a hill to live in, taking earth from the bed of the Severn, thus piling up the Wrekin. However, during a quarrel that soon broke out between them a raven pecked out the eyes of the one with the spade, making it easier for the other. The latter, determined to put his foe where he could never trouble him again, imprisoned him within a hill he quickly built up – Ercall Hill, beside the Wrekin, where the defeated giant remains to this day – his groans may be heard at the dead of night. In the second myth, the Wrekin was left by a wicked old giant from Wales trying to flood Shrewsbury. He was, however, thwarted by a local cobbler who feared to lose his customers and persuaded the giant that Shreswbury was so far away that it could not be reached for many days: although he himself had just left the town he had already worn out all the boots and shoes that he now carried with him. The giant's load of earth, intended to dam up the Severn, was thus dropped where he stood to become the Wrekin and the earth scraped off his boots the little Ercall by Wrekin's side (Briggs 1970–1, vol. 1, 618–19, citing Burne and Jackson 1883, 2–3).

Strange natural features such as caves, not surprisingly, attracted legend: Eldon Hole in the Peak District, for example, became the Devil's bolt-hole to Hell. It was described by Defoe as 'a frightful chasm, or opening in the earth, or rather in the rock, for the country seems thereabouts to be all but one great rock; this opening goes directly down perpendicular into the earth, and perhaps the centre; it may be about twenty foot over one way, and fifty or sixty the other; it has no bottom, that is to say, none that can yet be heard of' (Defoe 1724–6, 477). In Peak Cavern the 'beggar king' Cock Lorrel is said to have supped with the Devil.[3] Stones attracted wonder and the Whetstone on Hergest Ridge above Kington in Herefordshire is reputed to go down to the Buck Brook for a drink when it hears the morning cock crow.[4] In several places in Herefordshire and Worcestershire, natural holes in a river bed have sometimes been interpreted as the 'devil's footsteps', such as 'the Devil's leap' in Doddenham (Worcs.). Springs or 'wells' (from Old English *wealla*, 'spring') seem to have played a part in Celtic mythology, and were often associated with healing, but were readily taken over by Christianity and associated with special saints. The story of the murder of St Kenelm at the foot of the Clent Hills (Worcs.) goes back to medieval times.[5] As a boy king he is said to have been murdered by his sister in AD 821, his head rolling into the nearby bushes where it was discovered by a red cow. A spring gushed forth at the site of his murder and was chosen as the site of a church. The original spring lay beneath the church but the well now occupies another site near by and is still attributed with healing powers.

Another kind of wilderness that became the setting for folk tales and leg-ends was the forest, a backdrop which was also used for the medieval tales of *Sir Gawain and the Green Knight* and *Perle*. The forests encountered by Gawain have been placed in Cheshire, some way beyond 'the wilderness of Wirral':

> … a forest that was deep and fearsomely wild,
> with high hills at each hand, and hoar woods beneath
> of huge aged oaks by the hundred together;
> the hazel and the hawthorn were huddled and tangled
> with rough ragged moss around them trailing …

(*Sir Gawain and the Green Knight*, stanza 32, trans. Tolkien 1979, 33)

Here we meet folktale motifs such as the 'beheading context'; and the 'exchange of winnings', mixed with Arthurian imagery. Hunting legends are not infrequent and a particular group associated with hilly forested districts concerns 'the wild hunt', an item of folklore certainly as old as the early twelfth century, when sightings of the black huntsmen and their black hounds and the sound of their horns were recorded in the *Peterborough Chronicle*. Such demonic huntsmen, accompanied by phantom hounds, would be heard galloping across the sky by night, either in pursuit of dead sinners or as the damned souls themselves, but they were always an omen of death or war (Simpson and Roud 2000, 390). On the Lickey Hills, near Birmingham, the Devil and his chief huntsman would hunt the wild boar by night near Bromsgrove with a pack of hounds the Devil kept at Halesowen (Reader's Digest 1973, 321); Lickey was part of the mid-Worcestershire Forest of Feckenham. On the edge of the same forest, a large black dog is also reputed to have haunted the site of Bordesley Abbey after its dissolution. Rather better known is the pack that rides out across the Stiperstones betokening death, commemorated, again by Mary Webb, in her novel *Gone to Earth*.

Contested landscapes

Because the Midlands has been a 'busy' region of settlement and farming since way back in prehistory the relatively undeveloped regions have always exerted a particular fascination, but they have also been heavily contested landscapes. As land was being parcelled out as individual estates in the early medieval period, disputes might arise between the Crown and the grantees of such estates over such things as rights to swine pasture. A ninth-century Anglo-Saxon charter records, for instance, disputes over the right to mast in *Scyrhylte*, 'the shire wood', within Malvern Forest, which resulted in the safeguarding of the rights of the church of Worcester (Sawyer 1968, S 1437; Hooke 1990, 96–7). After the Norman Conquest, both kings and lords attempted to claim control of the 'waste', whether through the imposition of forest law under the Norman kings, the extension of grazing rights by abbeys, or the enclosing of parks and the claiming of sole right to game by manorial lords. There was often increased conflict between king and people over the right to resources.

In particular, forest law was extended across large parts of the country, the Midlands being no exception. This seriously limited the right to take game as food, a right now reserved for the king and his followers, although continued grazing by surrounding communities was normally allowed. The common folk frequently responded by determined poaching (below). Grants were also increasingly being made by manorial lords to abbeys and priories who thereby acquired grazing rights on the manorial commons. Vaccaries for cattle might be established which combined use of enclosed valley hay meadows with unenclosed upland grazing, but as sheep became increasingly profitable cells or farms (known as granges) were established, especially in upland regions, which made increasing use of the pastures for sheep rearing. Garendon Abbey (Leics.), for instance, acquired, along with other foundations, granges in the White Peak of Derbyshire (Figure 42). Some establishments set up cells to develop newly reclaimed land within wooded regions and some communities were themselves established in such regions, such as Stoneleigh Abbey and Combe Abbey (Warwicks); some lay at the heart of islands of clearance. Many Midland religious communities were able to augment their revenues by the assarting of woodland, often despite such land being subject to common rights (Bond notes the case of Evesham Abbey destroying woodland at Ombersley in the Severn valley of Worcestershire: 2004, 69).

'Squatting' around the waste was often tolerated by local lords for economic reasons, but squatters trod only too closely on a cultural privilege the rich wished to keep for themselves. A certain notoriety and glamour often accompanied the stealing of game, expressed in the tales of Robin Hood (where forests also provided sanctuary) and many a later folk ditty, within the Forest of the Peak. In Peak Cavern in northern Derbyshire bands of tinkers 'hung out', among them the infamous Cock Lorrel, who bested the Devil in an eating contest. Here, in the mid-seventeenth century, rope-makers lived in the cavern mouth in squalid conditions, making ropes for use in the lead mines and, allegedly, for the hangman. Other brigands are said to have occupied caves in Dovedale in the Dove valley. The Peak Forest was also the location for Scott's *Peveril of the Peak*, in which the Peveril family was portrayed as being esconced in their castle perched on the steep valley side above Peakshole Water like an eagle's eyrie. The Peverils had administered the forest but their estates were forfeited for alleged intrigue in the twelfth century; Scott, however, immortalised William Peveril as a royalist confronting Parliamentarian supporters.

It was often as poachers that the common man found a place in history books. Hay has researched the way in which local people reacted to the harsh game laws on Cannock Chase (Staffs.), observing acidly that 'True equality before the law in a society of greatly unequal men is impossible: a truth which is kept decently buried beneath a monument of legislation, judicial ingenuity and cant'. But the act of 1670 did not even try to hide the truth: under this act 'a man had to be lord of a manor, or have a substantial income from landed property, even to kill a hare on his own land' (Hay 1977, 189). It was argued

that the laws were 'to prevent persons of inferior rank, from squandering that
time, which their station in life requireth to be more profitably employed'
(Hay 1977, 191, citing Bacon quoted in Burn 1772, vol. 2, 218). The poor, on
the other hand, condoning their own actions with the notion that Genesis
said that animals were made for man, continued to poach with as much skill,
dexterity, determination and courage as they could command – there could
hardly be a better example of class conflict. Most of those caught were indeed
poor – many of them labourers, colliers and weavers – and were undeniably
needy and without sufficient food for their families, but some were poachers
by trade, gaining a certain notoriety in the local area; most of them came from
Rugeley and were poaching in the woods of the Paget family of Beaudesert.
One cannot but feel a sense of admiration for their audacity and pride: almost
every labourer had 'his cross bred, coney-cut long Dog' and some 'kept hidden in their cottages the heads and antlers of deer they had felled, trophies of
the chase' (Hay 1977, 202, citing Staff RO Q/SB 1786, Ep/12; Taplin 1772, 30).
At times there were actual riots, especially when the Earl of Uxbridge, upon
inheriting the Paget estates, attempted to extend his warrens at the expense of
the commons, and in 1753 the dragoons had to be summoned from Stafford
to keep the peace. The disorder resulted in the cottagers losing their homes,
which were torn down before their crops were gathered in.

This situation found its way into the ballads of the day, although it has
been estimated that only about 300 poachers in all were actually transported
to Australia:

Come all you gallant poachers, that ramble void of care,
That walk out on a moonlight night with dog, gun, and snare,
The lofty hare and pheasant you have at your command,
Not thinking of your last career upon Van Dieman's Land.

(nineteenth-century; quoted in Palmer 1988, 149–50)

Most forests had, however, been disafforested by late medieval times and
had given way to enclosed farmland, a fate that befell Needwood (Staffs.), the
private woods of the Ferrers family in medieval times, only in the early nineteenth century. Here, as elsewhere, the loss of the woodland was severe and
the landscape became one of monotonous farmland with only a few private
deer parks and woods retaining anything of the earlier nature of the landscape.
Cannock Chase, a private chase of the bishops of Lichfield, retains something
of its earlier appearance despite the vast ranks of conifers planted here after
the two World Wars: ancient pollard oaks can be found in the woods at
Brocton and deer still frequent the more open Sherbrooke valley (Figure 43).
Vast tracts of the remaining commons in the Midlands were enclosed in the
final stages of parliamentary enclosure. In the Welsh Borderland, the open
sheepwalks were replaced by huge enclosed fields to which only the owner
and his men had right of access. Much of this enclosure took place as late as
the nineteenth century. In the Peak District the open moorlands became the
hated grouse moors, conserved for the enjoyment of the few.

FIGURE 43.
Sherbrooke valley
on Cannock Chase,
Staffordshire, an area
still frequented by deer
today.

Another source of contention was the ownership of mineral rights. Studies of rights in the Forest of Dean (Gloucs.) reveal considerable conflict, over rights not only to timber but also to the exploitation of the region's coal and iron resources. Here iron had been worked since prehistoric times but by the late thirteenth century the region was producing about one-sixth of the country's iron. The inhabitants of the area held traditional rights to dig for iron ore, coal or stone. These were rights they guarded jealously, with the freeminers holding their own courts to settle disputes from the seventeenth century (a freeminer was defined as a man born and living within the hundred of St Briavels who had worked there a year and a day in a coal or iron mine). As the iron industy expanded, these restrictive rights of exclusion and protectionism became a source of contention, and miners were increasingly tempted to lease their holdings to outsiders, especially gentlemen of quality. Rival ironmasters, in any case, paid little heed to the customs of the freeminers and commoners, with ensuing riots. Only in 1838 did the freeminers admit that they held such rights by royal sufferance, thus weakening their position and opening up the way for the 'regulating [of] the opening and working of mines and quarries in the Forest of Dean' (*VCH* 1907, 222–32). Similarly, other small-scale delvings for coal or minerals by the poorer members of the community, as on the Clee Hills or in the Ironbridge region, were to give way to organised mining by large companies. Many of these people had combined seasonal mining with smallholding and communities had spread around the fringes of the commons in both regions, making use of the available free pasture to keep a few cattle, sheep or geese.

Landscapes of identity

Wilderness regions were often also to become the landscapes of nostalgia, remembered in times of adversity and exile, or in old age and periods of ill health. Others were to find that such landscapes fulfilled their need for a place of personal identity, a place they could feel was their 'homeland'. For the poet A. E. Housman it was 'the blue remembered hills' of Shropshire, seen in the distance from his home in north Worcestershire. The Malvern Hills, too, have been remembered with nostalgia by many, especially those away from home during the two World Wars, and have inspired a corpus of poetry of their own. These same hills also inspired the music of Elgar.

The wildness and harshness of the Peak District has symbolised the independence of spirit – the stoicism, strength and perseverance – which, it was felt, characterised the people of the North in contrast to those of the easier South (Tebbutt 2004, 142). This was a wild and elemental landscape, the kind of upland that served as a refuge against any invader and upheld 'British' values of freedom and liberty (Figure 44). Both peace and a sense of adventure were to be found in the untamed valleys and sweeping moorlands: 'the elemental grandeur of the barren moors and gritstone edges' (Baddeley 1908). This landscape provided a fitting backcloth for 'the military values of courage, a cool head, resolution, self-control, restraint and character', played out through sports such as mountaineering, in which the individual pitted himself 'against nature in a character building battle with self and the physical world' (Tebbutt 2004, 144–5). Farming, too, was often difficult and the gritstone farmhouses still cling to the edge of the hills, surrounded by their greener intake fields that have been wrestled only with difficulty from the surrounding moor. Several authors, among them Francis Brett Young (1932) and, more recently, Bruce Chatwin (1982), have written about the region straddling the border between Wales and England and have compared the harshness of Wales and the Welsh outlook with the tenderer 'softness' of England.

For Francis Brett Young, writing in the 1930s, it was the Wyre Forest that symbolised stability in a changing world. As industry was converting the Black Country into a living hell of fire, smoke and appalling living conditions, the woodland only a few miles away changed hardly at all. In his 'Werewood',

> the passage of time is so leisurely as to be barely perceived. The first quality of the forest is its timelessness. The growth of its close-ringed oaks is so gradual that the span of one human generation adds little to their girth or stature. Men are born and live and die among them without making much difference. It is only they who change. (Brett Young 1936, part I, ch. 5, ii)

Conservation landscapes: the healing landscape offering an escape from the everyday world

Perhaps it was the great loss of the commons in the enclosure movements from the eighteenth century onwards that brought home to the general populace the loss of a landscape they had until then generally felt was very much 'their own'. It had been the creation of royal and demesne deer parks that had first removed extensive areas of waste into private ownership, but even here, an ancient 'Law of Arden', quoted in a law suit of 1221, claimed to allow a lord to make enclosures only so long as sufficient common was left for his tenants (Stenton 1934, lxvi–ii, 448–9). This pre-dated the Statute of Merton which, in 1236, similarly attempted to protect the rights of landowners whose grazing rights were being diminished by the enclosure of grassland and woodland. Over the centuries, the commoners often had to be vigilant in protecting their various rights over the manorial wastes, whether these entailed rights to pasture (even, usually, protected within royal forests), common of turbary (the right to take turf and peat for fuel) or of estover (the right to take sufficient wood for fuel, making tools, houses and hedges), but these were among acknowledged rights over the waste generally enjoyed by most commoners everywhere. Gradual enclosure by lord or tenant had nibbled into the wastes, but it was the enclosure movement, gaining ground in the eighteenth century under the impetus of 'agricultural improvement', that caused the greatest losses, and the remaining wastes became the focus of enclosure in the nineteenth century. Vast tracts of marginal land were to pass into private ownership, especially the open sheepwalks of the Welsh Borderland or Derbyshire. Large acreages in the White Peak around Bakewell and Matlock were enclosed and subdivided by private act into the stone-walled fields that still dominate the modern landscape. In the Borderland, the Clun sheepwalks in south-western Shropshire were some of the last hill commons to disappear in this way, with over 6,000 acres (2,428 ha) enclosed under the general act of 1845. In the Dark Peak much of the open moorland had remained accessible for pasture by the poor after Peak Forest had ceased to exist in the seventeenth century, but by the end of the nineteenth extensive areas had become grouse moors.

It was in the latter area that public reaction was strongest, for the Dark Peak was very close to the growing industrial districts of northern England and had long served as a 'lung' for those attempting to escape such surroundings. The advent of the railway, trams, buses and bicycles had given the public increased mobility. Day trippers from Birmingham and the Black Country were able to access the Clent and Lickey Hills to the south and after the Open Spaces Acts of 1877 and 1881 the Birmingham Association for the Preservation of Open Spaces bought Rednal Hill on the Lickeys with the help of local philanthropic families to provide land for public enjoyment, land which was extended by further gifts. On the Malvern Hills, a Commons Society was set up in the late nineteenth century to protect the hills from encroachment and quarrying, and the Conservators were able to purchase the manor and manorial rights in 1925, giving them control over 1,700 acres (688 ha); another 1,200 acres (485 ha) were acquired by the National Trust in 1935. Elsewhere, the footpaths that had long served the rural countryside were upheld as rights of way. The northern grouse moors of the Dark Peak, however, enjoyed little similar benevolence.

FIGURE 44.
A view over Axe Moor in the Dark Peak.

FIGURE 45.
The view from
Mortimer's Way over
the Vale of Wigmore
in Herefordshire.

Rights of way here were few and when in 1877 landowners closed one of them to safeguard their shooting a struggle began with those responsible for managing the rights of way of ordinary folk that lasted for some twenty years. Even when the contested route was reinstated matters were not resolved and when walkers were prevented by gamekeepers from walking over the moors of Kinder Scout in 1930 a mass trespass was organised which involved as many as 400 protestors. Fortunately, the situation has improved immeasurably since then, with landowners able to claim reimbursement for providing access under a succession of government-aided schemes. Nationally, whole regions have been designated as National Parks, augmented by Areas of Outstanding Natural Beauty, and measures have been taken to encourage public enjoyment of open spaces. In the Midlands most of these areas include areas of upland or woodland. On a smaller scale, local councils have set aside Countryside Parks. In an attempt to extend the amount of land under woodland, additional areas have been designated as National or Community Forests; one of the latter lies to the north of the West Midland conurbation. New long-distance footpaths have been designated in every Midland county (Figure 45) and the 'right to roam' over open moorland has been established over much of such land in the region. Objectives are twofold: to preserve the environment and to provide 'wilderness' areas for public enjoyment. Such landscapes are seen as beneficial for health and enjoyment, acting as places for both exercise and relaxation.

Today 'wilderness' is no longer, then, the despised 'waste' of the nineteenth-century agricultural writers, who saw it as a grossly under-used resource, but is a rare and treasured environment offering a habitat for wild fauna and flora and an escape for people from the stress of the everyday world. Measures are taken to protect, conserve and manage what is left for the good of the nation. The 'weirdness' may have gone but the 'wonderful' lives on.

Notes

1. Most stories of malevolent rivers seem to come from nineteenth-century traditions (recorded, for example, for the Dart in Devon in 1850 and the Derwent in Derbyshire in 1903), with rivers sometimes being inhabited by water spirits who dragged people (especially children) into the water to drown them (Simpson and Roud 2000, 297, 381). Palmer (2002, 16) gives no date for the belief that the Herefordshire Wye required a victim, other than stating that it was 'a traditional belief', but quotes a late occurrence of the belief after a child was drowned near Bredwardine.

2. The dating of legends passed down through oral tradition can be difficult but stories of the Devil being thwarted by ordinary humans or by members of the Christian church probably hark back to medieval times. Medieval Christianity taught that the strategies of the Devil, although he persistently attacked individuals with temptations, were ultimately futile, since Christ had already defeated him (Simpson and Roud 2000, 94–5).

3. The ballad of Cock Lorrel is incorporated into Jonson's masque 'A Masque of the Metamorphosed Gipsies', first performed in 1621 (see Gifford 1875, 7, 392–4), but the figure pre-dates this, for he appears c.1510 in an anonymous poem 'Cocke Lorrelle's Bote'. Gifford (1875, 7, 391, n.7) notes that Cock Lorrel was said to be the head of a gang of thieves, by trade a tinker, in the time of Henry VIII. His swaggering pride remained a feature of Derbyshire folklore into modern times.

4. Palmer suggests that the name Whetstone here may be a corruption of 'wheat stone' and may derive from 'a time of plague in the fourteenth century when supplies of corn and other produce were left there for Kington people to collect' (Palmer 2002, 4).

5. Bodleian Library, Oxford, MSS Douce 368.

CHAPTER TWELVE

Tally-ho! The Making and Representation of the Hunting Landscape of the Shires

Nicholas Watkins

The evolution of the modern sport of foxhunting in the second half of the eighteenth century signalled a geographical and cultural retreat into the countryside. A metropolitan elite, followed by royalty, was drawn away from the fashionable centres of Bath and Brighton to spend the winters in the landscape of the East Midlands, foxhunting as many as six days a week with the five famous Shire packs the Quorn, its southern offshoot the Fernie (formerly known as the Billesdon, Mr. Tailby's and the South Quorn), the Belvoir, the Cottesmore and the Pytchley (Figure 46). Market Harborough, on the southern border of the Fernie and within easy reach of the Pytchley, and more particularly Melton Mowbray, on the eastern border of the Quorn at the junction with the Belvoir and Cottesmore, were transformed from obscure market towns into nationally renowned winter resorts dedicated to foxhunting. Charles James Apperley, who, under his *nom de plume* of Nimrod and with his favourite illustrator Henry Alken Senior, was the originator of foxhunting journalism, established a defining image of the sport and was partly responsible for its immense popularity, described the impact of hunting on the local economy of Melton Mowbray in the 1820s: 'The money, however, spent in this town alone by strangers, who resort to it for the purpose of hunting, cannot be computed at less than twenty thousand pounds per annum, as there are generally from two hundred and fifty to three hundred horses quartered in its stables' (Nimrod 1835, 133). To sustain a full season's hunting, with two hunters out each day and a covert hack to get to the meet, required a stable of an absolute minimum of nine horses with their grooms and second-horsemen, coupled with the support services of farriers, veterinary surgeons, horse dealers, saddlers, forage merchants, boot makers, tailors and hatters. Apart from the provision of hunt kennels, the accommodation of this annual influx of wealthy visitors, along with their horses and grooms, had a considerable effect on the built environment. Lodges, hunting boxes and stables sprang up in Market Harborough, Melton Mowbray and in the surrounding towns and villages, and farmhouses in the country were let during the season.

This chapter, however, is concerned with the actual landscape and its perception and not with the built environment, which scarcely features in representations of the hunting landscape. In the paintings discussed here no visual link is consciously established between the country mansion, aristocratic patronage and the hunt. The point, often missed, is that the modern sport of foxhunting was a radically new form of hunting, somewhat risqué in its origins and disturbingly democratic in its inclusiveness. Quite unlike previous forms of exclusively royal and aristocratic deer hunting, which took place in protected woodland and parks, modern foxhunting was the first form of organised hunting in which large numbers of subscribers crossed farmland with the permission of supportive landowners and their tenant farmers, who were obliged to preserve foxes and let the hunt over their land. Anyone with sufficient funds could hunt and farmers always went free. As it developed in the nineteenth century, foxhunting became the national, quintessential English sport, establishing in the process defining qualities of Englishness: it was robust, courageous, companionable and rooted in the traditions of the

FIGURE 46.
The Hunting Countries of the Shire Packs of the East Midlands. Detail from *Southern and Wales Showing the Fox Hunts, Baily's Hunting Directory 1921–1922.*

countryside. The Continentals, particularly the French, had hunting, but it was confined to forests and therefore did not test the nerve and skill of horsemen jumping fenced farmland at pace. Foxhunting in the Shires evolved its own mythology, with its legendary heroes, whose daring exploits and feats of stamina were chronicled by Nimrod and depicted by Alken and Ferneley, and the landscape itself came to be perceived as the 'Elysian Fields' (Blow 1983, 5) or as a veritable 'paradise of jumpable fences' (Sassoon 1928, 247). In comparison with the glamorous metropolitan image of the five Shire packs, the other 300 registered packs in the country were judged provincial. So persuasive and prevalent was the identification of Englishness with the mythology of foxhunting in the Shires that David, Prince of Wales, later Edward VIII, was keen to participate and adopt the image of the dashing foxhunter (Figure 47), and a sensitive poet such as Siegfried Sassoon, trapped in the trenches of the First World War, yearned for the certainties of English country life centred on foxhunting (Egremont 2005, 92).

Following on from the work of Hoskins (1955; 1957; 1978), Everett (1994), *The Geographies of Englishness: Landscape and the National Past 1880–1940* (Corbett *et al.* 2002) and de Belin (2004), this chapter sets out to examine the interaction of hunting, modernisation, landscape and national identity in the making and representation of the hunting landscape of the Shires, and focuses on the interwar art of Sir Alfred Munnings (1878–1959) and Lionel Edwards (1878–1966), the two leading artists of the twentieth century associated with hunting. Both painters appealed to and transformed traditions of representing the hunting landscape established by Henry Alken Senior (1785–1851) and John Ferneley Senior (1782–1806). The chapter seeks to show how their representation of the hunting landscape of the Shires was inseparable from its myth, and that their ways of representing the landscape evolved and changed along with the landscape itself.

Hunting, modernisation and the making of the landscape

But why was foxhunting so closely associated with the East Midlands and what effect, if any, did this have on the making of the landscape? The answer to the first question is that the modern sport of foxhunting was perfected in Leicestershire. Although the fox had been hunted regularly well before the eighteenth century, the development of the modern sport was largely due to Hugo Meynell, founder and Master of the Quorn, the first subscription pack, from 1753 to 1800. The Meynellian science involved a radically new form of foxhunting, based on the facts that the fox feeds at night but was to be hunted by day, and that the landscape itself was remarkable for the paucity of large areas of woodland. Instead of a local squire with a few friends meeting early in the morning and slowly hunting the fox back to its home covert, the process was reversed: the earths were stopped at night, when the fox was out hunting, and the hunt began by drawing its home covert, starting at the much later time of eleven o'clock in the morning, when the fox had had time to digest its evening meal. Once flushed the fox had to flee across open country in the direction of the next covert, thus affording the mounted followers, known as the 'field', the thrilling opportunity of a 'scurry', 'skim' or 'run' in their attempt to keep up with hounds. As Meynell did not own the land over which he hunted, he had to negotiate with all the landowners concerned (de Belin 2004, 54). However, in hunting circles, he is best remembered as an outstanding breeder of hounds. He learned about in-and-in breeding (brother to sister) from his near-neighbour Robert Bakewell at Dishley Hall and bred a much faster, deep scenting, hound (Ellis 1951, 9; Ridley 1990, 17). The pace of foxhunting speeded up. Improved hounds were matched in the Shires by faster, near-thoroughbred, horses and by a new style of quick riding, which included – much to Meynell's horror – jumping at pace, the 'flying leap' promoted by Mr Childe of Kinlet (Carr 1986, 40). Foxhunting became the downhill skiing of its age. The development of foxhunting as a fashionable metropolitan sport in Leicestershire could not, however, have taken place without the modernisation of the landscape, achieved firstly through a dramatic improvement in communications and secondly by the completion of the gradual process of enclosing large open fields into the patchwork of strongly fenced small fields we see today.

Prior to this modernisation nobody – let alone a large influx of outsiders

*The Making
and Representation
of the Hunting
Landscape
of the Shires*

– would have been able to get to a distant meet of a hunt because, before the building of the turnpike roads, which reached Leicestershire's southern border in 1721–2, the county was near-impassable in winter. Daniel Defoe reported on the dreadful state of Leicestershire's roads in the early eighteenth century (Defoe 1924–6, 407). By 1750 the Northampton to Derby turnpike passed through Market Harborough, Leicester and Loughborough, and by 1760 turnpike roads connected Leicester with Uppingham, Oakham and Melton Mowbray (Cross 2003, 31, 33). The extension of the turnpike system, coupled with the improvements of Telford and McAdam, resulted in journey times between London, Market Harborough, Leicester and Melton Mowbray being cut dramatically. Between 1811 and 1835 the speed of the mail coach from London increased by 40 per cent, averaging 9.68 mph (15.5 kph) on the 106-mile (170 km) trip to Melton Mowbray (Cross, 2003 18). With the advent of the railways, however, these times were soon eclipsed.

The railway revolution was central to the development of foxhunting as a metropolitan sport in the Shires. The Midland Railway line, linking Derby and Leicester with the London and Birmingham line at Rugby, opened in May 1839 and in 1861 Market Harborough and Leicester received a direct connection to London (Simpson 1927, 34). Branch lines meant that Melton Mowbray and Oakham were accessible by train from 1848; and the rail journey between London and Melton Mowbray was much improved in 1879 by a direct link from Market Harborough with through carriages from Euston (Ellis 1951, 94). Initially, foxhunters regarded the advent of the railways as a form of desecration. Brooksby, the *nom de plume* of Captain Pennell-Elmhirst, Nimrod's successor as the leading hunting correspondent of his age, commented on the 1876/7 season, 'You have heard, reader, that the bosom of Leicestershire is being scarred and seared by railways crossing it in every direction' (Brooksby 1883, 192). However, despite foxhunters prophesying the destruction of their sport at each technical innovation, they soon took full advantage, and special trains were laid on for them. During the 1877/8 season Brooksby, again, reported on a meet in the Pytchley country in which 'Hounds came by train; so did the Master; and so did a strong proportion of the field – from Leamington, Coventry, Birmingham and elsewhere' (Brooksby 1883, 220). As lines and speeds improved it became possible by the 1880s to have a day's hunting with a Melton pack from London, catching the 7.15 from King's Cross and reaching Melton at 10.32, and then return that evening (Ridley 1990, 63).

The East Midlands landscape was not so much made as adapted for foxhunting, as Hoskins pointed out (1978, 81). The classic account of its suitability was published by Nimrod in 1835:

Both nature and art have contributed to render Leicestershire the country for fox-hunting. To the former, it is indebted for the depth and richness of its soil – favourable to holding a scent; and to the latter, for the large size of its enclosures, for the general practicality of its fences, for the greatest portion of the land being old pasture, and for the numerous gorse coverts made

FIGURE 48.
Lionel Edwards,
Sheepthorns, 1928. By
courtesy of Rosenstiel's
Widow & Son Ltd

for the breeding and preserving of foxes. There is another circumstance also which gives Leicestershire a decided advantage over other countries; and that is, the few <u>large</u> coverts which the better part of it contains, thereby affording such <u>room</u> for sport, that if a fox once gets away, and is a good one, a run (barring accidents) must be the consequence. (Nimrod 1835, 1)

The enclosures of pasture, the stockproof but jumpable fences and the small coverts are the three crucial features of the hunting landscape of the Shires, and these will be taken in turn.

What singled out Leicestershire in the minds of foxhunters as the ideal hunting country was its grassland. Brooksby asked rhetorically, 'In what have we been taught to consider lies its first charm, and what does experience tells us is its ruling delight? Is it not its springy turf and firm elastic footing; the power of skimming lightly over the surface, and bounding gaily over its fences … ?' (Brooksby 1883, 59). Lionel Edwards summarised the attractions of Leicestershire in one word: 'grass' (Edwards 1947, 60). The heavy liassic clays of the East Midlands, as Hoskins pointed out, produced excellent grassland (Hoskins 1978, 82). Much of it was old pasture, particularly in the Melton area, where about a third of the land had always been devoted to grazing, but the lucrative nature of the business ensured that during the second half of the eighteenth century most of the parishes around the town were laid down to grass. Large enclosures of old pasture provided the ideal surface for a fast

*The Making
and Representation
of the Hunting
Landscape
of the Shires*

run, in contrast to post-enclosure pasture laid down over the old ridges and furrows. As Brooksby observed, 'How horses must, and do, always hate this relic of ancient agriculture! Nothing kills their pluck, or chokes their lungs, like being called upon to plunge and rise at top speed against these chopping seas of turf' (Brooksby 1883, 129–30). A further restriction to a fast gallop came with the gravitation from sheep to cattle, when the large enclosures of old pasture were often subdivided and the stock rotated between smaller fields of anything from about 7 to 24 acres (2.8–9.7 ha) (de Belin 2004, 13).

The parliamentary enclosure acts of the eighteenth and early nineteenth centuries in fact completed a process that had been going on since the fifteenth century. Goodacre's case study of the transformation of a peasant economy in the Lutterworth area documents the accelerating progress of enclosure from 1507 to 1797 (Goodacre 1994, 243), and Hoskins estimated that some 60 per cent of Leicestershire was subject to pre-parliamentary enclosure (Hoskins 1957, 86). Enclosure in the county generally entailed the conversion from arable to livestock and pasture. In his case study of the parish of Wigston, Hoskins demonstrated that the effect of the enclosure act of

FIGURE 49.
Henry Alken Senior,
*The Leicestershire
Covers*, 1824. Courtesy
of Roger Rixon,
Leicestershire County
Council

THE LEICESTERSHIRE COVERS
By Henry Alken Senior, 1824. Engraved by T. Sutherland.

Lent by Messrs. Walford Bros

The Cover   Whissendine Brook   Freeby Wood   Waltham Stonesby   Buckminster   Wymondham   Whissendine

FULL CRY: WHISSENDINE PASTURE

Mr. Crosses' House   Great Home Close   Kettleby Church   Road to Melton   Bilsdon Coplow

THE DEATH: VIEW OF KETTLEBY

157

1766 was so complete that only some 55 or 56 acres (22–22.5 ha), out of a total of just over 2,887 acres (1168 ha), escaped. In addition, the award stipulated that within four months the allotments to the two main beneficiaries, the Duke of St Albans and the vicar, were 'to be mounded and fenced round by ditches and quickset hedges guarded or fenced with good posts and double rails', which were to be paid for by the other proprietors. By 1832 two-thirds of the parish of Wigston was under pasture (Hoskins 1957, 250–4, 261–2). A very similar pattern was followed all over Leicestershire, Rutland and north Northamptonshire. De Belin points out that landholding patterns changed, with the landowning yeoman farmer giving way to an agricultural economy of landlord and tenant, and that by the late eighteenth century grassland farms brought better rents and reduced expenditure on buildings and maintenance. She also suggests that the prevalence of grassland may reflect the landowners' growing enthusiasm for foxhunting, as new tenancy agreements often included the obligation to admit the hunt and maintain coverts (de Belin 2004, 11–12).

The flying leap or jumping at pace was a singular attraction of the Shires for a foxhunter. As Brooksby put it:

> When jumping ceases to be a pleasure, then Leicestershire has ceased to be the place for us … The thrill of the flying leap is only a part of the joy of a good grass country. But it is a very large and leading part; while our nerve lasts and we are happy in our horseflesh. (Brooksby 1883, 229)

Strong thorn hedges are most commonly associated with the post-enclosure hunting landscape. However, as thorn hedges took at least twenty years to grow before they could be cut and laid, the newly planted saplings themselves had to be protected from stock by a wooden rail on either side. Foxhunters then had the choice to jump either in and out over the rails, hopefully missing the saplings, or to clear the whole obstacle. Hedges before laying looked like near-impenetrable screens, known as bullfinches, through which a bold horse had to crash its way, with the rider often emerging with a scratched face, a fate that the Empress Elizabeth of Austria, hunting with the Pytchley in 1877, instructed her 'pilot', the famous horseman Bay Middleton, to avoid: 'Remember, I do not mind the falls but I will not scratch my face' (Buxton 1987, 80). To make the enclosed fields additionally stockproof, the hedges were strengthened into oxers or the extra-strong double oxers, which came in with the import of boisterous Irish bullocks in the 1830s (Ellis 1951, 24, 26–7). Nimrod gives a detailed description of an oxer or oxe-fence: 'first, there is a wide ditch; secondly, a strong blackthorn hedge, which in this country generally grows luxuriantly; and about two yards beyond the hedge is a strong rail' (Nimrod 1835, 136). The double oxer had a rail on both sides of the hedge, and in some areas a second ditch. Brooksby complained that the farmers of Brooksby and Rotherby:

> would seem to have constructed their fences under some special contract

*The Making
and Representation
of the Hunting
Landscape
of the Shires*

with the fiend of destruction. An ox-rail is seldom a welcome addition to a stiff fence, still less is it nice to find it set a full horse's length beyond; but when all this combination is supplemented by a second ditch, the hope of getting over becomes a very forlorn one indeed. (Brooksby 1883, 82)

Another unwelcome variant was the 'rasper', which leant outwards from the fence with a considerable portion of the blackthorn left uncut (de Belin 2004, 18). If all this proved too daunting a foxhunter could, with any luck, find a gap in the hedge with an infilling post-and-rail fence to jump.

The scarcity of hedgerow timber and the comparative absence of wire were further features of the hunting landscape of the Shires. Hoskins noted that the few trees in the hedges were spaced out at wide intervals to allow plenty of room for jumping, a point substantiated by Costobadie: 'Owing to the numerous accidents which occurred to sportsmen about fifty years ago through their coming into collision with over-hanging boughs, a great many trees in the hedge-rows were cut down' (Hoskins 1955, 196; Costobadie 1914, 197). With fields on fashionable days of 300, or even on occasion as many as 500, such a development was also necessary to prevent riders crashing into each other. With numerous places to jump a large field could spread out and 'take their own line' across country. Lionel Edwards' picture of the Fernie at *Sheepthorns* (Figure 48) shows a typical hunting landscape with relatively few trees in the hedgerows. These hedgerows, with their subsidiary fencing, were expensive to build and maintain and so, from its introduction in the 1860s, wire, a much cheaper alternative, became increasingly prevalent. However, so important was traditional fencing for the mobility and enjoyment of the hunt that the Shire packs paid for the wire to be taken down in key areas during the hunting season and then put back in spring.

Even more crucial, though, to the development and continuance of foxhunting was the establishment and maintenance of small purpose-built fox coverts of some 2 to 20 acres (0.8–8 ha) across the country. This was an absolute necessity to ensure good runs and a sustainable, evenly distributed fox population (Ellis 1951, 60). The comparative scarcity of large woods was a prime condition for the conversion of the landscape of the Shires into a foxhunting paradise. It was very difficult to get a fox away quickly from a large wood of some 250 acres (101 ha), such as Owston Wood, as Brooksby makes clear:

Tell me, unbiased and experienced reader, what do you attach to the prospect of Owston Wood, Launde Wood, Tilton Wood, and such other sylvan resorts? Do you not connect the names with harassing hours of idleness, with many bitter disappointments, and many futile vows of future abstinence from thus tempting fate? (Brooksby 1883, 144)

The country was historically sparsely wooded. Anthony Squires and Michael Jeeves make the point that in the Domesday Book folios only 3.7 per cent of Leicestershire and 12.3 per cent of Rutland was woodland and that this remarkable shortage, first detectable at least 1,000 years earlier in the Iron

Age and possibly originating in Neolithic times, has endured to the present day (Squires and Jeeves 1994, 26). By the time of the publication of Combe's *Map of Leicestershire and the Surrounding Country* in 1834, in which, according to Nimrod, 'all the coverts belonging to the different hunts are laid down with great accuracy' (Nimrod 1835, 138), the East Midlands landscape was covered in a network of fox coverts. The process of adding and, where necessary, replacing coverts became a major responsibility of the hunts. These coverts, often located on the crests of hills, have become well-known landmarks. Several of them were named after their makers or owners, some after distinguished foxhunters and royalty, and others, such as the Waterloo covert in the Pytchley country, after battles or national events. Quite a number are named after nearby villages, such as the Billesdon Coplow, or after geographical features. Botany Bay, in the Quorn country, acquired its name from being far from human habitation, like the penal settlement in Australia.

These famous coverts entered hunting mythology and became familiar to foxhunters the world over through sporting literature, paintings and prints. Siegfried Sassoon gives a vivid description of a dedicated provincial foxhunter, Colonel Hesmon, who modelled himself on Whyte-Melville and mid-Victorian sporting novels and who, through the writings of Brooksby in *The Field*, 'knew the name of every gorse-covert and woodland in the Shires' (Sassoon 1928, 155). Colonel Hesmon was not unique. These coverts were central to foxhunting in the Shires. Alken was careful to name them in the captions below *The Leicestershire Coverts* (Figure 49). Ferneley often includes such notable landmarks as the Billesdon Coplow, which rises to more than 180 m above the surrounding countryside. Lionel Edwards features these coverts in his hunting scenes in both *My Hunting Sketch Book* and *A Leicestershire Sketch Book*, and describes their locations. In the former he selected *Sheepthorns* (Figure 48) to represent the Fernie country – 'A rolling, almost a hill country; all grass as far as the eye can see, the fields mostly ridge and furrow, few trees, and stiff fences' – and

FIGURE 50. John Ferneley Senior, *The Quorn Hunt Scurry at Billesdon Coplow*, 1831. Oil on canvas, 30.5 × 121.8 cm. Private collection, USA. Courtesy of Richard Green Gallery, London

*The Making
and Representation
of the Hunting
Landscape
of the Shires*

placed the covert in the centre 'depicted from the hillside below Carlton Clump [itself a landmark from miles around], looking towards Tur Langton Church' (Edwards 1935, 14). Each notable feature of the hunting landscape became associated with some equestrian event. Carlton Clump, for instance, was the finishing post of the race on 5 December 1829 between Squire Osbaldeston on Pilot and Captain Ross on Polecat (Cuming 1926, 55).

Sheepthorns is a typical purpose-built hunting covert: located in sight of the next covert on the horizon and yet isolated like an island within a sea of grass (the grass has now given way to plough). The actual construction of a blackthorn fox covert differs from a shooting covert. The objective is to provide a warm, dark sanctuary for a fox. According to Joe Cowen, the current Master of the Fernie, blackthorn is ideal because it sprouts off the roots and grows up thick from the bottom to provide a dense protective lair. The shooting fraternity dislike blackthorn coverts because it is difficult to get the birds out of them. Charles Simpson gives a detailed description of the method for planting or renovating a blackthorn covert:

> A few larches and a little privet may be planted at each corner – purely for ornament, as Isaac would say – but the covert itself (usually of from two to twenty acres) should be a square plot of low blackthorn surrounded by a whitethorn hedge. The difference between the two thorns is that live blackthorn … will spread and spring up from the roots extending to a considerable space underground, while whitethorn will not. (Simpson 1927, 106)

The purpose of the whitethorn hedge was to keep out the wind and provide a protective fence around the covert.

Royalty, national identity and the representation of the hunting landscape

The experience of modern foxhunting in the Shires brought a changed perception of the landscape orchestrated in terms of movement of the hunt across the
landscape, and presented artists with the challenge of finding ways of conveying this convincingly. Never before in peacetime had so many horsemen all
dedicated to a common pursuit appeared in the countryside. Henry Alken
Senior established the precedent of dividing the foxhunt into four stages, each
with its own distinctive character (Figure 49). *The Meet* provided the occasion
for an equestrian group portrait, with the hunt hierarchy of master, secretary, huntsman with his hounds and whippers-in competing for attention with
leading members of the field. *Breaking Covert* opened up a panorama of the
landscape over which the fox was expected to lead the field. *Full Cry* or *Scurry*,
the third and most challenging stage for the field, was the civilian equivalent of
a cavalry charge, with competitive sportsmen drawn out across the panorama
of the landscape. Seemingly inevitably, the landscape features some frighten-
ing hazard, such as Whissendine Brook or the Billesdon Brook, which brings
many a sportsman to grief. John Ferneley's *The Quorn Hunt Scurry at Billesdon
Coplow* (Figure 50), for instance, was commissioned to commemorate a desper-
ate incident when a group of hard riders in their eagerness to get a good start
followed the fox and overrode hounds (Morris 2005, 48–51; Cuming 1926,
48–51). *The Scurry* was the ultimate test of nerve and horsemanship. Dale, in
his account of the Belvoir in the period 1799–1828, notes 'how the struggle
with France stimulated Englishmen of all classes to take part in manly exer-
cises, and this favoured the rise of fox-hunting' (Dale 1899, 84). The equation
between hunting and the preparation for war continued to be advanced as a
defence of the sport during the First World War, and cavalry officers up to the
Second World War were encouraged to hunt, without it counting as leave.

The Death or *The Kill*, usually depicted in open country, was the occasion
for another, smaller group portrait of the select few with the skill, courage and
stamina to be up at the last. Such was the pace of modern foxhunting in the
grasslands of the Shires that two horses were needed and *Change of Horses*,
which generally took place at two o'clock, was a fifth, subsidiary, stage providing the setting for an equestrian portrait of an individual patron (see Figures
52 and 53). As it evolved into a national sport, foxhunting became identified
as an English tradition, an icon of national identity, to be defended against
cultural changes and the intrusion of modernity. This novel public perception
of foxhunting owed much to increased royal patronage.

Royalty had a defining cultural role in the evolution of foxhunting. The
Prince Regent, later George IV, set his seal of approval on the elevation of
the fox from despised vermin to honoured quarry in 1793, when he gave up
hunting the stag in Hampshire and took to foxhunting (Carr 1986, 41). Such
was the national popularity of foxhunting that on 5 December 1843 Queen
Victoria, who disliked the sport, felt obliged to attend a meet of the Belvoir
at Croxton Park, at which the Prince Consort hunted (Dale 1899, 41). She

*The Making
and Representation
of the Hunting
Landscape
of the Shires*

also, according to Hoyle, 'disliked the exclusive character of shooting and compared it unfavourably to hunting, whose openness was the source of its popularity, and encouraged her son to hunt more and shoot less' (Hoyle 2005, 10). The Prince of Wales, the future Edward VII (1841–1910), hunted intermittently with the Shire packs from 1866, when he first went out with the Belvoir at Piper Hole, and in 1871 a covert was named after him in the Quorn country by Baggrave Hall (Dale 1899, 233; Clayton 1993, 19). By comparison with his ancestors, Edward, Prince of Wales, the future Edward VIII (1894–1972), was by far the keenest royal foxhunter and had the greatest impact on the sport: the royal family had until then patronised shooting in Norfolk and, by switching to hunting in the Shires, Edward was striking out on his own (Hoyle 2005). The Prince first hunted with the Pytchley as the guest of George Drummond of Pitsford Hall, which had been the home of several previous masters of the hunt, including Mr Musters (1821–7), Squire Osbaldeston (1827–34) and Colonel Anstruther Thomson (1864–9) (Paget 1937, 12–13). After that the Prince hunted from Melton Mowbray, staying at Craven Lodge, where he was often joined by his brothers the Dukes of Kent and Gloucester (Clayton 1993, 123). Lionel Edwards was not alone in crediting him with the popularity of Melton Mowbray after the First World War (Edwards 1947, 59). The Duke of York (George VI) first hunted from Melton but after his marriage to Lady Elizabeth Bowes Lyon in 1923 he took a hunting box at Naseby Woollies for a couple of seasons and then after that at Thornby, both in the Pytchley country. In April 1931 the young Princess Elizabeth (Queen Elizabeth II) witnessed the last day of Frank Freeman (Figure 51), the celebrated huntsman of the Pytchley, who was painted by Munnings (Paget 1937, 19, 256).

Munnings achieved public recognition as the leading painter of hunting scenes at the Royal Academy Summer Exhibition of 1921, which featured his equestrian portrait *The Prince of Wales on Forest Witch* (Figure 47). The painting was presented by *The Field* to commemorate the Prince's first season hunting with the Pytchley and was initially shown at Munnings's Alpine Gallery exhibition in 1921, along with scenes of hounds and hunting painted during his stay in the winter of 1919/20 at Woolsthorpe with Major Tommy Bouch, Master of the Belvoir (Goodman 1988, 165). The Royal Academy stood for the nation, a defender of traditional values against modernism and foreign influence, and its agreement to have *The Prince of Wales on Forest Witch* removed from a commercial gallery, possibly at the instigation of King George V, and placed in a position of honour on an easel at the top of the staircase leading to the Summer Exhibition confirmed the status of foxhunting in the Shires as a symbol of Englishness and the Prince's wish to be identified publicly with this quintessential English rural pursuit (Taylor in Corbett *et al.* 2002, 173). The painting also embodied two important ideas: firstly, a perpetuation in the post-war period of what Everett defined as a Tory perception of landscape, 'a point of view opposed to a narrowly commercial conception of life and associated with a romantic sensibility to the ideas of continuity and tradition felt to be embodied in certain kinds of English landscape' (Everett 1994, 1);

FIGURE 51.
Sir Alfred Munnings,
Frank Freeman on
Pilot, 1925. Oil on
canvas, 39 × 40 in.
Private collection. By
courtesy of Rosenstiel's
Widow & Son Ltd

and, secondly, the reiteration of a theme familiar from the 1760s that sporting
competence and traditional ways of rural life were at the heart of the nation's
morale and leadership (Deuchar 1988, 159). The resurgence of foxhunting in
the landscape of the Shires after the devastation of the First World War was
therefore symbolic of the revival of the nation, with the Prince as its dashing
young leader.

In making a public icon out of the Prince as a foxhunter Munnings had to
graft concepts of status and leadership onto an essentially democratic sport and
reconcile the highest genre of equestrian royal portraiture with the lowly genre
of the provincial sporting picture. His solution was to isolate the Prince from
the social hierarchy and context of the hunt and pose him alone on Forest
Witch, the hunter lent him by George Drummond, his host at Pitsford Hall,
against a rural landscape background. Munnings, who had made his name
at the Royal Academy exhibition of Canadian War Records in the spring of
1919 with his equestrian portrait of *Major General Seely on Warrior*, coolly
posed alone at the front in sight of the German guns, now presented Edward
as the debonair prince to lead the peace, attired ready to hunt in the Shires,
complete with cutaway scarlet coat, top boots, and top hat rakishly adjusted
at an angle (Baily 1921, 94). The positioning of the Prince beside a gnarled old
oak tree was intended, Munnings later maintained, to convey 'Future King

– British Oak', a restatement of Van Dyck's celebrated equation of horseman-ship, leadership and the oak in the portrait of *Charles I on Horseback* (1635) (Munnings 1951, 149–50).

Despite the artist's later reservations about the oak being too large and the horse too distracting as it faced towards the spectator with its ears pricked, *The Prince of Wales on Forest Witch* was an unqualified success, described by one critic as 'an admirable equestrian portrait of the most popular sportsman in the United Kingdom by our greatest living sporting artist' (McConkey 2001, 18). The painting supplied a glamorous, studiedly stylish image to foxhunt-ing in the Shires that was of enormous appeal to a moneyed cosmopolitan set who followed the Prince of Wales to the Shires, bought into the hunting culture and patronised Munnings. Ambrose Clark, the Singer sewing machine heir, kept up a stable of fifty thoroughbred hunters at Warwick Lodge. The Marahanee of Cooch Behar stayed at the Spinnies in Thorpe Road and then at Stavely Lodge (Blow 1983, 105, 121; Clayton 1993, 126). Ronnie Tree, an heir of the Marshall Field fortune, married Nancy (later Lancaster), the widow of his late cousin Henry Field, and became joint master of the Pytchley in 1926, renting first Cottesbrooke Hall and then Kelmarsh (Wood 2005, 13, 31–2). Without roots in the English landscape, Munnings's cosmopolitan patrons wanted to be portrayed alone (as in his equestrian portrait of the Prince of

Wales), stylishly dressed in hunting clothes and mounted on thoroughbred hunters against a landscape background, as the fashionable new leaders of an international smart set in which royalty rubbed shoulders with the heirs of industrial tycoons. As part of the myth, the huntsman and his pack of hounds were also elevated and featured by Munnings as sporting heroes, posed on a promontory overlooking the hunting landscape (Figure 51). Munnings's representation of the hunting landscape in his equestrian portraits is both highly selective and idealised.

From George Stubbs, then unfashionable, Munnings learnt how to restrict the landscape to a narrow band at the bottom of the canvas. In *Changing Horses* (Figure 52) his wife Violet, a brilliant horsewoman, is stylishly silhouetted above the Vale of Belvoir with the landscape, consisting of two horizontal bands of the top of the hill in the foreground and the vale below, only occupying a quarter of the whole canvas area. Frank Freeman (Figure 51), one of the most famous huntsmen of his day, is similarly posed, with the Pytchley hounds, on the hill by the hunt kennels at Brixworth (Northants) with the ground dropping sharply away towards Cottesbrooke Hall. The placement of the second horseman doing up the girth of the horse turned inwards along the diagonal in *Changing Horses* recalls John Ferneley Senior's portrait *The Hon. George Petre with the Quorn at Rolleston 1814* (Figure 53). Munnings affirmed that he could not look at one of Ferneley's large hunting pictures 'without thinking how well that son of a Leicestershire wheelwright could put Leicestershire and the lie of its land on canvas' (Munnings 1952, 23–4). When painting the American Mr Strawbridge, a former Master of the Cottesmore (1913–15), with the well-known covert Lack's Gorse in the background, Munnings remembered being taken to see the place, stopping 'on the top of a hill looking across that magnificent country' and thinking of 'Osbaldeston and his field, and of the artists Alken and Ferneley' (Munnings 1952, 23–4).

The perpetuation of a specifically English tradition stemming from Stubbs, Henry Alken Senior and John Ferneley Senior was but one aspect of Munnings's art. Part of his success also lay in his ability to bring traditional subjects subtly up to date. The hunting landscape was changing, along with the social composition of the field. While working within an established tradition he managed to provide an appealing, updated image of hunting. His hunting landscapes are painted with the broad brushstrokes and the sensitivity to light, atmosphere and colour learnt from French *plein air* naturalism. He cast his wife in the liberated role of a modern Diana of the chase, whereas the poor design of side-saddles had previously precluded women from jumping at pace across country. It took three revolutionary innovations – the leaping head (or third pommel) on the side-saddle, the safety skirt and the balance strap – coupled with the example of the Empress Elizabeth of Austria, to make hunting fashionable for women (Buxton 1987, 63–7, 80). What Munnings chose to ignore was the intrusion of modernity into the hunting landscape.

Lionel Edwards, on the other hand, recognised that the hunting landscape had changed, along with the ethos and social composition of the hunt, and he

The Making
and Representation
of the Hunting
Landscape
of the Shires

evolved a seemingly artless 'natural' style to represent it. His evocations of the hunt moving across a landscape have as little to do with Alken and Ferneley as the hard-riding masculine world of Squire Osbaldeston's autobiography has with Sassoon's sensitive hero recalling his feelings about his hunting experiences. Edwards's hunting scenes of the Shires are in no way concerned with registering the fierce competition between leading horsemen. From G. D. Giles (1857–1941) in particular he learned how to spread the field across the landscape. In *Sheepthorns* (Figure 48) the hunting hounds occupy the foreground, the scarlet coat of the huntsman takes the eye to the left, the whipper-in behind him asserts a line going back to the steeple of Tur Langton church on the horizon, and then two small flashes of scarlet draw our attention to the main body of the field coming into sight on the right. In comparison with his predecessors Edwards kept the figures small. For him the landscape came first and he remained unrivalled in his ability to capture it in all its changing appearances and moods. While crediting Alken with the public perception of hunting as dangerous, Edwards recognised that Alken depicted a very different Leicestershire: 'The Oxers are newly erected and the hedges freshly planted in many pictures, and it puzzles me that the obstacles are often so provincial in character, the fences appearing to be banks such as one sees in Dorset, and other Western countries' (Edwards 1947, 194). In both Alken's and Ferneley's pictures the enclosures of old pasture are large and the fences comparatively low, which ties in with Nimrod's and Brooksby's descriptions of the ideal hunting landscape. His reference to banks accords with Hoskins's account of the Wigston enclosure stipulation that the allotments should be 'mounded and fenced around by ditches'. Guy Paget, writing at the end of the 1930s, thought that if two former masters of the Pytchley, Osbaldeston (1827–34) and George Payne (1835–8, 1844–8) were to return to the country, 'they would be appalled at the strength of the thorn fences, which have grown stronger and larger in a hundred years, but they would rejoice in the disappearance of the double oxer, which in those days stopped as many people as wire does to-day', and George Payne would 'rejoice in the better going brought about by the improvement in land drainage' (Paget 1937, 5).

In the final analysis, Edwards's art in the interwar period was distinguished by his ability to represent the fast-changing interaction between hunting, modernisation and the landscape. If modernity intruded on a particular scene, he depicted it. His picture *The Quorn, The Hoby Vale 1934* includes the Asfordby Iron Works and a glimpse of the Leicester–Melton railway. In his books he would specifically draw attention to these changes. He writes in the text alongside *Sheepthorns* (Figure 48):

> You will notice in the foreground the posts of an old oxer in front of the fence. These oxe fences (oxers), for which this part of Leicestershire was once famous, have now almost disappeared. Such extensive post and rail fences are, at the present price of labour, beyond the purse of most agriculturists; so wire now replaces the rails. The scourge of wire afflicts

the Midland Hunts more than most, for they are purely bullock-grazing countries. (Edwards 1935, 14)

He would on occasion sketch from a car, and in his sketch of the opening meet of the Quorn at Kirby Gate in *A Leicestershire Sketch Book* he focuses on all the vehicles bringing the public rather than on the horses and hounds. His modern version of 'the return from the Chase' depicts the horses being 'boxed' for the homeward journey by the light of the motor lamps. This ability to adapt to changed circumstances is a distinguishing feature of both Edwards's art and the hunting community he represents in its efforts to preserve both the legacy of foxhunting in the Shires and its landscape, long after the international set, the fashionable birds of passage, had departed.

Acknowledgements

I would like to thank Charles Phythian-Adams, Mandy de Belin, Richard Hoyle, Jenny Dancey, Melton Carnegie Museum, Diane Rowe, The Sir Alfred Munnings Art Museum, Ann Williamson, The British Sporting Art Trust, Roy Heron, Meriel Buxton, Joe Cowen, Jonathan Brankin Frisby, Susan Morris, Richard Green Gallery, Captain MacDonald Buchanan, Richard Cazenove and David Bragg.

FIGURE 53.
John Ferneley Senior, *The Hon. George Petre with the Quorn at Rolleston*, 1814.
Oil on canvas, 103.6 x 136 cm. Private collection, USA.
Photograph courtesy of Richard Green Gallery, London

CHAPTER THIRTEEN

'An Angel-Satyr[1] Walks these Hills': Landscape and Identity in Kilvert's Diary

Philip Dunham

In recent years there has been a tendency, among historical geographers at least, to supplement the study of the material 'making of landscape' with an appreciation of its cultural significance. Accordingly, landscape is now widely understood not only as a tangible palimpsest, made up of layers of material human imprints, but also in relation to particular ways of 'seeing', 'experiencing' and 'ordering' the spatial environment, and of understanding one's position within it (for a review, see Seymour 2000). A popular theme in this cultural history of landscape has been the study of the relationship between landscape and identity, a theme which has revealed that, far from representing a neutral or passive backdrop to human activity, landscape can play an active role in the construction and expression of particular ideas of the self, from the scale of the nation (e.g. the Cotswolds landscape as a symbol of England) to that of the subject (Short 1991; Matless 1998; Brace 1999; 2003).

Largely taking its lead from developments in poststructuralist theory, recent work in this area has attempted to convey a sense of the complex and unstable connections between landscape and identity. On the one hand, there has been a growing fascination with different imaginations or representations of landscape which has challenged the power relationships that have tended to elevate certain constructions, and their related identities, above those of others. As a result, a conventional emphasis on elite (usually white, male, high-status) 'ways of seeing' landscape has given way to an exploration of various neglected alternatives, often linked to the expression of 'other' kinds of identity position, such as those experienced by women, the disabled and ethnic and sexual minorities. For example, analyses by Kinsman (1995), Halfacree (1996) and others have recovered some of the landscape histories of the late twentieth-century countryside otherwise obscured by the powerful symbolism of an English rural idyll (for a comprehensive review, see Halfacree 2003). On the other hand, several writers have begun to rediscover the materiality of landscape, replacing an emphasis on interpretation and representation with ideas of movement, mobility and embodiment, and the fragile, shifting and mutually constitutive nature of the relationship between landscape and identity. Building upon phenomenological notions of 'being-in-the-world' (Heidegger 1962), this work has placed the sentient subject firmly back into a physical topography of landscape, regarding both landscape and identity as historically contingent 'outcomes' of actual encounters with, and movements through, particular kinds of terrain, even though the subject invariably brings to these situations an established set of cultural and cognitive repertoires. For example, recent studies of the Victorian urban *flâneur* (e.g. Nead 2000; Parsons 2001) and the countryside walker of the nineteenth and twentieth centuries (e.g. Matless 1998; Edensor 2000; Wylie 2003; 2005) have revealed how certain spatial practices – literally a movement through the landscape – can be vital to the performance of particular kinds of identity at different times and places. And this suggests that, far from being fixed, identities linked to landscape need continually to be reproduced in order to achieve a sense of stability or coherence.

It follows from this that those interested in unravelling the complex entanglements of landscape and identity in particular historical contexts need to bring together concerns with the physical, embodied experience of landscape as well as its representation, thus shedding light on '... the formation and undoing of self and landscape *in practice*' (Wylie 2005, 245, my emphasis). This chapter contributes to the task by examining the relationship between landscape and identity in Kilvert's Diary, the journal of an obscure mid-Victorian clergyman. It is set in the Welsh Border country of the 1870s, and much of its present-day appeal lies in its ability to feed a strong public appetite for rural nostalgia. Early critical notices (see, for example, O'Brien 1943, and reviews in Toman 2001) rhapsodised about Kilvert's ability to capture a period of apparent harmony and tranquillity, which contrasted sharply with the turmoil of the middle decades of the twentieth century. One of countless similar passages in the text will begin to illustrate why:

> *Sunday, 14 April [1872]:* The beauty of the view, the first view of the village, coming down by The Brooms this evening was indescribable. The brilliant golden poplar spires shone in the evening light like flames against the dark hillside of the Old Forest, and the blossoming fruit trees, the torch trees of Paradise, blazed with a transparent green and white lustre up the dingle in the setting sunlight. The village is in a blaze of fruit blossom. Clyro is at its loveliest. What more can be said? (Plomer 1977, vol. 2, 182)

Largely on the strength of prose idylls such as this, something of a Kilvert cult has developed since the 1940s. It is reflected in the international membership of the Kilvert Society, and in the emergence of a fledgling tourism industry centred on the bold and dramatic contrasts of what is rapidly becoming known as 'the Kilvert Country' (Barber 2004) (Figure 54). In what follows a look is taken beneath the surface of entries such as that above to reveal how Kilvert's experiences and detailed accounts of the Clyro landscape can tell us much about the connections between landscape and identity in the

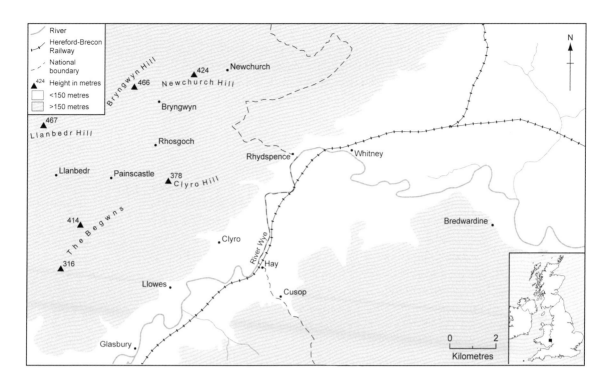

FIGURE 54.
'Kilvert Country':
the Radnorshire/
Herefordshire
borderland.

Victorian countryside. The chapter is presented in two parts. In the first are some introductory comments about the production of the diary. There follows an exploration of the relationships between landscape and identity that emerge from it. Specifically here, the metaphor of the 'borderland' is used to show how Kilvert's movements through the countryside (and his vivid descriptions of encounters with landscapes and figures) supported not only his deliberate construction of an idealised 'self', but also enabled a series of 'other', more surprising and sometimes disturbing, identities to be revealed. In this way, it will be illustrated how, by walking through the Clyro landscape and writing about his experiences in journal form, Kilvert effected an unfolding and interweaving of different narratives of self and landscape, one which repeatedly invokes concerns with movement, embodiment and performance as well as their cultural representation.

Entering the borderland: Kilvert and his diary

First published in three volumes between 1938 and 1940, Kilvert's Diary is now widely recognised as a minor classic. Its author, Francis Kilvert, was born in Wiltshire in 1840. He took holy orders in the early 1860s, serving first as his father's curate in his home village of Langley Burrell before moving, in the spring of 1865, to take up a position as curate to the Rev. Richard Lister Venables at Clyro (Radnor.), a small village close to present-day Hay-on-Wye in the English–Welsh Borders. There he began to write a daily record of his life, which he kept assiduously from the spring of 1870 until his premature death in 1879, aged thirty-eight. The diary remained in private hands until 1937, when it was sent by a nephew of Kilvert to William Plomer, a minor poet and novelist, and a reader for the Jonathan Cape publishing company. Enthralled by its contents, Plomer immediately set about editing the diary for publication, and the three volumes he produced contain roughly one-third of the contents of the manuscript notebooks in which it was originally written. All but three of these were destroyed sometime in the 1950s by a niece of the diarist, who felt that they contained 'objectionable material'. However, the three surviving notebooks – which cover the spring and early summer of 1870 – have since been published in full (Hughes and Ifans 1982; Ifans 1989; Maber and Tregoning 1989). This means that, for one year at least, an extended section of Kilvert's original text can be set alongside Plomer's abridgement (Newman 1982).

The notion of the borderland – with its pervading sense of 'liminality' or 'betweenness' (Johnston 2000) – is a persistent motif in Kilvert's Diary.[2] For example, almost like an ethnographer, Kilvert assumed the role of a stranger moving into the Clyro community and studying it intensively from the inside. His role as curate also placed him in the social borderlands of contemporary rural life, affording him access to the social gatherings of the local elite, yet bringing him into regular contact with the poor, the infirm and the destitute. The diarist's ambiguous social position was further complicated by his unmarried state: his typically Victorian idealisation of family and home – and his own lack of both – undoubtedly compounding his sense of social marginalisation and 'betweenness' (Toman 2001). Perhaps most importantly, however, Kilvert's Clyro was part of a quintessentially borderland landscape (Lewis 1967), one which straddled the physical, cultural and political boundaries of England and Wales. As the distinguished Kilvert scholar Grice put it:

> East of Clyro the land falls away abruptly. As we move into Herefordshire, the hills diminish and dwindle, and within a few miles we find ourselves in a rich pastoral landscape of lush pastures, picturesque villages, hop-fields, cider orchards and half-timbered farmsteads … But west of Clyro lies another landscape, the Welsh landscape of massive hills, bare fells, sombre brown mountains, small fields, hidden waterfalls [and] impoverished hill farms … Here the landmarks have retained their difficult Welsh names and Whitney and Clifford have given way to Aberedw, Bryngwyn and Llanbedr … Here England and Wales met, and still meet, in a colourful fusion of culture, language and behaviour. (Grice 1998, 53–4)

The Clyro landscape was, and of course remains, one of outstanding natural beauty and distinct cultural contrast (Figure 55). The Anglicisation of Welsh culture had arguably reached its zenith by the 1870s (Lewis 1967), and this had produced a curious juxtaposition and intermixing of different dialects and traditions. For example, the border landscape was characterised by the strong demarcation of English and Welsh identities (e.g. through an opposing of Church and Chapel) and a blurring of their boundaries (e.g. through the

FIGURE 55.
The Black Mountains,
from Clyro Hill.

Anglicisation of Welsh place-names). Furthermore, this ambivalent cultural geography was inscribed on to a physical territory of equal richness and diversity. Just to the east of Clyro, the national boundary bisected the landscape from north to south, its somewhat arbitrary route separating the English and Welsh inns on either side of the road at Rhydspence, and cutting straight through the middle of a cottage (now demolished) called 'the Pant'.[3] To the south, between Clyro and the border town of Hay, the Wye negotiates its slow, meandering course along the valley floor, then sharing the flatlands with the main Brecon road and the Hereford–Brecon railway (now dismantled), which made travel into this part of Wales considerably easier than it is today. Behind Hay to the south rises the formidable ridge of Hay Bluff, the northernmost edge of the Black Mountains, the stark, brooding presence of which looms over the soft, pastoral landscape of the valley below. And north of Clyro lie the gentler slopes of the Radnorshire hills, over which thread the roads to Painscastle, Newchurch and Rhos-Goch. Dotted with the whitewashed farmsteads of Clyro and its outliers, and cut into by secret *cwmau* and dingles, these eventually open out on to further expanses of high country, completing the rich gamut of landscapes afforded by this relatively compact area of border countryside.

This physical and cultural borderland provided Kilvert with much of his inspiration as a rural diarist. The production of his diary involved him in a succession of long solitary wanderings, physically traversing the landscape along the network of footpaths that criss-crossed the countryside. Kilvert enjoyed something of a reputation as a walker, even by the standards of a time when it was the most common form of transport. For instance, in 1870 Kilvert recorded pastoral visits to over sixty households scattered over Clyro parish (Figure 56). And he frequently supplemented these with longer excursions that extended far beyond the confines of his own parish. That Kilvert was proud of his prowess as a walker is confirmed by the self-congratulatory narratives that occasionally creep into his diary. For example, on 23 March 1872, he recorded that '... two men walking down the Cwm after me tried to overtake me but it was more than they were able to do' (Plomer 1977, vol. 2, 157). We know something about Kilvert's appearance from surviving photographs. In the clearest of these (Figure 57) he is shown to be tall and slim with a full black beard, and wears the clerical frock coat and trousers characteristic of his profession. In moving through the landscape, Kilvert therefore embodied elements of his own identity as clergyman and gentleman, and this undoubtedly influenced how he interacted with others and how they responded to him.

Kilvert's penchant for movement was linked to a particular fondness for writing. In keeping a journal he was not unusual, as diary-keeping was a popular pastime in Victorian England, especially among the clergy. But the volume, detail and style of Kilvert's text are remarkable. Perhaps most importantly, a strong relationship existed between his movement and his writing, with a tendency to move through the landscape more frequently and extensively appearing to coincide with the start of his journal in the spring of 1870.[4] The importance of this relationship cannot be overstated. Not only does it emphasise the extent to which Kilvert's journal represented a material and embodied engagement with landscape as much as it did a more reflective enterprise, it also underscores the close parallels between the forms of narration of self and landscape made possible by walking through the countryside on the one hand and by compiling a countryside diary on the other. Both forms of narrative are dynamic, transient and uncertain, and both engender the sense of perpetual suspense and betweenness invoked by the idea of the borderland. Indeed, Wylie's (2005, 237) remark that the countryside walker lies continually '... poised between the country ahead and the country behind, between one step and the next ... perpetually caught in an apparitional process of arriving/departing' is equally true of the transient, momentary narrative of Kilvert's journal. Most of the diary was written during short, intensive periods in the evenings in his Clyro lodgings. However, we know that Kilvert took a pocket book with him on his travels, and that many entries combined the 'on-the-spot' reportage of his pocket book with subsequent, more considered, reflection. The diary is therefore a complicated text, one which repeatedly unsettles the distinctions between past and present (yet another 'borderland'), and which chronicles a succession of unfolding 'double moments' of writing and remembered experience.

The borderlands of the self: Kilvert, landscape and identity

Friday, St. Swithin's Day [1870]: Familiar as this place is to me I am always noticing some fresh beauty or combination of beauties, light or shade, or a view from some particular point, where I had never been before, at some particular hour and under some particular circumstances. (Ifans 1989, 95)

In this otherwise unremarkable passage, Kilvert hints at a unifying purpose to his movement and his writing: namely, to experience and record particular moments of encounter with the Clyro countryside. Moreover, his use of the word 'fresh' here suggests that the Diarist had a particular desire to encounter novelty, newness and change. Through time, the diary seems to have played an increasingly important role in satisfying this urge. In March 1865, when he first moved to Clyro (and was, as he later admitted, 'in a transport of delight and enthusiasm': Plomer 1977, vol. 2, 161), Kilvert did not require the discipline of writing in order to do this, as his experiences were, by definition, entirely fresh. By 1870, though, once he had become more familiar with the landscape and its people, his desire for novelty demanded that he not only move through the countryside more frequently and extensively, but that he utilise his considerable powers of observation and description in order to capture the freshness of each new experience. This suggestion of an inherently 'restive' quality to Kilvert and his journal sits uncomfortably with the many present-day readings of the diary that associate it with the constancy and security of an English rural idyll. It is not so much 'the strain of keeping things fixed' – the desire to hold back time which several writers have detected in Kilvert as much as in his readers (Toman 2001) – as it is the 'strain of fixing': the struggle to be worthy, through writing, of manifold encounters with the Border country he loved. One of the most striking features of Kilvert's journal is its consistently slow tempo, which gives the impression of things being 'suspended' or 'frozen' in time. The diary proceeds at the same slow pace throughout, taking as its focus the careful delineation of *moments* of encounter with landscapes and figures. For instance:

Tuesday, 26 March [1872]: At Wernewydd ... Mrs. Lloyd ... came to the door with ... a kindly welcome. She got the round table and put it by me, cut some sweet home-made bread and butter and made some tea into which I am sure she put some spirit, rum I think ... Lloyd the farmer came in and sat down by the fire taking his youngest child on his knee. Phoebe was ironing at a table in one deep thick-walled window, Carrie sewing in another ... Yellow Mint [the farm dog] sat tall and upright in the hearth with his back to me and looking into the fire ... The setting sun shone in warm and cheerful through the West window, lighting up the old fashioned large kitchen and glowing upon the warming pan hanging on the wall. (Plomer 1977, vol. 2, 160–1)

This is a description so vivid and intimate it is almost as if we are there. The

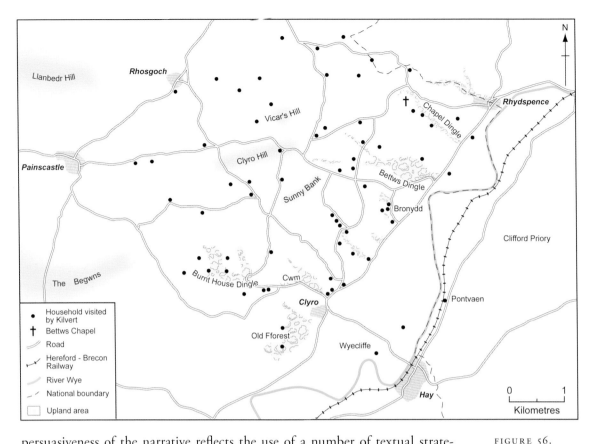

FIGURE 56.
Pastoral visits by the
Diarist, 1870.

persuasiveness of the narrative reflects the use of a number of textual strategies. For instance, Kilvert's descriptions carry a great deal of detail, much of
it trivial and mundane. In vignette after vignette, it is the small and insignifi-
cant details (e.g. 'the warming pan hanging on the wall') which help draw the
reader into a scene. Kilvert's prose is also characterised by an abundant use
of adjectives. This is again indicative of a desire to 'capture' and to 'celebrate'
the moment, and it is illustrated well by the diarist's struggle to describe the
playing of the sunlight on the leaves of the poplar trees that dominated the
view from his bedroom window:

> *Wednesday, 7 October* [*1874*]: For some time, I have been trying to find
> the right word for the shimmering, glancing, twinkling movement of the
> poplar leaves in the sun and wind. This afternoon I saw the word written
> on the poplar leaves. It was 'dazzle'. The 'dazzle' of the poplars. (Plomer
> 1977, vol. 3, 91)

What is of interest is not so much the extent to which Kilvert succeeded
in his careful descriptions of momentary encounters and experiences, but that
he was continually engaged in the struggle to produce them. In entries like
these, Kilvert displays a remarkable capacity to let himself go, to indulge the
moment of experience and to struggle to be worthy of it through the medium
of writing. It is this which makes him such an effective writer of landscape

and identity. In constructing his diary around particular instances of writing and remembered experience, Kilvert opened up a space in which his own identity, and its relationship to the landscape, could become equally 'momentary'. The transience of the diary narrative meant that any shifts in identity could be thoroughly chronicled as they were described and indulged to the full, before being quickly transformed or discarded. And his tendency to 'give way to the moment' meant that the identities he revealed could be surprising, even disturbing. In this way, the diary provides a practical demonstration of the suggestion made earlier that constructions of landscape and identity shift over time and from one moment to the next, based on the context at hand.

Kilvert's movements through the countryside, and his writing, were linked to the production of at least two different narratives of self and landscape. First, there is considerable evidence to suggest that Kilvert deliberately approached, interpreted and wrote about the border landscape in ways that supported the development of a desired self-identity: one that he wanted to construct for himself and, if only indirectly or sub-consciously through the diary, to present

FIGURE 57.
The Rev. Francis
Kilvert, *c.*1869.

177

to the world. In this sense, the diary emerges as a structured narrative of self and landscape, linking moments of experience together and charting the progress made by the diarist towards his desired self-image.[5] That this represented another important motivation behind the production of his diary is indicated by Kilvert's fondness for similar kinds of narrative in his own choice of reading material (Toman 2002). For example, we know from his diary that he read, and was delighted by, an 1869 book called *Stepping Heavenward* by one Elizabeth Prentiss.[6] According to Toman (2002, 2–3), the similarities between the timing and format of this publication and Kilvert's own journal are too close to be entirely coincidental: 'the book's heroine, Kate Mortimer, monitors her spiritual progress through her diary entries, and it is not inappropriate to see Kilvert's Diary as a record of his [own] spiritual progress'.

Such a reading of the diary helps us to locate Kilvert in time as well as space, as a discourse of self-improvement, both moral and spiritual, was central to the development of middle-class Victorian values (Thompson 1988; Briggs 2000). However, more pertinent to the argument being developed here is the fact that, for Kilvert, the typically Victorian quest for self-improvement reflected in his diary was bound up with his experience of the Clyro landscape, and in this respect he also borrowed heavily from established nineteenth-century *mores*, aesthetics and sensibilities. Perhaps the best examples of this 'self-improvement-through-landscape' at work in the diary relate to Kilvert's engagements with the Welsh Border country as expressions of his Christian faith and his romanticism. In terms of the former, Kilvert frequently interpreted the Clyro landscape as a divine creation, and clearly felt that a constant discovery of 'God-in-nature' was crucial to his own spiritual development as a Christian. Accordingly, he took pains to record experiences that brought him closer to God through nature, and which served to confirm and intensify his faith. For instance, a typically detailed and idyllic account of the Clyro landscape on Easter Sunday, 1870, was prefaced with the remark: 'My first thought was, Christ is risen' (Plomer 1977, vol. 1, 96), while the following entry highlights the almost revelatory qualities that Kilvert attributed to particular combinations of light and scenery in the northernmost reaches of the Black Mountains:

> *Tuesday, 14 March [1871]:* ... the Black Mountains were invisible, being wrapped in clouds, and I saw one very white brilliant dazzling cloud where the mountains ought to have been. The cloud grew more white and dazzling every moment, till a clearer burst of sunlight scattered the mists and revealed the truth. This brilliant white cloud that I had been looking and wondering at was the mountain in snow ... I stood rooted to the ground, struck with amazement and overwhelmed at the extraordinary splendour of this marvellous spectacle ... One's first involuntary thought in the presence of these magnificent sights is to lift up the heart to God and humbly thank Him for having made the earth so beautiful ...' (Plomer 1977, vol. 1, 308–9)

Elsewhere in the diary, Kilvert cast himself in the role of the romantic wanderer, consciously living out what Grice (1983) memorably called his 'Wordsworthian dream' by imbuing the Clyro poor with the qualities of honesty, robustness and diligence so cherished by the Lakeland poet, and constantly seeking the spiritual and moral benefits of a solitary communion with nature afforded by particular kinds of landscape encounter. These romantic interludes represented rare occasions in which Kilvert, normally 'the least egocentric of all English diarists' (Lockwood 1990, 17), articulated a sense of social and cultural 'aloofness'. This was reflected in his predilection for deserted roads and 'lonely, waste and ruined places' (e.g. Plomer 1977, vol. 1, 307), and in his occasional tirades against tourists (e.g. Plomer 1977, vol. 1, 79; Maber and Tregoning 1989, 64). And it represents another example of how Kilvert could develop his narration of landscape in ways that supported the construction of an idealised self:

> *Whitsun Monday, 29 May, Oakapple Day [1871]*: A letter came yesterday from Mr. Webb of Hardwick describing the opening of the tumulus Twyn y beddau on the Black Mountain last Friday and urging me to go and see it before it is filled up ... So I made a pilgrimage to the place today starting at 3pm. Imagine my delight to find the place perfectly silent and solitary except for the sheep. It was so much grander to visit the old-world resting place of the wild warriors alone in the silence of the summer afternoon with no-one to look on but the great mountains than to be stunned by the prattle of the Woolhope Club, or to be disgusted by the sight of a herd of Hay holiday makers ... It is a fine thing to be out on the hills alone. A man can hardly be a beast or a fool alone on a great mountain. There is no company like the grand, solemn, beautiful hills. (Plomer 1977, vol. 1, 349)

However, by virtue of his capacity to let himself go – to be swept up by the moment and to struggle to be worthy of it through writing[7] – Kilvert's interpretations and experiences of the Clyro landscape also enabled his identity (and that which he ascribed to the landscape) to develop and unfold in different, unexpected and sometimes troubling ways. Throughout its pages, a series of 'other' Francis Kilverts are permitted to surface momentarily in the diary which contrast sharply with the image of the conscientious and compassionate clergyman, or the romantic wanderer seeking physical and moral improvement through nature. These 'other' Francis Kilverts found expression in his recording of the 'darker' sides to contemporary rural life: '... the acts of gratuitous savagery, of cruelty towards the young, the unfortunate and the deranged' (Grice 1983, 41). Examples of this include his account of the confinement of 'the madwoman of Cwmgwanon', and the appalling abuse suffered at the hands of their father by the children of a local farm labourer:

> *Thursday, 29 June [1871]*: How unkindly their father uses them. The neighbours hear the sound of the whip on their naked flesh and the poor girls

crying and screaming sadly sometimes when their father comes home late at night … It is said that sometimes Corfield strips the poor girls naked, holds them face downwards across his knees … and whips their bare bottoms so cruelly that the blood runs down their legs. (Plomer 1977, vol. 1, 367–8)

Kilvert was no detached observer of these 'other' border landscapes. Instead, in entries like this he indulged the darker sides to his character, effectively 'working the hyphens' (Fine 1998) between self and other in a transient, auto-biographical narrative. Perhaps the most powerful of these 'darker' sides was a pronounced susceptibility to youthful feminine beauty. Although Le Quesne (1978, 134) was almost certainly correct in his assessment that Kilvert's fanta-sies were '… erotic in origin and innocent in fact', there is no doubt that he was sexually attracted to both women and girls. This undoubtedly influenced his movement through the landscape, and his writing, resulting, for instance, in a peculiar form of topophilia in which places became revered for their associations with particular children (Figure 58):

Saturday, 9 July [1870]: It is a pretty lane this Bird's Nest lane, very shady, quiet, narrow and overbowered here and there with arching wyches and hazels. Sometimes my darling child Gipsy comes down to School this way, but more often she comes down Sunny Bank when the days are fine, then over the stile by Little Wern y Pentre. Yet often and often must those tiny feet have trodden this stony, narrow green-arched lane, and those sweet blue eyes have looked down on this vista to the blue mountains, and those little hands have gathered flowers along these banks. O my child if you did but know. If you only knew that this lane and this dingle and these fields are sweet to me and holy ground for your sweet sake. But you can never know, and if you should ever guess and read the secret, it will be but a dim, misty suspicion of the truth – Ah Gipsy. (Ifans 1989, 75–6)

Tuesday, 3 May [1870]: By Tynycwm meadows to Newchurch village … Shall I confess that I travelled ten miles today over the hills for a kiss, to kiss that child's sweet face? Ten miles for a kiss. (Hughes and Ifans 1982, 19–20)

That Kilvert experienced some guilt about his sexuality is certain, as the diary contains several remorseful references to his own sinfulness which endorse the orthodox view of Victorian sexuality as something to be expunged and repressed (Mason 1994). However, in reality Kilvert's moral identity was more complicated, and this is reflected in the diary. His capacity to let himself go meant that Kilvert could wallow in a moment of sexual excitement to the full, allowing his own identity to shift from moral self to immoral other as the mood, quite literally, took him. For instance, his account of a visit to a local farm in the summer of 1871 concluded with the words:

Wednesday, 23 August [1871]: … I was lost to everything but love and the embrace and the sweet kisses and caresses of the child … I am exhausted with emotion. (Plomer 1977, vol. 2, 18)

Indeed, Kilvert's identity, and its relationship to the landscape, could sometimes change mid-way through the same entry, especially if he found himself becoming excited at the moment of writing. For example, in the following passage (which concerns a sixteen-year-old farm girl) Kilvert allowed his identity to change almost in mid-sentence, as what begins as a straightforward description of the view from his bedroom window turns first into an erotic fantasy before culminating, as he checks himself, in a puritan celebration of work and duty:

Monday, 11 July [1870]: The view from my bedroom window looking up the dingle always reminds me of Norway, perhaps because of the spiry dark fir tops which mark Pentwyn … Often when I rise I look up to the white farmhouse of Penllan and think of the sweet grey eyes that have long been open … The sun looks through her window … And before the sun has touched the sleeping village in the shade below … he has stolen into her bedroom and crept along the wall from chair to chair till he has reached the bed, and has kissed the fair hand and arm that lies upon the coverlet, and the whiter bosom that heaves half uncovered after the restlessness of the sultry night … Then, when she has dressed and prayed towards the east, she goes out to draw water from the holy spring … After which she goes about her honest holy work, all day long, with a light heart and a pure conscience. (Ifans 1989, 78–9)

One woman who remembered Kilvert from her youth remarked that if he had not been such a good man, he could have been a very wicked one. And it is not difficult to see what she was getting at here. However, Kilvert's identity, and its relationship to the landscape, could never be described as *either* 'good' *or* 'bad', 'self' *or* 'other'. It always contained elements of both: elements which could be either indulged or repressed, depending on the context at hand. One of Kilvert's great strengths as a diarist is that he was acutely aware of the tensions and ambiguities of his 'borderland self', and he made strenuous efforts to record them. Nowhere is this better illustrated than in the strange, autobiographical entry he made for 20 June 1871 – 'An Angel-Satyr walks these hills' (Plomer 1977, vol. 1, 363). Here, perhaps more clearly than anywhere else in the diary, Kilvert revealed the full complexity of his landscape-identity, one which could range from 'angel' (the compassionate clergyman) to 'satyr' (the hybrid man-beast, driven by sensuous desire) as he moved through the Clyro countryside.

Conclusion

Although he is most often remembered as a historian of the material landscape, Hoskins was only too aware of the ways in which landscape is conditioned by human 'ways of seeing' and could therefore 'act back' on us. A good example of this is the introduction to the second edition of *The Making of the English Landscape*, which ends with a paean to romanticism that Kilvert would have applauded:

Many parts of the English landscape remain just as our forefathers left them a long time ago. It is to these quiet solitudes … that we can still gratefully turn for refreshment and sanctuary from noise and meaningless movement. (Hoskins 1977, 16)

Recent work on the relationship between landscape and identity has striven to highlight the complexity and fluidity of the links between them. In particular, it has emphasised the extent to which they are produced through material and embodied engagements with particular kinds of terrain as much

as through more detached and considered reflection. Using the 'borderland'
as a metaphor for self as well as for landscape, this chapter has contributed
to this debate by examining the narration of self and landscape in Kilvert's
Diary. It has been argued that Kilvert and his journal embodied many of
the tensions and contradictions so characteristic of borderland spaces, and
that this was reflected in the diarist's performance and representation of both
landscape and identity. On the one hand, Kilvert's encounters with, and
representations of, the Border landscape have been shown to have supported
the deliberate construction of idealised narratives of the self, especially those
linked to a conscious expression of Victorian theology and romanticism. On
the other hand, and reflecting Kilvert's capacity to give way to, and indulge,
individual 'moments' of encounter with landscapes and figures, they have also
been shown to have sometimes taken quite a different form. In particular,
it has been suggested that Kilvert's encounters with the borderland reflected,
and occasionally celebrated, a darker erotics of landscape as much as they
did more conventional forms of contemporary landscape aesthetic. And it
has been argued that the narrative form of the diary – with its characteristic focus on movements through the landscape and 'moments' of encounter
and experience – lent itself well to the performance and representation of
such fleeting and hybrid identities. Further work involving different kinds
of diary narrative could arguably enrich the study of landscape history by
connecting the traditional focus on the material 'making of landscape' with
those more recent cultural histories which have implicated landscape in the
practices and politics of identity construction. For it is only by bridging this
divide that the splintered trajectories of landscape history after Hoskins can
be meaningfully brought together.

Notes

1. *Satyr*: a lustful and excessively sensual man-beast, usually depicted (in Greek and
   Roman mythology) as a woodland God with a human head, arms and torso, and a
   goat's ears, tail and legs.
2. That Kilvert, of course, remains in a state of 'betweenness' is underlined by the word-
   ing of his tombstone inscription: 'he being dead, yet speaketh'.
3. Kilvert's account of a pastoral visit to this cottage in November 1870 underlines the
   significance that this particular boundary had for the people of Anglicised mid-
   Victorian Clyro: '*Friday, 18 November [1870]:* ... Next to the Pant ... We were talking
   about parishes and boundaries ... the extraordinary story which old Betty Williams of
   Crowther used to tell me about the birth of a child in this house and the care taken to
   ensure that the child should be born in ... the English corner of the cottage. "Stand
   here Betsey, in this corner," said the midwife. And the girl was delivered of the child
   standing' (Plomer 1977, vol. 1, 262, emphasis in original).
4. This is indicated by the number of entries which confirm that, in the early months
   of 1870, Kilvert was either discovering new places (e.g. Rhos-Goch Mill; Plomer 1977,
   vol. 1, 67–8) or revisiting them for the first time in several years (e.g. Llanthony Priory;
   Plomer 1977, vol. 1, 79).
5. For further discussions of the connections between diary-keeping and the self, see
   Meth (2003) and Weiner and Rosenwald (1993).

6. The importance of this book to Kilvert is underlined by the fact that he occasionally gave copies to parishioners (especially young girls) in the belief that they would benefit from reading it. For example, on hearing about the love affairs of his vicar's servant, Kilvert recorded in his diary, '… I must give her a copy of *Stepping Heavenward*. I think it will do her good' (Plomer 1977, vol. 2, 85).

7. This essentially inductive account of 'otherness' resonates closely with some of the writings of poststructuralist geographers (see, for example, Doel 1998; 2004). Doel (1998, 1–2), for instance, sees 'otherness' as a product of an aleatory (or 'chance-like') materialism of encounter, one in which the writer-researcher '… has to be willing to let go … in the hope of being swept up by what is coming. For that is the only way in which something 'other' will ever have a change of happening'.

Acknowledgements

I would like to thank Lewis Holloway, John Toman and David Watts for their helpful comments on an earlier version of this chapter. Grateful thanks are also extended to Stuart Gill for producing the maps.

CHAPTER FOURTEEN

Ways of Seeing: Hoskins and the Oxfordshire Landscape Revisited

Kate Tiller

W. G. Hoskins completed *The Making of the English Landscape* at Steeple Barton in Oxfordshire in January 1954. He was to recollect that 'when I wrote the concluding pages of this book ... I described the landscape as seen from the windows of a Victorian vicarage in deepest Oxfordshire' (Hoskins 1988, 13). *The Making of the English Landscape* was intended as a new way of seeing England, a reading of its past from the present landscape. North Oxfordshire was clearly a potent setting in which to do this, and Hoskins used its landscape both to demonstrate his method and to frame his ideas. His concluding chapter, written overlooking this 'epitome of gentle unravished English landscape', contains some of Hoskins's most lyrical unravellings of rural landscape and some of his most frequently quoted and most vehemently anti-modern sentiments. It is here that he writes of:

> those long gentle lines of the dip-slope of the Cotswolds, those misty uplands of the sheep-grey oolite, how they have lent themselves to the villainous requirements of the new age! ... England of the arterial by-pass, treeless and stinking of diesel oil, murderous with lorries; England of the bombing range wherever there was once silence, as on Otmoor or the marshlands of Lincolnshire ... Barbaric England of the scientists, the military men, and the politicians; let us turn away and contemplate the past before all is lost to the vandals. (Hoskins 1988, 238)

In such a vision there was limited room for the twentieth century: '... since the year 1914, every single change in the English landscape has either uglified it or destroyed its meaning, or both ... It is a distasteful subject but it must be faced for a few moments.' Hoskins also turns to north Oxfordshire elsewhere in the book. An earlier chapter, on the landscapes of communications – roads, canals and railways – is based on his reading of the area surveyed in the Banbury sheet 145 of the one-inch Ordnance Survey map.

This chapter revisits those same Oxfordshire landscapes and their apparent influence on Hoskins's work in order to reassess his approach in three inter-related ways. Firstly, the ways in which he interpreted this particular tract of countryside in 1953–4, and what he did and did not see or write about, will be considered; secondly, the ways in which others, Hoskins's contemporaries and successors, have investigated and explained the same local societies and landscapes will be examined; and, thirdly, the changes in this countryside in the fifty years since publication of *The Making of the English Landscape*, and the reasons for those changes, will be assessed.

The Hoskins family moved to their new, rented, home in the Vicarage at Steeple Barton in December 1952 and lived there until May 1955 (Robert Peberdy pers. comm.). To Hoskins it was 'a sanctuary from noise and meaningless movement'. Although only 12 miles (19.2 km) from Oxford, Steeple Barton was certainly remote, and his daughter, Susan, has vivid memories (Susan Hewitt pers. comm., 2005) of sometimes hair-raising journeys down twisting lanes when her mother had to drive her father (not a driver himself) through winter fogs to the nearest station on the Cherwell valley railway line so that he could travel into Oxford, where he was Reader in Economic History. Hoskins's own introspection and his position not as a college fellow but a member of the Senior Common Room of All Souls' College, which meant he was 'cut off from the routine, everyday contact with colleagues working in the same field' (Thirsk 1994, 348), made his Oxford years somewhat unhappy. Steeple Barton offered a very different setting.

The Vicarage is a fine example of the solid and comfortable grandeur in which the reformed and resident parochial clergy of the mid-nineteenth century expected to live (Figure 59). It was built in 1856 to the designs of S. S. Teulon. The local historian and land agent William Wing commented in 1866 that 'The architect being a Londoner, overlooked the necessity of providing a country clergyman with a stable and piggery. Notwithstanding this

FIGURE 59. Steeple Barton Vicarage, built in 1856 to the designs of S. S. Teulon (from a contemporary engraving). It was here that Hoskins wrote *The Making of the English Landscape*, a book in which the surrounding landscapes play a significant part.

oversight the design and execution ... possesses considerable merit' (quoted in Martin 1999, 50).

Visiting Steeple Barton today, embowered still in lush grassland and woodland, with banked lanes and streams, a shrunken and closed settlement away from main roads, it does indeed seem an environment to foster Hoskins's strong feelings for what he had already called, in *Chilterns to Black Country* (1951), 'essentially English countryside, the very heart of it all' (Hoskins 1951, 43). Equally it evoked, as we have seen, what Thomas, in a fiftieth-anniversary edition of *The Making of the English Landscape*, has called Hoskins's 'violently anti-modern sentiments' (Hoskins 2005, xvi).

Steeple Barton lies near the centre of the canvas chosen by Hoskins to analyse the imprint of communications on the landscape. So Chapter 8 of *The Making of the English Landscape* takes sheet 145 of the post-war, sixth edition of the one-inch Ordnance Survey (Figure 60), which covers an area stretching from the northern edge of Oxford up to a few miles beyond Banbury, and from Chipping Norton on the west to beyond Brackley in Northamptonshire in the east. The terrain runs from the Oxford Clay Vale (with Wychwood Forest on the west and the marshland of Otmoor to the east), up on to limestone uplands (in which Steeple Barton lies), and then into the rich Redlands of Banburyshire (in the north of Oxfordshire and the adjoining parts of Warwickshire and Northamptonshire). The whole is bisected from north to south by the river Cherwell; of this Hoskins had previously written, in *Chilterns to Black Country*, 'to some the valley of the Cherwell between Oxford and Banbury offers some of the most satisfying valley scenery in the whole of England' (Hoskins 1951, 43). It had also historically been a conduit of communications from river to road and canal to railway.

It was in this chapter that Hoskins was also able to demonstrate in practice the excitement and the local character of his proposed methods of landscape study. As he put it, 'there are certain sheets of the one-inch Ordnance Survey maps which one can sit down and read like a book for an hour on end, with growing pleasure and imaginative excitement' (Hoskins 2005, xviii). By following this through in the case of just one such sheet he deliberately set out to avoid unoriginal and dull generalisations: 'Let us take instead one comparatively small piece of country, which contains every variety of road from the prehistoric trackway to the modern by-pass ... the interest of an enquiry such as this, and one cannot say it too often, lies in the detail of the subject'.

Hoskins began with the roads and trackways of the north Oxfordshire landscape, taking the ancient Banbury Lane as a particularly strong example of his theme. He emphasised the continuities, from Saxon or earlier periods to the eighteenth century, of routes on direct lines and significantly associated with archaeological features and boundaries. Major routes are thus portrayed as being used and reused with the effect of concentrating communications. Some (like Banbury Lane) are of great antiquity, originating as 'a more or less open corridor ... bounded on either side by dense forest'.

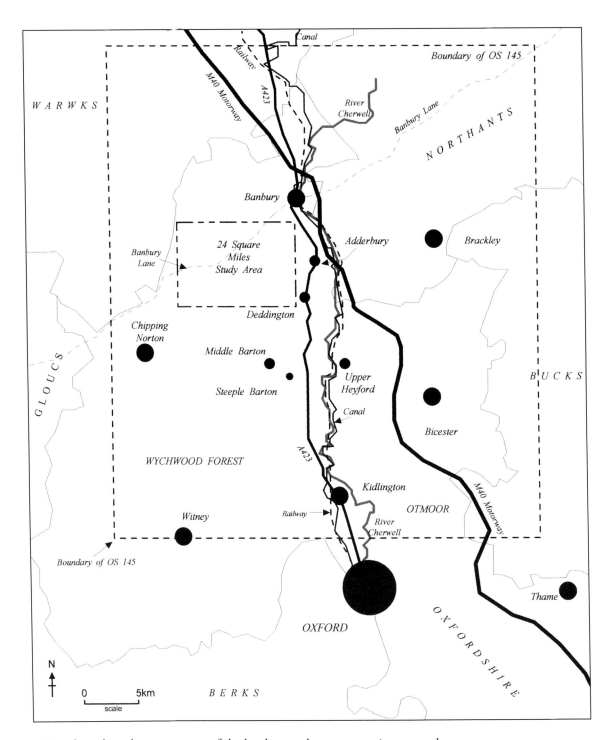

Roads and trackways are one of the landscape elements now interpreted very
differently as a result of expanded and revised archaeological evidence. Much
earlier clearance of forest, intensive settlement, cultivation and ritual activity
are all recognised as features of the English landscape from the Neolithic

period onwards. Thus Taylor (as in his 1988 edition of *The Making of the English Landscape*) points not to dominant and continuously important roads but rather to multiple routes through a cultivated landscape, with particular roads fluctuating in importance at different periods. Trackways like Banbury Lane cannot any longer be seen as of exclusive or continuous significance. 'Spiders' webs of local roads' played an important part in communication. New elements, like a toll house on a road turnpiked in the eighteenth century, injected fresh activity and sometimes settlement into the landscape (in Hoskins 1988, 200).

The other main post-1955 commentator on Hoskins's Oxfordshire landscape has been Emery, an historical geographer and author of *The Oxfordshire Landscape* (1974). This was a volume in the series of individual county volumes 'The Making of the English Landscape', for which Hoskins's 1955 book had been conceived as an introductory overview. Emery, like Taylor, pointed to the changed interpretations which had followed from realisations of much earlier, pre-Saxon clearance, cultivation and settlement of the Oxfordshire landscape, but he also emphasised the continuing making of that landscape. The study and acceptance of the significance of later periods were essential to understanding its history. A few reluctant and distasteful moments of consideration would not be enough.

Specifically, Emery argued that more needed to be done to relate the history of the landscape to modern influences of planning, conservation and development. For example, he made direct links between historical patterns and twentieth-century planning in Oxfordshire. Its Victorian landscape has striking examples of open and closed villages. In post-war Oxfordshire, with its rapidly growing population and changing patterns of economic activity, this legacy of contrasting settlement types fed directly into public policy on development control. The closed villages were difficult to develop 'because their appearance is so coherent, traditional and therefore worthy of protection from modern designs and materials'. In open villages, on the other hand, planning authorities 'still find plenty of odd corners for infilling and rounding off, while it does not amount to an intrusion if new housing estates are tacked on to these "specified villages"' (Emery 1974, 231). Such contrasts were nowhere more apparent than in Hoskins's Steeple Barton and the adjoining larger and very open village of Middle Barton. Emery used Middle Barton as his example of an archetypical open village, contrasting it with the closed settlement pattern and social structure of Sandford St Martin, adjoining it to the west, rather than the also very closed Steeple Barton to the east (Figure 61).

Middle Barton's infill and expansion would undoubtedly have offended Hoskins's eye, but it has produced a relatively affordable place to live for Oxfordshire people in the late twentieth century. Since the 1960s Oxfordshire's planning policies have featured particular villages designated for development, urban growth deliberately concentrated in the four towns of Banbury, Bicester, Witney and Didcot, and elsewhere green belt, conservation areas and other controls on development. The importance of public policy and of changing

FIGURE 60.
The area chosen by
Hoskins to discuss
the imprint of
communications on
the landscape. Also
shown are the line of
the M40, completed
in 1991, and the study
area of the *Twenty-four
Square Miles* survey of
1944.

economic circumstances have indeed proved key to the continuing evolution of this landscape. Hoskins seems to have ignored such factors, although they were already emergent in the Oxfordshire of 1955 and before.

Indeed, such influences had been prefigured, nationally and locally, during the Second World War. Hoskins himself had been recruited, in 1941, by Nuffield College, Oxford, as a statistician and local investigator into the 'Social Reconstruction of the East Midlands Area', but instead was required to do war work as a statistician for the Board of Trade in London (Thirsk 1994, 342–3). It was in 1943, as part of the preparation for post-war reconstruction, that a national study of what should happen to English rural society was undertaken. That survey, which was to be highly relevant to the north Oxfordshire landscape, was undertaken by Oxford University's Agricultural Economics Research Institute (AERI), under its director, the distinguished agrarian historian C. S. Orwin, whose classic study of *The Open Fields* had been published in 1938. The survey appeared in book form as *Country Planning. A Study of Rural Problems* (AERI 1944) and was soon followed by the film of the book – *Twenty-four Square Miles* (COI 1946). The area chosen for this national example of rural life was that of one six-inch OS sheet just south of Banbury. It encompassed twenty-two settlements, five of them large villages, most of them in 1943 'farm' villages. There was little employment outside agriculture. The population of the area had fallen, by about a quarter, between 1881 and 1931. The survey revealed the relative deprivation of the country dweller – in terms of standard of living, housing conditions, educational and medical services and social opportunities. This was a landscape of declining population, dilapidated agricultural buildings and farming methods fossilised by economic depression in a traditional mixed husbandry carried out in units (average farm size 109 acres (44 ha)) and field patterns derived from an earlier era. Rural crafts had declined to the point where only three smiths worked in the area. Community activities were marked by apathy and a lack of leadership. The centre of village life was the pub. These were the landscape and social consequences of prolonged agricultural depression, which (as the first Land Utilisation Survey of 1933 revealed) had left Oxfordshire a 'green' county with 55 per cent of land under permanent grass and a little over 30 per cent arable, presenting 'a general picture of neglect' (Scargill 1989, 9).

The authors of *Country Planning* argued that mains water, gas, electricity, metalled roads, a bus past the door, and active citizenship should be brought to these neglected areas. They were aware of likely opposition:

> There is evidence of a certain reluctance on the part of many country lovers to contemplate any serious change to the rural scene. But it is sufficient to look at any village street to realise that there has been a continuous evolution and change through the centuries, not only in the village but in the face of the country-side too. A static village is dead, and 'the preservation of rural England', must not be interpreted in the museum sense. (AERI 1944, 274)

The corollary of this was a recognition that 'the village of a few hundred people cannot survive as a healthy organism …'. A minimum size for health was a population of between 1200 and 2400. This could not be based on an unrealistic revival of traditional crafts and trades: 'three out of four boys born on the land must seek other employment'. The survey's answers came in the form of planned decentralisation of employment, for example in light industry, with adequate road communication and transport playing a vital role. As to farming, old field layouts and agricultural buildings should be replanned. In the villages old houses should be reconditioned and some new ones built. Communal facilities should be created. All this could be achieved by careful planning, if necessary taking villages together to achieve a critical mass for viability. One such proposal from *Country Planning* suggests how in two villages with an existing population of 239, 'eighty-nine additional houses could be incorporated without upsetting the present form and character of the villages, and pulling them together at the same time, by the provision on a central site of a new School and School-house, a Community Centre and a Sports Ground' (AERI 1944, chapter 14) (Figure 62).

Rural north Oxfordshire was shown by the survey to be decayed, deprived and disadvantaged, suffering from isolation and a lack of communications. Yet this is a reality absent from Hoskins's treatment of the same area, either in portraying the countryside as recent history had made it, or in engaging with the forces and ideas already at work in shaping its future. Eva Taylor, reviewing *The Making of the English Landscape* in the *Geographical Journal* in 1955, had commented that Hoskins seemed unaware of the work of geographers (quoted in Matless 1993, 188). She compared Hoskins's work to that of Stamp, whose New Naturalist volume *Man and the Land* was also published that year (Stamp 1955). The attitudes of the two to the modern world and to the role of planning were in striking contrast, with Stamp concluding that 'Land planning is here to stay and so the landscape of Britain is destined to be moulded as never before by the hand of man'. Matless has found this difference indicative of two distinct directions in landscape studies to be seen in 1955:

> Stamp's narrative of English landscape is one of ongoing planned progress; Hoskins' is not. And it is perhaps here that the important novelty of Hoskins' work lies, in allying the pursuit of knowledge regarding landscape and place (indeed almost allying landscape and place *per se*) to a specifically anti-modern and anti-planning outlook. (Matless 1993, 189)

Hoskins saw from his Oxfordshire window a 'rich and favoured countryside … The cultural humus of sixty generations or more lies upon it' (Hoskins 1988, 242). This vision, and the methods of studying landscape as a palimpsest which Hoskins developed from it, have transformed the awareness and understanding of vast numbers of readers. It is an irony, however, that, whilst continuing change is a central feature of the book, Hoskins was unable to acknowledge and describe facts and trends which were unavoidably to be seen around him. This is strikingly apparent in the Oxfordshire evidence. It was others, his contemporaries and successors, who both built on and bridged gaps in Hoskins's approach. This, too, can be seen in the subsequent history of the making of our Oxfordshire landscapes.

Thirty years on from *Country Planning* there was a restudy, again by Oxford University AERI, of the same 24 square miles (9 km²) (Bates and Cudmore 1975). It showed that Oxfordshire had continued to suffer population loss into the 1950s. From the 1960s growth had become rapid, but with a good deal of in and out migration movement. In 1973 5 per cent of the workforce was in agriculture and the rest was in industry and services, often in the towns. There was extensive travel from villages to work and school. If anything, rural facilities had declined – seven of twenty-two villages were now without a shop; fourteen schools in 1943 were now reduced to seven primary schools and one secondary school. But mains water and sewerage had reached the villages of north Oxfordshire and housing conditions and standard of living had improved: 'Deprivation in the 1970s was much less to do with quality of housing, much more to do with the level of service provision and the isolation of those without cars' (Scargill 1989, 12). It was to tackle problems of this kind that local authority development plans identified key or specified villages with concentrations of services and of building development.

The story of the landscape of communications also proves to have been a fuller and a changing one. This is reflected in two themes, one which Hoskins did not discuss (air), and another which he did at length (roads). In 1952, when Hoskins moved to Steeple Barton, north Oxfordshire was littered with airfields, nearly all military. Nearest of all was one of the largest, RAF Upper Heyford, a flying base since 1916. In 1950 the USAF had arrived and the runway was extended to 10,000 feet (3050 m). In June 1953 Strategic

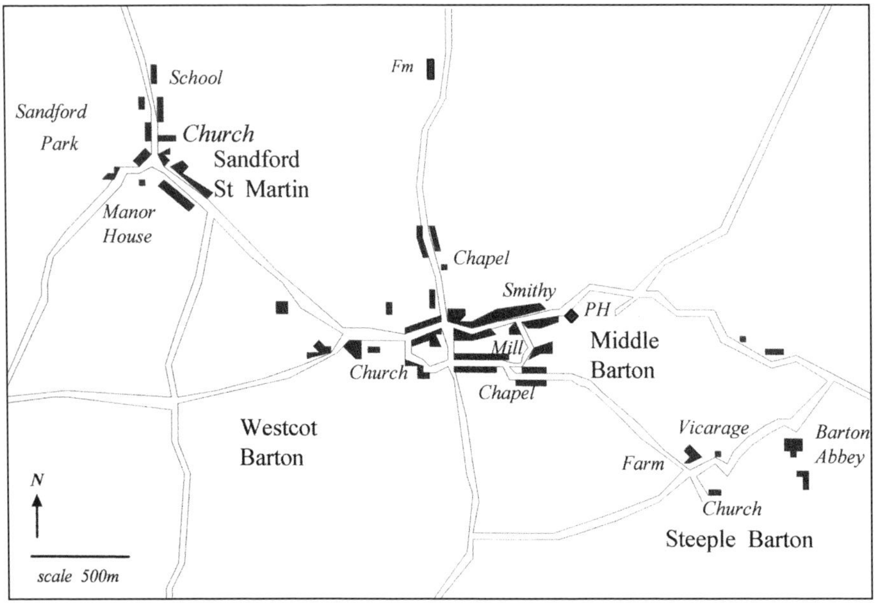

FIGURE 61.
The contrasting characters of Sandford St Martin, a closed settlement, and Middle Barton, an open village, as identified by Emery (1974) from the Ordnance Survey map of 1900. The difference persists, now more marked following the building of post-war housing in Middle Barton. Steeple Barton, immediately to the east, presents another striking, closed village contrast.

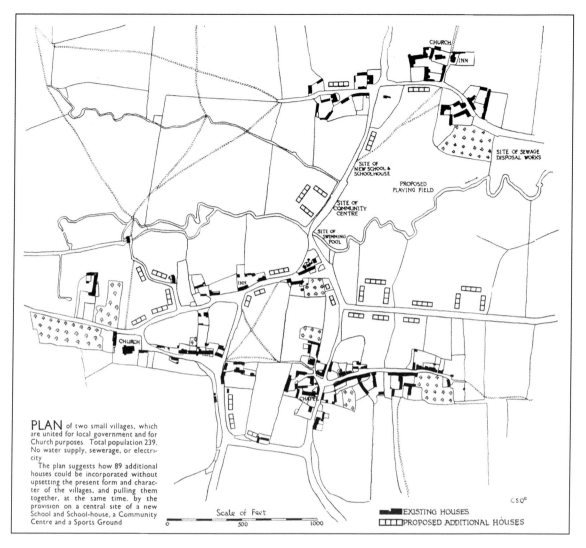

PLAN of two small villages, which are united for local government and for Church purposes. Total population 239. No water supply, sewerage, or electricity

The plan suggests how 89 additional houses could be incorporated without upsetting the present form and character of the villages, and pulling them together, at the same time, by the provision on a central site of a new School and School-house, a Community Centre and a Sports Ground

Scale of Feet

0   500   1000

■■ EXISTING HOUSES
▢▢▢ PROPOSED ADDITIONAL HOUSES

FIGURE 62.
Villages replanned, from the 1944 north Oxfordshire survey *Country Planning.* Reproduced by permission of the Delegates of Oxford University Press.

Air Command moved to the base (remaining until 1965, to be succeeded by Tactical Air Command). They operated from Upper Heyford and surrounding satellite bases until the USAF withdrew in 1994. During the Tactical Air Command era the 20th Tactical Fighter Wing flew F111 swing-wing fighters out of Upper Heyford, which was the largest station of its kind in Europe. These followed the nuclear-armed Stratojets of the mid-1950s (Bowyer 1988, 116–29; Davison 1990, 6).

So the aeroplane, and particularly the military jet, played a major part in the life of north Oxfordshire which could not be ignored. This provoked some of Hoskins's fiercest polemic: 'Airfields have flayed it [the immemorial landscape of the English countryside] bare ... Over [it] drones, day upon day, the obscene shape of the atom-bomber, laying a trail like a filthy slug upon Constable's and Gainsborough's sky' (Hoskins 1988, 238). Certainly the ground shook, and 'the windows of local houses were well and truly rattled'

(Davison 1990, 6). More and more runways, military buildings, dispersed bomb-proof shelters, communications aerials and domes and dishes, along with the schools, stores, hospital, sports grounds and housing of an American town, appeared in the middle of Oxfordshire. Away from the base the local economy was significantly affected, with increased demand for goods and services. This included housing for families living or visiting off base, with consequent pressure on the housing market and rental prices. Americans were to be seen in the streets of Banbury and local villages; the sights and sounds of the landscape changed; and the airspace was restricted (Figure 63).

The closure of RAF Upper Heyford has brought a new perspective to the landscape. One consequence has been to reopen the airspace, enabling archaeological flying to take place from the civilian airfield at Kidlington just north of Oxford. This (along with the exceptionally good conditions for cropmark formation in 1995 and 1996) has led to a transformation of our knowledge of early sites in the Cherwell valley (Figure 64). Bowden (1999, fig. 56) takes north Oxfordshire as an example of how modern techniques of landscape investigation can, in a very short period, transform our understanding of the landscape.

The fabric of the Upper Heyford base remains, seeking a new use. A new town for north Oxfordshire has been mooted. This has not happened, although some ex-military housing has been put to local use. In 2005 falling new car sales saw thousands of unsold vehicles parked along the runways. Meanwhile, in the local and national press debate flowed about the longer-term future of the base. Under the headline 'English Heritage could list airbase at Upper Heyford', the local MP was quoted (*Oxford Times* 15 July 2005): '[It] wants to list a number of rather battered bunkers at the former … base. This is probably one of the largest brownfield sites in Oxfordshire, and such sites are much needed for redevelopment for housing, including affordable housing'. On the opposite side of the argument a correspondent to *The Guardian* (10 September 2005) pleaded for preservation:

> At Upper Heyford … there is an intact USAF base which … remains as the most important monument to the Cold War in western Europe. The Cold War landscape, comprising security fence, runways, underground facilities and fifty-six hardened aircraft shelters, was specifically designed to remain operational under a bombing or missile attack. In terms of its historical and cultural importance, there is no doubt Upper Heyford should be a prime candidate for the list of sites to be protected under the 1954 Hague convention.

Hoskins airbrushed jets out of his idyllic view from Steeple Barton but the then landscape of north Oxfordshire could not be understood without reference to the Cold War, and, subsequently, to such far-flung factors as the fall of the Berlin Wall and the break-up of the USSR, the fortunes of the motor industry, and international conservation provisions. It is hard to imagine Hoskins supporting the case to preserve its Cold War landscape, yet the opposed views of 2005 perhaps echo the two approaches to the history of the landscape discernible fifty years earlier.

As regards roads in the landscape, a great deal has changed since 1955, both because evidence for earlier periods has been reinterpreted and because significant new layers have been added to the palimpsest. By 1974, when Emery wrote, there was keen anticipation of the likely impact of the proposed M40 London–Birmingham motorway, which was finally completed in early 1991. In the intervening years the prospect of this greatest change to communications and landscape since the arrival of the canal and railway – and some argued ever – generated new interest and extensive activity in the history and archaeology of the Oxfordshire landscape. The motorway was planned to pass near Oxford, cutting through the green belt and crossing parts of Bernwood and Otmoor and the surrounding seven towns. The prospect mobilised highly vocal opposition which argued, through years of planning enquiries and legal process, for a rerouting of the motorway further to the east of Oxford, and of Bernwood and Otmoor, before it turned west to join the river, canal and railway on the valley route north to Banbury. As the collective of campaigners known as the Otmoor Group awaited the planning inspector's ruling in 1984 they published a collection of writings and drawings on the nature of Otmoor (Otmoor Group 1984). This included surveys of how local residents used the moor, lists of its birds and insects, its literary associations and historical accounts, and technical arguments on the propensity of the area to fog and on anticipated traffic flows. The aim of the booklet was to encapsulate the distinctive character of the place and, in doing so, to show what the new road and its associated motorway corridor would destroy. Its title, *Otmoor for Ever!*, echoed the cry of the Otmoor rioters of 1830, famously quoted by the Hammonds and other historians as examples of popular opposition to the enclosure of their landscape and the extinction of common rights (Hammond and Hammond 1911, 64–72). One feels that Hoskins would have approved of this historical echo, and also of the investigations of place, albeit spurred by threat of change. As the opening sentences of *Otmoor for Ever!* put it: 'Man is a spiritual as well as a material being and clear evidence has been presented of the way in which this place, Otmoor, provides for the inner man. It is a place with a remarkable history and a capacity to inspire.' Such eloquence, combined with local authority support, led to the motorway route being moved to the east (see Figure 60).

The prospect of motorway building had already transformed knowledge of north Oxfordshire's landscape in another way. It triggered a major programme of archaeological survey and excavation along the proposed route in the 1970s. Large numbers of sites of prehistoric, Roman, Saxon and medieval dates were recorded (Hinton and Rowley 1974), providing a striking example of the threat of enforced change injecting new energies and resources into landscape study; a paradoxical, positive and now regular spin-off.

People throughout north Oxfordshire, whatever their views for or against the new motorway and its routing, expected that once opened it would

FIGURE 63.
A USAF F-III swing-
wing fighter at RAF
Upper Heyford in the
1980s: Hoskins'
'filthy slug' above the
English landscape
personified. Courtesy
of Jon Davison/Eye in
the Sky
(www.eyeinthesky.
com.au)

significantly change landscapes and lives, not just along the lines of its car-
riageways, embankments, bridges, plantings, slip roads and service areas, but
in a wider corridor of adjoining countryside and settlements. Some fifteen
years on we can now see the impact of this most recent major road in the
landscape of sheet 145. Large villages like Adderbury and Deddington on the
old A423 described by Hoskins are now relieved of the through traffic of the
former trunk road. Yet the motorway, crossing and recrossing the eighteenth-
century canal and the nineteenth-century railway with which it shares the
Cherwell valley barely a mile east of Adderbury, has had other effects. It has
generated building, both residential and commercial, and new patterns and
intensities of traffic coming to and from new factories, warehouses, offices,
out-of-town shops, homes and schools. The influence of the M40 reaches far
beyond the noise of the lorries speeding back and forth from the West Midlands and north of England to London and Southampton. Nowhere can this
be better seen in the early twenty-first-century landscape than at Banbury, the
main town and focal point of the landscape of sheet 145.

Banbury was chosen by Everitt (1985) as archetypical of his 'primary towns'

FIGURE 64.
Archaeological sites in
the Cherwell Valley,
many discovered by
aerial photography
following the opening
of the local airspace
when the USAF
withdrew from Upper
Heyford in 1994. From
Bowden 1999, fig. 56.
© Crown copyright
NMR

of England, which were characteristically ancient in origin and usually associated with prehistoric or Roman roads, or both. Certainly, communications
had always been key to Banbury's development as a major market town and
the centre of a hinterland of influence stretching into the neighbouring counties of Northamptonshire and Warwickshire. By 1830 fifty-four coaches a week
left the town, their destinations including London, Birmingham, Leicester,

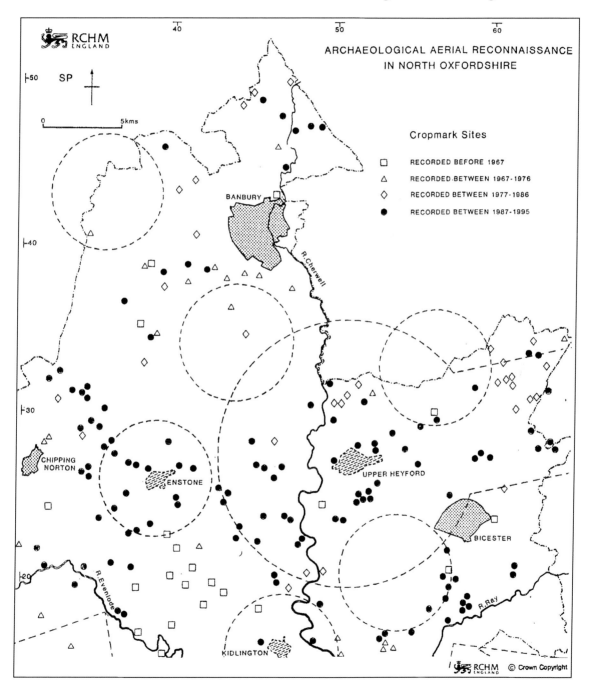

ARCHAEOLOGICAL AERIAL RECONNAISSANCE
IN NORTH OXFORDSHIRE

Cropmark Sites

□ RECORDED BEFORE 1967

△ RECORDED BETWEEN 1967-1976

◇ RECORDED BETWEEN 1977-1986

● RECORDED BETWEEN 1987-1995

© Crown Copyright

Oxford, Northampton and Cheltenham. More locally, in 1843 Banbury 'was the metropolis for 140 places within a circuit of 10 miles' by dint of its network of carriers' carts (VCH 1972, 12–13). In addition to the road network, the Oxford Canal was opened from Coventry to Banbury in 1778, and was extended from there to Oxford by 1790. In the 1850s Banbury was reached by the Great Western and the North Western Railway Companies, and by 1901 lines radiated from the town in six directions (Little 2003).

This transport base contributed significantly to the growth of new enterprises. Notably, Samuelson's agricultural implement making at the Britannia Works was linked by a tramway to the railway which transported products nationally and, *via* other links, internationally. Much of Banbury's economic activity remained linked to agriculture, and here, too, communications were as important as ever. For Emery, writing of towns in the Oxfordshire landscape, it was Banbury's cattle market, then the largest in Europe and, significantly, next to the railway station, that deserved comment, for 'In this we see a modern expression of the town's place in the English network of drove roads for cattle, especially the great midland thoroughfare of Banbury Lane, much used between 1600 and 1800' (Emery 1974, 199).

Today the great Midland thoroughfare is the M40. A new link road joins Banbury to the motorway at junction 11, just to the east of the town. Along the link and around the junction clusters of sheds and 'pagodas' fill previously open countryside, housing storage and distribution, processing and service industries. Products handled include foodstuffs, plastics, mobile phones, car components, and in one case world championship-winning rally cars. Few of these have links to the indigenous market functions of Banbury. The cattle market described by Emery opened in 1925 and closed in 1998.

The arrival of the motorway has accelerated existing trends. Large-scale, non-agricultural industry had come to the town as early as 1931, when the Northern Aluminium Co. Ltd (a Canadian-owned company, later Alcan), supported by members of the town corporation keen to see added diversity in Banbury's static economy, opened their factory on former green fields on Southam Road (VCH 1972, 68). The *Country Planning* survey confirmed how this provided jobs not only in the town but for workers bussed in from surrounding villages. In 1950 Banbury became the subject of a further major sociological survey led by Margaret Stacey, in which 'the social structure and culture of Banbury with special reference to the introduction of large-scale industry' (Stacey 1960, v) was studied. However, growth, new industry and incomers were to become even more significant parts of the Banburyshire experience. In the early 1960s Banbury Council applied, under the Town Development Act (1952), to be designated for expansion and made agreements to take overspill from Birmingham and London. More large-scale industry was relocated there, including, in the 1960s, the Bird's Custard factory from Digbeth in Birmingham. Their workers came with them and, by the late 1960s, the areas where they lived had been named The Aviary and Little London (Stacey *et al.* 1975, 15).

Public policy and economic development had moved Banbury in changed directions, physically and socially. The period 1950–68 was intensively observed, recorded and analysed by the sociologist Stacey and her co-workers in the study already mentioned, and then in another based on fieldwork in the town in 1966–8 (Stacey 1960; Stacey *et al.* 1975). The returning researchers found that 'Banbury by 1966 had much more the air of an industrial town than a market town' (Stacey *et al.* 1975, 8). In landscape terms, 'All the country walks, at one time so close to the town centre, seem to have disappeared … There are no longer tongues of open country penetrating wedge-shaped behind the ribbon development which fronted each main road in the thirties, forties and early fifties' (Stacey *et al.* 1975, 10). The study concluded that whereas in 1950 Banbury had had a discernible social class basis with a dominant group drawn largely from people born and brought up in the town, by the late 1960s no such core group was found. Traditional class demarcations had lessened and a number of influential groupings existed, not a single powerful elite. By the time the M40 opened Banbury was already an expanded and changed town, its centre including a large shopping centre (albeit hidden behind the preserved façades of older buildings on the Market Square), and a regenerated canal and waterfront.

The present study has reconsidered the north Oxfordshire landscapes so richly described and so deliberately used by Hoskins in 1955 to demonstrate new ways of looking at the English landscape. His emphases and his prejudices come across very clearly. His was a partial account of the post-war Oxfordshire countryside and its communities. The state of the landscape – its settlements and its people – was far from prosperous, peaceful or sustainable, as was apparent in contemporary print and film (notably *Country Planning* and *Twenty-four Square Miles*) and in the appearance of the places themselves. It is hard to believe that Hoskins was altogether unaware of such studies, or of what was to be seen around him. Whilst there is never enough space in a general study for every detail these gaps in Hoskins's analysis speak of a more fundamental lack in his approach. The few distasteful moments he felt able to allow for the contemplation of the recent past, the present and the future were simply not enough to realise in full the methods of landscape study and the understanding of landscape for which he strove. The Oxfordshire evidence reviewed here gives different perspectives and added reality and depth to the account, and demonstrates powerful formative influences already at work on the landscape when he wrote: notably planning, conservation and development.

To revisit the Oxfordshire scene also demonstrates the range and extent of additional evidence available to those now unravelling the landscape. This comes not only from additional techniques of survey and recording, but also from the large amount of professional and local archaeological and historical work undertaken in the last fifty years, often inspired by Hoskins's example. Equally, the value of including the insights and methods of other disciplines, including geography, social science and anthropology, is very clear.

As methods of studying these Oxfordshire landscapes have changed, with neglected perspectives recognised and fresh techniques applied, so the results have modified some of Hoskins's conclusions, as in the case of roads and their role in the landscape. This is an inevitable and positive part of the development of all subjects. More generally, Taylor (in Hoskins 1988, 237) has argued the benefits of a more distanced and objective view than Hoskins was sometimes able to bring:

> ... if aesthetic pleasure is separated from objective study the most dreadful landscapes can come alive after close research and bring with them their own form of satisfaction ... the English landscape has never been static but has always been changing, for better or worse. Today we are passing through a period which can perhaps be regarded as a disaster. Yet it is not the faceless planners, mindless civil servants, wild military men or politicians who are always to blame. Ultimately they merely carry out what we as a democratic society demand. It is we who want broad motorways, cheap coal, instant electricity, subsidised food, and protection from alleged enemies without care for the past or indeed thought for the future. Perhaps we have achieved in our landscape what we deserve.

In the fifty years since the publication of *The Making of the English Landscape*, the north Oxfordshire landscape has altered greatly. The military jets have gone, the motorway has come; Steeple Barton remains picturesque, whilst Middle Barton is larger and busier than ever; mobility and work patterns are transformed, as the case of Banbury eloquently demonstrates. At least two more generations of cultural humus now lie upon this land, layers of the palimpsest to be studied by landscape historians still inspired by Hoskins but now needing to engage with a wider body of knowledge and some different ways of seeing.

Acknowledgements

Robert Peberdy, Joan Thirsk and Liam Tiller (who also drew Figures 60 and 61) made valuable comments on earlier drafts. I am grateful to them, and to Paul Barnwell, for their help and guidance.

CHAPTER FIFTEEN

Conclusion:
Discovering the Post-Medieval
Landscape – After W. G. Hoskins

....

P. S. Barnwell

In the year that he wrote *The Making of the English Landscape*, W. G. Hoskins gave three talks on the BBC Third Programme on the theme of 'The Rediscovery of England', an adapted version of which was published in 1963 (Hoskins 1963). The first talk sketched the history of the 'discovery' of England's landscape, which started with Leland's topographical account of 1535–43 and matured during the reign of Elizabeth I with the drawing of county maps and the writing of the first county histories. Hoskins then moved, in the second talk, to the awakening of interest in the archaeology, architecture, history and place-names of the landscape which had begun between the two World Wars, and which he and other scholars were furthering at the dawn of what was, at the time, often optimistically called the 'new Elizabethan age', though the link between the two queens was only implied. He concluded the series with an outline of some of the large projects he thought might usefully be undertaken in the ensuing years. Half a century later, considerable progress has been made in many of the fields Hoskins identified – particularly Anglo-Saxon topography and landscapes, vernacular architecture or what he preferred to call 'peasant buildings' (though still with less emphasis on town buildings and on integration with other disciplines than he desired), urban topography, and the history of building materials.

The scholarly careers of the contributors to the present volume have been conducted entirely within the second Elizabethan age and in the period following the publication of *The Making of the English Landscape* – some, indeed, entirely after Hoskins's death in 1983 – and, although this is not always explicitly acknowledged, the influence of that book can be seen in almost every essay presented here. The most obvious continuities from topics which interested Hoskins lie in the chapters by Longcroft and Hoyle. The former analyses the landscape of one county, Norfolk, and suggests that different forms of landscape, supporting differing agrarian regimes, underlie varying patterns of the 'rebuilding of rural England', the subject of Hoskins's major contribution to the study of vernacular architecture, written only a year after the study of England's traditional buildings came of age with the foundation of the Vernacular Architecture Group (Hoskins 1953). The latter builds on Hoskins's earlier work on Market Harborough, first published in 1949 (Hoskins 1963), and assesses the reasons for the creation of new market towns in the early modern period, examining the economic ties between the urban and rural lands of the lords who developed them, and touching upon their physical environment. That thematic strand is pursued into the eighteenth century by Stobart's exploration of the influence of the local gentry on the development of Chester, which emphasises the social and cultural influence of the rural gentry in the developing economy, street plan and buildings of the city. The impact on the landscape of the sectional concerns of particular social groups is also reflected by Hey and Silvester when they discuss the ways in which the sharply contrasting social groups involved in grouse shooting and in creating squatter communities shaped the management and appearance of the land, sometimes on a large scale, and at the same time affected other members of society, for example by restricting access to the grouse moors. Similar themes are explored in Goddard's discussion of competing interests of industry, health, amenity and leisure in the rapidly expanding urban environment of nineteenth-century Croydon.

In these chapters, landscape is seen primarily as a product of economic, social and cultural influences, but it is also a source of evidence for economic, social and cultural history. That has always been implicit in landscape studies, but at the start of the twenty-first century some scholars are shifting the focus more clearly onto this topic. In this volume, the approach is exemplified by Finch, the only contributor to paint with an avowedly theoretical brush. Using broad strokes, he seeks to understand great estates as landscapes with multiple layers of significance: an estate was at once economic and cultural artefact, which served, and was perceived differently by, differing communities (land-owners, visitors, tenant farmers, labourers and servants), while at the same it created its own single landscape which integrated the varied interests into a single estate community. Each estate was the product of a unique set of cir-cumstances which forged its own particular landscape containing evidence for its peculiar culture and society: landscape and way of life are inseparable.

All the chapters so far mentioned proceed from foundations already laid by the mid-1950s, though not all with a form of superstructure which could have been anticipated. The building on one particular set of foundations, how-ever, has been arrested, as Sheail shows in his discussion of the integration of understanding of the historic environment and ecology which began to be sig-nificantly developed in the 1960s and 1970s. The work was largely conducted by staff of the government agencies involved in understanding and managing the historic and natural landscape, and fell victim to changes in bureaucratic culture in the 1980s which made cross-fertilisation of ideas between agen-cies more difficult than it had been. At the start of the twenty-first century there is a new recognition of the inter-relationship between archaeology (in its widest sense), historical ecology and today's natural environment, and of the importance of integrated land management. It remains to be seen whether that realisation leads to a revival of connections between agencies and to a new generation of scholarship.

In other fields of enquiry the last fifty years have seen a broadening of the appreciation of the kinds of landscape which are thought to contain evidence for past human activity. One such area is the landscapes of industrial activity, the study of which developed almost entirely in the second half of the twentieth century. In this volume, it is a field of study represented by Roe, who introduces to his discussion of lead mining in the Yorkshire Dales the idea that the invisible underground 'landscapes' of mine workings contain evidence which can radically alter conventional understanding of the industry. The landscape created in the twentieth century, which Hoskins openly despised, is now an important subject, as here exemplified by Tiller in her elegant revisiting of the part of north Oxfordshire in which Hoskins wrote *The Making of the English Landscape*. The relationship between the nature of the land, economic and cultural forces, and human activity is as important for the present age as for previous times, not least since the landscape provides evidence for government action and for changing ways of life which are often so ephemeral as to fall rapidly from the conscious memory of those who live through them.

If perceptions of the kinds of landscape and landscape feature which are historically significant have evolved, so too has the scope of landscape history itself, for the scholars of today may be as interested in past perceptions of landscape as in the landscape itself. Historians of art and literature have for long been interested in this subject, though usually from the perspectives of their own disciplines rather than in ways which would sit comfortably in a collection of papers about the landscape itself. The increasing interest in integrating all forms of evidence relating to past landscapes is here exemplified in the chapter on the East Midlands hunting landscape by Watkins, in which the physical creation of one of the most evocative landscapes of England is discussed alongside both the creation of the image of that landscape in painting and the way in which that image has influenced the way in which the landscape is perceived today. Similarly, as Dunham implies, anyone who has read Kilvert's diary may have his or her perception of the central Welsh Marches coloured by the creative writing and psychological condition of its author. Appreciation of the landscape may also be affected – deepened and enhanced – by myths and stories about it, some, as demonstrated by Hooke, forged many generations ago – myth, like landscape, putting us in contact with distant ancestors.

While not reflecting all the developments in landscape studies since Hoskins wrote of the 'rediscovery' of England, nor even being systematically representative of them, the papers gathered in this volume illustrate some of the trends of the last fifty years in relation to the post-medieval landscape: the building upon ideas and techniques pioneered by Hoskins and his contemporaries, the extension of established fields of enquiry, the expansion into new ones. The same trends can be seen in the work of the Society for Landscape Studies, founded in 1979, and in the scope of the articles published annually in its journal, *Landscape History*, and its more recent sister, *Landscapes*, the very existence of which would have seemed unlikely in the 1950s. Starting from the 'archaeological' discovery of the landscape in the middle of the twentieth century, the second Elizabethan era has seen an awakening and expansion of interest in the English landscape which may prove to be as significant as that of the first Elizabethan age.

Contributors

....

Dr P. S. Barnwell is Director of Studies in the Historic Environment at Oxford University Department for Continuing Education, having previously worked for the Royal Commission on the Historical Monuments of England and, latterly, for English Heritage as Head of Medieval and Later Rural Research Policy. He has published on a wide range of subjects, including vernacular houses, farm buildings and medieval parish churches.

Dr Philip Dunham is Senior Lecturer in Human Geography at Coventry University. He has published several articles on the philosophy and practice of geography and on aspects of rural economic change. He is currently working on further studies of the Rev. Francis Kilvert and landscape history, including 'Kilvert and the Borderland' and 'Madness, Cloud and Delirium: Francis Kilvert and the Emotional Narration of Landscape'.

Dr Jonathan Finch is Lecturer in Archaeology at the University of York. He has published articles on topics ranging from medieval regional landscapes to the development of foxhunting and landscape change. He is currently co-editing a volume on estate landscapes for the Society for Post-Medieval Archaeology, and is working with seven country houses in Yorkshire to explore the role of the estate within the modern landscape.

Nicholas Goddard was until recently Professor of Agrarian and Environmental History at Anglia Ruskin University. He is the author of the history of the Royal Agricultural Society of England, *Harvests of Change* (1989). He has contributed to the *Agrarian History of England and Wales* Vols VI (1750–1850) and VII (1850–1914) and written widely on nineteenth-century rural and environmental affairs.

Dr David Hey is Emeritus Professor of Local and Family History at the University of Sheffield and a former postgraduate student of William Hoskins. He is currently President of the British Association for Local History. His most recent books are *Journeys in Family History* (The National Archives, 2004) and *A History of Yorkshire* (Carnegie, 2005).

Dr Della Hooke is an Honorary Fellow in the Institute for Advanced Research in the Arts and Social Sciences at the University of Birmingham, having previously been a Research Fellow in the School of Geography there and subsequently a Senior Lecturer at Cheltenham and Gloucester College of Higher

Education. She works as a freelance consultant in historical landscapes and has published widely, especially on the early medieval landscape. Her latest book concerns the evolution of the West Midlands landscape, published as part of English Heritage's *Landscapes of England* series.

Richard Hoyle is Professor of Rural History at the University of Reading. He has published extensively on early modern economic history, sixteenth-century political history and the history of northern England. He is currently a British Academy Research Reader and is engaged in writing the *Oxford Economic and Social History of Britain, 1500–1700*. Amongst other duties, he also serves as editor of *Agricultural History Review*.

Dr Adam Longcroft is a Lecturer in Local and Regional Studies in the School of Education and Lifelong Learning at the University of East Anglia. He is the founding chair of the Norfolk Historic Buildings Group and a member of the Council of the Norfolk and Norwich Archaeological Society.

Professor Marilyn Palmer is a history graduate who has most recently been Head of the School of Archaeology and Ancient History in the University of Leicester, where she is also the Professor of Industrial Archaeology. She serves on committees concerned with historical and industrial archaeology for English Heritage, the Council for British Archaeology and The National Trust. She is Chairman of the Association for Industrial Archaeology and jointly edited *Industrial Archaeology Review* for twenty years as well as publishing widely on industrial archaeology, historical archaeology and local history. Her most recent book, with Peter Neaverson, is *The Textile Industry of South-west England: a Social Archaeology* (Tempus, 2005).

Martin Roe has had an interest in mining landscape since the age of 12. He is a freelance archaeologist specialising in the archaeology of the extractive industries, with a particular interest in recording underground landscapes, and is working on a PhD study of lead-mining landscapes in the Yorkshire Dales.

Dr John Sheail is a Research Fellow of the Centre for Ecology and Hydrology (Natural Environment Research Council) at Monks Wood, where he was, prior to his retirement, Deputy Head of the site. An environmental historian, he has published widely in the areas of historical ecology and the interface between public policy-making and the environmental sciences. In 2002 he published *An Environmental History of Twentieth-Century Britain* (Palgrave, Basingstoke).

Bob Silvester studied archaeology at Exeter, was an archaeological field officer in Devon and then Norfolk and, since 1989, has been deputy director of the Clwyd-Powys Archaeological Trust in east Wales. Recent publications include several on the archaeology of the Welsh uplands, and his main research interests centre on medieval and post-medieval settlement and landscape, church archaeology and the use of estate maps in historic studies.

Contributors

Jon Stobart is Professor of History at the University of Northampton. His research interests encompass industrial, regional and urban development, social and business networking, and leisure, consumption and shopping in eighteenth-century England. Recent publications include: *The First Industrial Region. North-west England, 1700–1760* (Manchester University Press, 2004) and 'Leisure and shopping in the small towns of Georgian England', *Journal of Urban History* **31** (2005). He is currently working on a new book entitled *Spaces of Consumption*.

Dr Kate Tiller is Reader Emerita in English Local History at Oxford University and a Visiting Fellow in English Local History at the University of Leicester. A second edition of her *English Local History: An Introduction* was published in 2002. She has published extensively on rural Oxfordshire, including *Wychwood Forest in the nineteenth century, enclosure and rural change in south Oxfordshire*, and (with James Bond) *Blenheim: Landscape for a Palace* (1997). Her latest book is *Dorchester Abbey: Church and People 635–2005* (2005).

Nicholas Watkins BA (Hons), MPhil, PhD is Emeritus Reader, Fellow in the Department of the History of Art and Film at the University of Leicester. His recent publications include: *Bonnard Colour and Light* (1998), Tate Gallery Publishing, London, and 'The Genesis of a Decorative Aesthetic' in G. Groom, *Beyond the Easel: Decorative Painting by Bonnard, Vuillard, Denis and Roussel, 1890–1930* (2001), The Art Institute of Chicago and Yale University Press. He is a regular contributor to *The Burlington Magazine, Apollo, The Times Literary Supplement* and other leading journals. He is currently working on a book on the equestrian image in nineteenth- and twentieth-century art and culture.

Bibliography

AERI (Agricultural Economics Research Institute Oxford) (1944) *Country Planning. A Study of Rural Problems*, Oxford University Press, Oxford.

Aikin, J. (1795) *The Country from Thirty to Forty Miles round Manchester*, John Stockdale, London.

Alcock, N.W. (1993) *People at Home. Living in a Warwickshire Village, 1500–1800*, Phillimore, Chichester.

Allen, D.E. (1971) 'Hedges and local history', *Watsonia* **8**, 425–6.

Anderson, J.C. (1882) *A Short Chronicle Concerning the Parish of Croydon*, Reeves and Turner, London.

Andrews, M. (1989) *The Search for the Picturesque*, Stanford University Press, Stanford.

Anon. (1970) 'Hedges and local history', *Nature* **223**, 5 July 1970, 18.

Anon. (1971) *Hedges and Local History*, Standing Conference for Local History, London.

Anon. (2000) 'Obituary: M.R.G.Conzen, 1907–2000', *Urban Morphology* **4**, 90–5.

Arkell, T. (2003) 'Identifying regional variations from the Hearth Tax', *The Local Historian* **33**, 148–74.

Arnold, D. (2004) *Rural Urbanism: London Landscapes in the Early Nineteenth Century*, Manchester University Press, Manchester.

Ashcroft, M.Y. (1984) *Documents Relating to the Swaledale Estates of Lord Wharton*, North Yorkshire Record Office, Northallerton.

Baddeley, M.J.B. (1908; 9th edn) *The Peak District of Derbyshire and Neighbouring Counties*, Nelson, London.

Baily (1921) *Baily's Hunting Directory 1921–1922*, Vinton and Co., London.

Baker, A.R.H. and Butlin, R.A. eds (1973) *Studies of Field Systems in the British Isles*, Cambridge University Press, Cambridge.

Banks, S. (1988) 'Nineteenth-century scandal or twentieth-century model? A new look at "open" and "close" parishes', *Economic History Review* 2nd ser. **41**, 51–73.

Barber, C. (2004) *Exploring Kilvert Country*, Blorenge Books, Abergavenny.

Barfoot, P. and Wilkes, J. (1794; 2nd edn) *Universal British Directory of Trade and Commerce*, 3 vols, Champante and Whitrow, London.

Barnes, F.A. (1970) 'Settlement and landscape changes in a Caernarvonshire slate quarrying parish' in ed. R.H.Osborne, *Geographical Essays in Honour of K.C.Edwards*, University of Nottingham, Nottingham, 119–30.

Barrett, J. (1994) *Fragments from Antiquity*, Blackwell, Oxford.

Barringer, J.C. (1993) 'Tanners and tanning' in ed. P.Wade-Martins, *An Historical Atlas of Norfolk*, Norfolk Museums Service, Norwich, 152–3.

Baskerville, S. (1980) 'The establishment of the Grosvenor interest in Chester, 1710–48', *Journal of the Chester Archaeological Society* **63**, 59–84.

Bateman, J.F. (1877; reprinted 1895) *Report on the Waterworks at Croydon*, Croydon Corporation, Croydon.

Bates, M. and Cudmore, B.V., ed. G.P.Hirsch (1975) *Country Planning. A Re-study*, Institute of Agricultural Economics, Oxford.

Beckett, J. (2005) *City Status in the British Isles, 1830–2002*, Ashgate, Aldershot.

de Belin, M. (2004) 'The Landscape of Foxhunting: Leicestershire, Northamptonshire and Rutland 1750–1900', unpublished MA dissertation, University of Leicester.

Beresford, M.W. (1957) *History on the Ground. Six Studies in Maps and Landscapes*, Lutterworth Press, London.

Beresford, M.W. (1967) *New Towns of the Middle Ages: Town Plantation in England, Wales and Gascony*, Lutterworth Press, London.

Bermingham, A. (1987) *Landscape and Ideology: The English Rustic Tradition, 1740–1860*, Thames and Hudson, London.

Blackmore, D.W. (1952) 'The re-birth of Croydon in 1851', *Proceedings of the Croydon Natural History and Scientific Society* **12**, 95–114.

Blow, S. (1983) *Fields Elysian*, Dent, London.

Bond, J. (2004) *Monastic Landscapes*, Tempus, Stroud.

Borsay, P. (1989) *The English Urban Renaissance. Culture and Society in the Provincial Town, 1660–1770*, Clarendon Press, Oxford.

Borsay, P. (2003) 'The landed elite and provincial towns in Britain 1660–1800', *The Georgian Group Journal* **13**, 281–94.

Bovill, E.W. (1959) *The England of Nimrod and Surtees 1815–1854*, Oxford University Press, London.

Bowden, M. ed. (1999) *Unravelling the Landscape. An Inquisitive Approach to Archaeology*, Tempus, Stroud.

Bowen, E.G. (1971) 'The dispersed habitat of Wales' in eds R.H. Buchanan, E. Jones and D. McCourt, *Man and his Habitat. Essays presented to Emyr Estyn Evans*, Routledge and Kegan Paul, London, 186–201.

Bowyer, M.J.F. (1988) *Action Stations. Military Airfields of Oxfordshire*, Patrick Stephens, Wellingborough.

Brace, C. (1999) 'Gardenesque imagery in the representation of regional and national identity: the Cotswold garden of stone', *Journal of Rural Studies* **15**, 365–76.

Brace, C. (2003) 'Landscape and identity' in eds I. Robertson and P. Richards, *Studying Cultural Landscapes*, Arnold, London, 121–40.

Bradley, R. (1998) *The Significance of Monuments. On the Shaping of Human Experience in Neolithic and Bronze Age Europe*, Routledge, London.

Brayshaw, T. and Robinson, R.H. (1932) *A History of the Ancient Parish of Giggleswick*, Halton and Co., London.

Brett Young, F. (1932) *The House Under the Water*, Heinemann, London.

Brett Young, F. (1936) *Far Forest*, Heinemann, London.

Briggs, A. (2000; 2nd edn) *The Age of Improvement*, Longman, Harlow.

Briggs, K.M. (1970–1) *A Dictionary of British Folk-Tales*, 4 vols, Routledge and Kegan Paul, London.

Brighton, T. (1981) *Royalists and Roundheads in Derbyshire*, privately published, Bakewell.

Britnell, R.H. (1993) *The Commercialisation of English Society, 1000–1500*, Cambridge University Press, Cambridge.

Britnell, R.H. (1996) 'Boroughs, markets and trade in northern England, 1000–1216' in eds R.H. Britnell and J. Hatcher, *Progress and Problems in Medieval England*, Cambridge University Press, Cambridge, 46–67.

Britnell, W.J., Silvester, R.J., and Suggett, R. (forthcoming) 'Ty-draw, Llanarmon Mynydd Mawr'.

Brooksby (Elmhirst, E.P.) (1883) *The Cream of Leicestershire. Eleven Seasons Skimmings*, Routledge, London.

Broster, P. (1782) *The Chester Guide*, P. Broster, Chester.

Brown, A. (1999) *The Rows of Chester*, English Heritage, London.

Brown, S.V. (?1983) *Castle, Kings and Horses. An Illustrated History of Middleham*, Old School Arts Workshop, Middleham.

Burn, R. (1772; 12th edn) *The Justice of the Peace, and Parish Officer*, T. Cadell, London.

Burne, C.S. and Jackson, G.F. (1883) *Shropshire Folk-Lore*, Trübner, London.

Butterworth, K. and Butterworth, A. (2002) *Leyburn Long Ago. A Social History of a Town in Wensleydale*, privately published, Preston-under-Scar.

Buxton, M. (1987) *Ladies of the Chase*, The Sportsman's Press, London.

Carpenter, A. (1859) *The History of Sanitary Progress in Croydon: A Lecture*, Warren, Croydon.

Carr, R. (1976) *English Fox Hunting: A History*, Weidenfeld and Nicolson, London.

Carr, R. (1981) 'Country Sports' in ed. G. Mingay, *The Victorian Countryside*, 2 vols, Routledge and Kegan Paul, London, vol. 2, 475–87.

Carr, R. (1986) *English Fox Hunting A History*, Weidenfeld and Nicholson, London.

Carson, C. (1976) 'Segregation in vernacular buildings', *Vernacular Architecture* **7**, 24–9.

Carter, A. (1986) 'Dereham inventories', unpublished typescript, Centre of East Anglian Studies, University of East Anglia, Norwich.

Carus-Wilson, E.M. (1965) 'The first half-century of the borough of Stratford-upon-Avon', *Economic History Review* 2nd ser. **18**, 46–63.

Chalklin, C. (1974) *The Provincial Towns of Georgian England. A Study of the Building Process, 1740–1820*, Edward Arnold, London.

Chalklin, C. (2001) *The Rise of the English Town, 1650–1850*, Cambridge University Press, Cambridge.

Chapman, J. (2004) 'Parliamentary enclosure in the uplands' in eds I. Whyte and A. Winchester, *Society, Landscape and Environment in Upland Britain*, Society for Landscape Studies Supplementary Series 2, Society for Landscape Studies, Birmingham, 79–88.

Chatwin, B. (1982) *On the Black Hill*, Jonathan Cape, London.

Chaytor, M.H.F. (1962) *The Wilsons of Sharrow: The Snuff-Makers of Sheffield*, Northend, Sheffield.

Clark, J., Darlington, J. and Fairclough, G. (2004) *Using Historic Landscape Characterisation*, English Heritage, London.

Clayton, M. (1993) *Foxhunting in Paradise*, John Murray, London.

Clemenson, H.A. (1982) *English Country Houses and Landed Estates*, Croom Helm, London.

Clement, C.O. (1997) 'Settlement patterning on the British Caribbean island of Tobago', *Historical Archaeology Journal* **31**, 93–106.

COI (Central Office of Information) (1946) *Twenty-four Square Miles*, film.

Colman, S. (1971) 'The Hearth Tax returns for the Hundred of Blackbourne, 1662', *Proceedings of the Suffolk Institute of Archaeology* **32**, 168–92.

Coombs, D. (1978) *Sport and the Countryside*, Phaidon Press, Oxford.

Corbett, D.P., Holt, Y. and Russell, F. eds (2002) *The Geographies of Englishness: Landscape and the National Past 1880–1940*, Yale University Press, New Haven and London.

Cornforth, J. (1998) *The Country Houses of England 1948–1998*, Constable, London.

Costobadie, F.P. de (1914) *Annals of the Billesdon Hunt (Mr. Fernies) 1856–1913*, Chapman and Hall, London.

Cousins, S. (2004) 'Why hedge dating doesn't work', *Landscape History* **26**, 77–85.

Cowdroy, W. (1789) *The Directory and Guide for the City and County of Chester*, J. Fletcher, Chester.

CPR (1907) *Calendar of Patent Rolls, Henry VI, vol. 3*, HMSO, London.

CPR (1982) *Calendar of Patent Rolls, Elizabeth I, vol. 7, 1575–8*, HMSO, London.

CPR (2002) *Calendar of Patent Rolls, 27 Elizabeth I (1584–5)*, ed. L.J. Wilkinson, List and Index Society, Kew.

CPR (2003) *Calendar of Patent Rolls, 29 Elizabeth I (1586–7)*, ed. L.J. Wilkinson, 2 vols, List and Index Society, Kew.

Crawford, W.H. (2002) 'The creation and evolution of small towns in Ulster in the seventeenth and eighteenth centuries' in eds P. Borsay and L. Proudfoot, *Change, Convergence and Divergence. Provincial Towns in Early Modern England and Ireland*, Proceedings of the British Academy 108, British Academy, London, 97–120.

Cross, A. (2003) *The Turnpike Roads of Leicestershire and Rutland*, Kairos Press, Newton Linford.

CSPD (1937) *Calendar of State Papers Domestic, William III, vol. 10*, ed. E. Bateson, HMSO, London.

Cuming, E. ed. (1926) *Squire Osbaldeston: His Autobiography*, The Bodley Head, London.

Currie, C.R.J. (1972) 'Smaller Domestic Architecture and Society in North Berkshire c.1300–1650, with Special Reference to Steventon', unpublished DPhil thesis, University of Oxford.

Currie, C.R.J. (1988) 'Time and chance: modelling the attrition of old houses', *Vernacular Architecture* **19**, 1–9.

Currie, C.R.J. (2004) 'The unfulfilled potential of the documentary sources', *Vernacular Architecture* **35**, 1–11.

Dale, T. (1899) *The History of the Belvoir Hunt*, Constable, London.

Daniels, S. (1988) 'The political iconography of woodland in later Georgian England' in *The Iconography of Landscape*, eds D. Cosgrove and S. Daniels, Cambridge University Press, Cambridge, 43–82.

Davies, A.E. (1976) 'Enclosures in Cardiganshire, 1750–1850', *Ceredigion* 7, 100–40.

Davis, S. and Corbett, S. (2004) 'Classic wildlife sites: the natural history and conservation of Porton Down', *British Wildlife* **15, 6**, 381–90.

Davison, J. (1990) *Superbase 11. Upper Heyford*, Osprey Publishing, London.

Dawson, W.H. (1882) *History of Skipton*, Edmundson, Skipton.

Defoe, D. (1724–6) *A Tour Through the Whole Island of Great Britain*, ed. P. Rogers (1971), Penguin, Harmondsworth.

Delle, J.A. (1999) 'The landscapes of class negotiation on coffee plantations in the Blue Mountains of Jamaica: 1790–1850', *Historical Archaeology Journal* 33, 136–58.

Deuchar, S. (1988) *Sporting Art in Eighteenth-Century England*, Yale University Press, New Haven and London.

Doel, M. (1998) 'Sudden theory', archived at *Critical Geography Forum*, http://www.mailbase.ac.uk/lists/crit-geog-forum/files/marcus.htm.

Doel, M. (2004) 'Waiting for geography', *Environment and Planning* 36, 451–60.

Done, A. and Muir, R. (2001) 'The landscape history of grouse shooting in the Yorkshire Dales', *Rural History* **12**, 195–210.

Douglas, A. (2001) *Stories of Shropshire*, Coughing Dog Music 2001 CDF 004.

Dransfield, J.N. (1906) *History of Penistone*, Wood, Penistone.

Duffey, E. (1971) 'The management of Woodwalton Fen: a multidisciplinary approach' in eds E. Duffey and A.S. Watt, *The Scientific Management of Animal and Plant Communities for Conservation*, Blackwell, Oxford, 581–97.

Duncumb, J. (1805) *General View of the Agriculture of the County of Hereford*, Richard Phillips, London.

Dyer, A.D. (2002) 'Small towns in England, 1600–1800' in eds P. Borsay and L. Proudfoot, *Change, Convergence and Divergence. Provincial Towns in Early Modern England and Ireland*, Proceedings of the British Academy 108, British Academy, London, 53–68.

Dymond, D. (1985) *The Norfolk Landscape*, The Alastair Press, Bury St Edmunds.

Edensor, T. (2000) 'Walking in the British countryside: reflexivity, embodied practices and ways to escape', *Body and Society* 6, 81–106.

Edmonds, J. (1998–9) 'Events at the Theatre Royal, Chester, 1807–10', *Cheshire History* 38, 55–70.

Edmonds, J. (2001–2) 'The patent and patent holders at the Theatre Royal, Chester', *Cheshire History* 41, 70–7.

Edmonds, M. (1999) *Ancestral Geographies of the Neolithic: Landscapes, Monuments and Memory*, Routledge, London.

Edwards, L. (1935) *A Leicestershire Sketch Book*, Eyre and Spottiswoode, London.

Edwards, L. (1947) *Reminiscences of a Sporting Artist*, Putnam, London.

Egremont, M. (2005) *Siegfried Sassoon*, Picador, London.

Ellis, C. (1951) *Leicestershire and the Quorn Hunt*, Edgar Backus, Leicester.

Ellis, J. (2001) *The Georgian Town, 1680–1840*, Palgrave, Basingstoke.

Emery, F. (1974) *The Oxfordshire Landscape*, Hodder and Stoughton, London.

English, B. (2000; 2nd edn) *The Great Landowners of East Yorkshire*, Hull Academic Press, Howden.

English Heritage (1999) *London Suburbs*, Merrell Holberton, London.

English Heritage (2000) *Power of Place*, London.

Estabrook, C. (1998) *Urbane and Rustic England. Cultural Ties and Social Spheres in the Provinces, 1660–1780*, Manchester University Press, Manchester.

Evans, N. (1984) 'Farming and landholding in wood-pasture East Anglia 1550–1650', *Proceedings of the Suffolk Institute of Archaeology and History* 35, 303–15.

Evans, N. (1993) 'Worsted and linen weavers' in ed. P. Wade-Martins, *An Historical Atlas of Norfolk*, Norfolk Museums Service, Norwich, 150–1.

Everett, N. (1994) *The Tory View of Landscape*, Yale University Press, New Haven and London.

Everitt, A. (1979) 'Country, county and town: patterns of regional evolution in England', *Transactions of the Royal Historical Society* 5th ser. **29**, 79–108.

Everitt, A. (1985) 'The Primary Towns of England' in A. Everitt, *Landscape and Community in England*, Hambledon Press, London, 93–107.

Everitt, A. (2000) 'Common land' in ed. J. Thirsk, *The English Rural Landscape*, Oxford University Press, Oxford, 210–35.

Everson, P. (1995) 'The survey of complex industrial landscapes' in eds M. Palmer and P. A. Neaverson, *Managing the Industrial Heritage*, Leicester Archaeology Monographs 2, Leicester, 21–8.

Everson, P. and Williamson, T. eds (1998) *The Archaeology of Landscape*, Manchester University Press, Manchester.

Farey, J. (1817) *General View of the Agriculture of Derbyshire*, 3 vols, Board of Agriculture, London.

Fieldhouse, R. and Jennings, B. (1978) *A History of Richmond and Swaledale*, Phillimore, Chichester.

Fiennes, C. (1685–1712) *The Journeys of Celia Fiennes*, ed. C. Morris (1947), Cresset Press, London.

Finch, J. (2004) '"Grass, grass, grass": fox-hunting and the creation of the modern landscape', *Landscapes* 5, 41–52.

Finch, J. (2007) 'Pallas, Flora and Ceres: landscape priorities and improvement on the Castle Howard estate, 1699–1880' in eds J. Finch and K. Giles, *Estate Landscapes*, Society for Post Medieval Archaeology Monographs **4**, Boydell and Brewar, Leeds.

Fine, M. (1998) 'Working the hyphens: reinventing self and other in qualitative research' in eds N. Denzin and Y. Lincoln, *The Landscape of Qualitative Research*, Sage, London, 130–55.

Fleming, A. (1998) *Swaledale: Valley of the Wild River*, Edinburgh University Press, Edinburgh.

Forster, W. (1883; reprinted 1985) *A Treatise on a Section of the Strata From Newcastle upon Tyne to Cross Fell*, Davies Books Ltd, Newcastle.

Fothergill, C. (1805) *The Diary of Charles Fothergill, 1805*, ed. P. Romney (1984), Yorkshire Archaeological Society Record Series 142, Yorkshire Archaeological Society, Leeds.

Fowler, P. J. (1970) 'Old grassland', *Antiquity* **44**, 57–9.

Frankel, M. S. and Seaman, P. J. eds (1983) 'Norfolk Hearth Tax assessment. Michaelmas 1664', *Norfolk Genealogy* 15.

Frazer, W. M. (1950) *History of English Public Health 1834–1939*, Ballere Tindall and Cox, London.

Fuller, H. A. (1976) 'Landownership and the Lindsey landscape', *Annals of the Association of American Geographers* **66**, 14–24.

Gale, G. J. (1916; 9th edn) *A Treatise of the Law of Easements*, Sweet and Maxwell, London.

Geertz, C. (1993; 2nd edn) 'Thick description: toward an interpretive theory of culture' in C. Geertz, *The Interpretation of Cultures. Selected Essays*, Fontana, London, 3–30.

Giddens, A. (1984) *The Construction of Society: Outline of the Theory of Structuration*, Cambridge University Press, Cambridge.

Gifford, W. (1875) *The Works of Ben Jonson*, 9 vols, Bickers and Son, London.

Gill, M. C. (1988) 'Yorkshire lead mining-before 1700', *British Mining* 37, 46–62.

Gill, M. C. (1989) *Customary Mining Law in Yorkshire*, International Mining History Conference, Bochum.

Gill, M. C. (1993) *The Grassington Mines*, Northern Mines Research Society, Keighley.

Gill, M. C. (1998) *The Greenhow Mines*, Northern Mines Research Society, Keighley.

Gill, M. C. (2000) 'Recreating mining landscapes', *British Mining* 67, 44–51.

Gillis, J. R. (1975) 'The evolution of juvenile delinquency in England 1890–1914', *Past and Present* 67, 96–126.

Gilpin, W. (1782) *Observations on the River Wye, and Several Parts of South Wales, etc., relative chiefly to Picturesque Beauty; made in the Summer of the Year 1770*, London.

Girouard, M. (1990) *The English Town*, Yale University Press, New Haven.

Goddard, N. (1996) '"A mine of wealth?": the Victorians and the agricultural value of sewage', *Journal of Historical Geography* **22**, 270–96.

Goddard, N. (2005a) '"Pestilential Swamps"?: the politicization of Victorian sewage farming' in eds M. Agnoletti, M. Armiero, S. Barca and G. Corona, *History and Sustainability*, Istituto di Studi sulle Società del Mediterraneo, Naples, 245–9.

Goddard, N. (2005b) '*Sanitate Crescamus*": water, sewage and environmental values in a Victorian suburb' in eds D. Schott, W. Luckin and G. Massard-Guilbaud, *Resources of the City*, Ashgate, Basingstoke, 132–48.

Goddard, N. and Sheail, J. (2001) 'Victorian sanitary reform: where were the innovators?' in ed. C. Bernhardt, *European Cities in the Nineteenth and Twentieth Century*, Waxman, Munster, 87–103.

Goodacre, J. (1994) *The Transformation of a Peasant Economy. Townspeople and Villagers in the Lutterworth Area 1500–1700*, Scolar Press, Aldershot.

Goodman, J. (1988) *What A Go! The Life of Alfred Munnings*, Collins, London.

Gore, A. and Carter, G. (2005) *Humphry Repton's Memoirs*, Michael Russell, Norwich.

Gosden, C. (1999) *Anthropology and Archaeology: A Changing Relationship*, Routledge, London.

Grenville, J. ed. (1999) *Managing the Historic Rural Landscape*, Routledge, London.

Grice, F. (1983) *Francis Kilvert and his World*, Caliban Books, Horsham.

Grice, F. (1998) 'Kilvert: a neglected genius' in ed. M. Sharp, *Jubilee Praise*, Kilvert Society Publications, Leamington Spa, 52–67.

Halfacree, K. (1996) 'Out of place in the country? Travellers and the rural idyll', *Antipode* **28**, 42–72.

Halfacree, K. (2003) 'Landscapes of rurality: rural others/other rurals' in eds I. Robertson and P. Richards, *Studying Cultural Landscapes*, Arnold, London, 141–64.

Hall, L. J. (1983) *The Rural Houses of North Avon and South Gloucestershire, 1400–1720*, City of Bristol Museum and Art Gallery, Bristol.

Hammond, J. L. and Hammond, B. (1911) *The Village Labourer*, Longman, London.

Harrington, D., Pearson, S. and Rose, S. eds (2000) *Kent Hearth Tax Assessment Lady Day 1664*, British Record Society Hearth Tax Series 2, British Record Society, London.

Harrison, B. and Hutton, B. (1984) *Vernacular Houses in North Yorkshire and Cleveland*, John Donald, Edinburgh.

Hartley, M. and J. Ingleby (1953) *Yorkshire Village*, Dent, London.

Hay, D. (1977) 'Poaching and game laws on Cannock Chase' in eds D. Hay, P. Linebaugh, J. G. Rule, E. P. Thompson and C. Winslow, *Albion's Fatal Tree. Crime and Society in Eighteenth-Century England*, Penguin/Peregrine, Harmondsworth, 189–253.

Hayfield, C. (1998) 'Vessey Pasture: the development of a Yorkshire Wold Farmstead', *Yorkshire Archaeological Journal* **70**, 109–23.

Heidegger, M. (1962) *Being and Time*, Blackwell, Oxford.

Hemingway, J. (1831) *History of the City of Chester*, 2 vols, J. Fletcher, Chester.

Herson, J. (1996) 'Victorian Chester: a city of change and ambiguity' in ed. R. Swift, *Victorian Chester*, Liverpool University Press, Liverpool, 13–51.

Hey, D. (2000) 'Moorlands' in ed. J. Thirsk, *The English Rural Landscape*, Oxford University Press, Oxford, 188–209.

Hey, D. (2002a) *Historic Hallamshire: History in Sheffield's Countryside*, Landmark, Ashbourne.

Hey, D. (2002b) *A History of Penistone and District*, Wharncliffe, Barnsley.

Hinton, D. A. and Rowley, T. eds (1974) *Excavations on the Route of the M40*, Oxfordshire Architectural and Historical Society, Oxford.

Holderness, B. (1972) '"Open" and "close" parishes in England in the eighteenth and nineteenth centuries', *Agricultural History Review* **20**, 126–39.

Holderness, B. A. (1984) 'East Anglia and the Fens: Norfolk, Suffolk, Cambridgeshire, Ely, Huntingdonshire, Essex and the Lincolnshire Fens' in ed. J. Thirsk, *The Agrarian History of England and Wales, vol. 5: 1640–1750*, 2 vols, Cambridge University Press, Cambridge, vol. 1, 197–238.

Hooke, D. (1990) *Worcestershire Anglo-Saxon Charter-Bounds*, Boydell Press, Woodbridge.

Hooke, D. (2006) *England's Landscape, Volume VI, West Midlands*, Harper Collins, London.

Hooper, M. D. (1970) 'Hedges and birds', *Birds* **3**, **5**, 114–17.

Hooson, W. (1747; reprinted 1979) *The Miners Dictionary*, Institute of Mining and Metallurgy, London.

Hoskins, W. G. (1951) *Chilterns to the Black Country*, Collins, London.

Hoskins, W. G. (1953) 'The rebuilding of rural England 1570–1640', *Past and Present* **4**, 44–59; reprinted in Hoskins, W. G. (1963b) *Provincial England. Essays in social and economic history*, Macmillan, London, 209–29.

Hoskins, W. G. (1955) *The Making of the English Landscape*, Hodder and Stoughton, London.

Hoskins, W. G. (1957) *The Midland Peasant*, Macmillan, London.

Hoskins, W. G. (1963a) 'The origin and rise of Market Harborough' in W. G. Hoskins, *Provincial England. Essays in social and economic history*, Macmillan, London, 53–68.

Hoskins, W.G. (1963b) 'The rediscovery of England' in W.G.Hoskins, *Provincial England. Essays in social and economic history*, Macmillan, London, 209–29.

Hoskins, W.G. (1964) 'Harvest and hunger', *The Listener* 72, 831–2.

Hoskins, W.G. (1967) *Fieldwork in Local History*, Faber and Faber, London.

Hoskins, W.G. (1977; 2nd edn) *The Making of the English Landscape*, Penguin, London.

Hoskins, W.G. (1978) *One Man's England*, BBC Publications, London.

Hoskins, W.G. (1988; 3rd edn) *The Making of the English Landscape*, with introduction and commentary by C.Taylor, Penguin, Harmondsworth.

Hoskins, W.G. (2005; new edn) *The Making of the English Landscape*, with introduction by K.Thomas, Folio Society, London.

Howe, G.M. and Thomas, P. (1968) *Welsh Landforms and Scenery*, Macmillan, London.

Howell, D.W. (1977) *Land and People in Nineteenth-Century Wales*, Routledge and Kegan Paul, London.

Howell, D.W. (2000) *The Rural Poor in Eighteenth-Century Wales*, University of Wales Press, Cardiff.

Howse, W.H. (1955) 'Encroachments on the king's waste in Cantref Maelienydd in 1734', *Transactions of the Radnorshire Society* 25, 27–33.

Hoyle, R. (2005) 'Royalty and the Diversity of Field Sports, *c.*1840–*c.*1981', unpublished manuscript.

Hudson, P.J. (1986) *Red Grouse: The Biology and Management of a Wild Gamebird*, The Game Conservancy Trust, Fordingbridge.

Hughes, K. and Ifans, D. eds (1982) *The Diary of Francis Kilvert, April–June 1870*, National Library of Wales, Aberystwyth.

Hughes, R.E., Dale, J., Williams, I.E. and Rees, D.I. (1973) 'Studies in sheep population and environment in the mountains of north-west Wales', *Journal of Applied Ecology* 10, 113–32.

Hunter, J. (1828–31) *South Yorkshire*, 2 vols, Nichols and Son, London.

Hunter, J., ed. A.Gatty (1869), *Hallamshire*, Virtue, London.

Ifans, D. ed. (1989) *The Diary of Francis Kilvert, June–July 1870*, National Library of Wales, Aberystwyth.

Ingold, T. (2000) *The Perception of the Environment: Essays on Livelihood, Dwelling and Skill*, Routledge, London.

Jackson, A.A. (1973) *Semi-Detached London*, George Allen and Unwin, London.

James, D. (2003) 'An investigation of the orientation of timber-framed buildings in Herefordshire', *Vernacular Architecture* 34, 20–31.

Jennings, L.J. (1880) *Rambles Among the Hills in the Peak of Derbyshire and the South Downs*, Murray, London.

Jennings, N. (2003) *Clay Dabbins: Vernacular Buildings of the Solway Plain*, Cumberland and Westmorland Antiquarian and Archaeological Society Extra Series 30, Cumberland and Westmorland Antiquarian and Archaeological Society, Kendal.

Johnston, R. (2000) 'Borderland' in eds R.Johnston, D.Gregory, G.Pratt and M.Watts, *The Dictionary of Human Geography*, Blackwell, London, 49–50.

Jones, N.W. (2003) *Y Graig, Abergavenny, Monmouthshire*, Clwyd-Powys Archaeological Trust, Welshpool.

Kennett, A. ed. (1987) *Georgian Chester*, Chester City Record Office, Chester.

Kent, N. (1775) *Hints to Gentlemen of Landed Property*, London.

King, A. (2005) 'Settle and John Lettsom', *Journal of the North Craven Heritage Trust* 2005, 17–19.

King, T.J. (1981) 'Ant-hills and grassland history', *Journal of Biogeography* 8, 329–34.

Kinsman, P. (1995) 'Landscape, race and national identity: the photography of Ingrid Pollard', *Area* 27, 300–10.

Lancaster, B. (2001) 'The "Croydon Case": dirty old town to model town', *Croydon Natural History and Scientific Society Proceedings* 18, 7, 145–206.

Latham, B. (1870) *Report on the Influence of Sewage Irrigation Works at Beddington on the Health of the Inhabitants of the Neighbourhood*, J.W.Ward, Croydon.

Le Quesne, L. (1978) *After Kilvert*, Oxford University Press, Oxford.

Leland, J. (1535–43) *The Itinerary of John Leland in or about the years 1535–1543*, ed. L.Toulmin-Smith (1907), 5 vols, Bell, London.

Lennie, S. (2001) *Market in the Hills*, privately published, Hawes.

Leone, M. (1984) 'Interpreting ideology in historical archaeology: using the rules of perspective in the William Paca Garden in Annapolis, Maryland' in eds D.Miller and C.Tilley, *Ideology, Power and Prehistory*, Cambridge University Press, Cambridge, 25–36.

Letheby, H. (1872) *The Sewage Question*, Spon, London.

Letters, S., with Fernandes, M., Keene, D. and Myhill, O. (2003) *Gazetteer of Markets and Fairs in England and Wales to 1516*, List and Index Society Special Series 32–3, 2 vols, List and Index Society, Kew.

Lewis, G. (1967) 'The geography of cultural transition: the Welsh borderland, 1750–1850', *National Library of Wales Journal* 11, 131–44.

Little, B. (2003) *Banbury. A History*, Phillimore, Chichester.

Llangynidr Local History Society (2000) *Shadows in a Landscape. Llangynidr: The Evolution of a Community*, Gomer Press, Llandysul.

Lockwood, D. (1990) *Francis Kilvert*, Seren Books, Bridgend.

Longcroft, A. (1989) 'Explaining Differing House and Messuage Survival Rates in Norfolk Sheep-Corn and Wood-Pasture Parishes: The Documentary and Early Map Evidence 1570–1640', unpublished MA dissertation, University of East Anglia, Norwich.

Longcroft, A. (1995) 'Service rooms in Norfolk farmhouses: some observations', *Annual of the Norfolk Archaeological and Historical Research Group* **4**, 36–43.

Longcroft, A. (1998) 'The Development and Survival of Post-Medieval Vernacular houses: A Case Study from Norfolk', unpublished PhD thesis, University of East Anglia, Norwich.

Longcroft, A. (2002) 'Plan-forms in smaller post-medieval houses: a case study from Norfolk', *Vernacular Architecture* **33**, 34–56.

Longcroft, A. ed. (2005) *The Historic Buildings of New Buckenham, Journal of the Norfolk Historic Buildings Group* **2**.

Lyne, M. (1938) *Horses, Hounds and Country*, Eyre and Spottiswoode, London.

Maber, R. and Tregoning, A. (1989) *Kilvert's Cornish Diary*, Alison Hodge, Penzance.

McConkey, K. (2001) 'English the scene … English the atmosphere' in Anon., *An English Idyll: Works from Private and Public Collections and the Sir Alfred Munnings Art Museum*, Sotheby's, London, 8–27.

McKelvie, C. (1985) *A Future for Game?*, Routledge, London.

McKie, D. (2004) *Jabez: The Rise and Fall of a Victorian Rogue*, Atlantic, London.

Mandler, P. (1997) *The Fall and Rise of the Stately Home*, Yale University Press, New Haven and London.

Martin, A. (1999) *The Changing Faces of the Bartons*, Robert Boyd Publications, Witney.

Martin, D. (2003) 'The configuration of inner rooms and chambers in the transitional houses of eastern Sussex', *Vernacular Architecture* **34**, 37–51.

Martin, E.A. (1900; 2nd edn) *Croydon: New and Old*, Saint Brides Press, London.

Mason, M. (1994) *The Making of Victorian Sexual Attitudes*, Oxford University Press, Oxford.

Matless, D. (1993) 'One Man's England: W.G. Hoskins and the English culture of landscape', *Rural History* **4**, 187–207.

Matless, D. (1998) *Landscape and Englishness*, Reaktion Press, London.

Mercer, E. (1975) *English Vernacular Houses*, HMSO, London.

Mercer, E. (1997) 'The unfulfilled wider implications of vernacular architecture studies', *Vernacular Architecture* **28**, 9–12.

Meth, P. (2003) 'Entries and omissions: using solicited diaries in geographical research', *Area* **35**, 195–205.

Miller, P. (1760; 12th edn) *The Gardeners Kalendar; Directing what Works are Necessary to be Performed every Month in the Kitchen, Fruit, and Pleasure-Gardens, as also in the Conservatory and Nursery*, Rivington, London

Mills, D.R. (1980) *Lord and Peasant in Nineteenth Century Britain*, Croom Helm, London.

Moore, N.W. (1962) 'The heaths of Dorset and their conservation', *Journal of Ecology* **50**, 369–91.

Moore, N.W. (1987) *The Bird of Time*, Cambridge University Press, Cambridge.

Moran, M. (2003) *Vernacular Buildings of Shropshire*, Logaston Press, Almeley.

Morris, J.N. (1989) 'A disappearing crowd? Collective action in late nineteenth-century Croydon', *Southern History* **11**, 90–113.

Morris, S. (2005) *British Sporting Paintings*, Richard Green Galleries, London.

Moses, G. (1999) 'Proletarian labourers? East Riding farm servants c.1850–75', *Agricultural History Review* **47**, 78–94.

Munnings, A. (1951) *The Second Burst*, Museum Press, London.

Munnings, A. (1952) *The Finish*, Museum Press, London.

Munsche, P.B. (1981) *Gentlemen and Poachers: The English Game Laws, 1671–1831*, Cambridge University Press, Cambridge.

Musson, C.R. and Spurgeon, C.J. (1988) 'Cwrt Llechrhyd, Llanelwedd: an unusual moated site in central Powys', *Medieval Archaeology* **32**, 97–109.

National Park Committee (1931) *Report*, HMSO, London, 77–9.

Nead, L. (2000) *Victorian Babylon*, Yale University Press, London.

Nevell, M.D. ed. (2003) *Farmer to Factory Owner; Models, Methodology and Industrialisation. The Archaeology of the Industrial Revolution in North-West England*, Archaeology North-West vol.16, Council for British Archaeology North West Industrial Archaeology Panel, Chester Archaeology and the University of Manchester Archaeological Unit.

Newman, C. (1982) 'Kilvert unabridged: a review', *Transactions of the Radnorshire Society* **52**, 80–90.

Nimrod (1835; reprinted 1926) *Nimrod's Hunting Tours*, The Bodley Head, London.

O'Brien, K. (1943) *English Diaries and Journals*, William Collins, London.

Ormerod, G. (1819) *The History of the County Palatine and City of Chester*, Lackington, London.

Orser, C.E. (1996) *A Historical Archaeology of the Modern World*, Plenum, New York.

Orwin, C.S. and Orwin, C.S. (1938) *The Open Fields*, Clarendon Press, Oxford.

Otmoor Group (1984) *Otmoor for Ever! A Case Against the Motorway*, privately published, Oxford.

Paasi, A. (1986) 'The institutionalisation of regions: a theoretical framework for understanding the emergence of regions and the constitution of regional identity', *Fennia* **164**, 105–46.

Paget, G. (1937) *The History of the Althorp and Pytchley Hunt 1634–1920*, Collins, London.

Palmer, M. (2005) 'Industrial Archaeology: constructing a framework of inference' in eds E. C. Casella and J. Symons, *Industrial Archaeology: future directions*, Springer, New York, 59–76.

Palmer, M. and Neaverson, P. A. (1998) *Industrial Archaeology: Principles and Practice*, Routledge, London.

Palmer, R. (1976) *The Folklore of Warwickshire*, Batsford, London.

Palmer, R. (1988) *The Sound of History. Songs and Social Comment*, Pimlico, London.

Palmer, R. (2002) *Herefordshire Folklore*, Logaston Press, Almeley.

Parsons, D. (2001) *Streetwalking the Metropolis*, Sage, London.

Pearson, S. (1994) *The Medieval Houses of Kent: An Historical Analysis*, HMSO, London.

Pennant, T. (1778–81) *A Tour in Wales, 1770*, 2 vols, H. Hughes, London.

Penoyre, J. (2005) *Traditional Houses of Somerset*, Somerset Books, Tiverton.

Penoyre, J. and Penoyre, J. (1978) *Houses in the Landscape. A Regional Study of Vernacular Building Styles in England and Wales*, Faber and Faber, London.

Peterken, G. F. (1969) 'Development of vegetation in Staverton Park, Suffolk', *Field Studies* **3**, 1–39.

Peterken, G. F. (1974a) 'Development factors in the management of British woodland', *Quarterly Journal of Forestry* **68**, 141–9.

Peterken, G. F. (1974b) 'A method for assessing woodland flora for conservation using indicator species', *Biological Conservation* **6**, 239–45.

Peterken, G. F. (1981) *Woodland Conservation and Management*, Chapman and Hall, London, 310–24.

Peterken, G. F. and Hubbard, J. C. E. (1972) 'The shingle vegetation of Southern England: the holly wood on Holmstone Beach, Dungeness', *Journal of Ecology* **60**, 547–71.

Peterken, G. F. and Tubbs, C. R. (1965) 'Woodland regeneration in the New Forest, Hampshire, since 1650', *Journal of Applied Ecology* **2**, 159–70.

Philip, L. J. (2005) 'Planned villages in south-west Scotland, 1730–1855: analysing functional characteristics', *Landscapes* **6**, 83–107.

Pidgeon, D. (1899) 'The Bacterial Treatment of Sewage', *Journal of the Royal Agricultural Society of England* **60**, 249–67.

Pitt, W. (1796; 2nd edn) *General View of the Agriculture of Staffordshire*, Board of Agriculture, London.

Plomer, W. ed. (1977) *Kilvert's Diary*, 3 vols, Cape, London.

Pollard, E., Hooper, M. and Moore, N. (1974) *Hedges*, Collins, London.

Portman, D. (1973) 'Vernacular building in the Oxford region' in eds C. W. Chalkin and M. A. Havinden, *Rural Change and Urban Growth: Essays in Regional History in Honour of W. G. Hoskins*, London, Longman, 134–68.

Pound, J. (1988) *Tudor and Stuart Norwich*, Phillimore, Chichester.

Proudfoot, L. (2002) 'Markets, fairs and towns in Ireland, c.1600–1853' in eds P. Borsay and L. Proudfoot, *Change, Convergence and Divergence. Provincial Towns in Early Modern England and Ireland*, Proceedings of the British Academy 108, British Academy, London, 69–96.

Pulsipher, L. M. (1994) 'The landscapes and ideational roles of Caribbean slave gardens' in eds N. F. Miller and K. L. Gleason, *The Archaeology of Garden and Field*, University of Pennsylvania Press, 202–21.

Rackham, O. (1967) 'The history and effects of coppicing as a woodland practice' in ed. E. Duffey, *The Biotic Effects of Public Pressures on the Environment*, The Nature Conservancy, Monks Wood, 82–93.

Rackham, O. (1971) 'Historical studies and woodland conservation' in eds E. Duffey and A. S. Watt, *The Scientific Management of Animal and Plant Communities for Conservation*, Blackwell, Oxford, 563–80.

Rackham, O. (1976) *Trees and Woodland in the British Landscape*, Dent, London.

Rackham, O. (1986) *The History of the Countryside*, Dent, London.

Rackham, O. (2000) 'Prospects for landscape history and historical ecology', *Landscapes* **2**, 3–15.

Raistrick, A. (1970) *The West Riding of Yorkshire*, Hodder and Stoughton, London.

Ratcliffe, D. A. (1977) *A Nature Conservation Review*, 2 vols, Cambridge University Press, Cambridge.

Rawding, C. (1992) 'Society and place in nineteenth-century north Lincolnshire', *Rural History* **3**, 59–85.

Rawlinson, R. (1882; reprinted 1895) *Report on the Waterworks at Croydon*, Croydon Corporation, Croydon.

RCHME (1985) *Rural Houses of the Lancashire Pennines*, S. Pearson, HMSO, London.

RCHME (1986) *Rural Houses of West Yorkshire 1400–1830*, C. Giles, HMSO, London.

RCHME (1992) *English Houses 1200–1800; the Hertfordshire Evidence*, J. T. Smith, HMSO, London.

Reader's Digest (1973) *Folklore, Myths and Legends of Britain*, Reader's Digest Association, London.

Redwood, P. and Redwood, M. (2002) 'Four hundred years on the Ffawydog: a landscape history in miniature', *Brycheiniog* **34**, 31–66.

Ridgway, C. and Warren, A. (2005) 'Collaborative opportunities for the study of the country house: the Yorkshire Country House Partnership', *Historical Research* **78**, 162–79.

Ridley, J. (1990) *Fox Hunting*, Collins, London.

Rieuwerts, J. H. (1998) *A Glossary of Derbyshire Lead Mining Terms*, Peak District Mines Historical Society, Matlock Bath.

Roberts, B. K. and Wrathmell, S. (2000) *An Atlas of Rural Settlement in England*, English Heritage, London.

Roberts, E. (2003) *Hampshire Houses 1250–1700. Their Dating and Development*, Hampshire County Council, Southampton.

Roe, M. (2000) 'The brighter the light the darker the shadows: how we perceive and represent underground spaces', *Cave Archaeology and Palaeontology Research Archive* **2**, http://www.capra.group.shef.ac.uk.

Roe, M. (2003a) 'Greenhow Hill lead mines survey', *British Mining* **73**, 89–103.

Roe, M. (2003b) 'Lead mining archaeology in the Yorkshire Dales', *Landscapes* **4**, 65–78.

Roe, M. and A. Davies (2002) 'A survey of the area around Jamie Mine, Sun Side Allotment, Appletreewick, North Yorkshire', *British Mining* **71**, 68–81.

Ronksley, J. G. ed. (1908) *An Exact and Perfect Survey and View of the Manor of Sheffield, with other Lands, by John Harrison, 1637*, Northend, Sheffield.

Ruskin, J. (1873) *The Works of John Ruskin, 6: The Crown of Wild Olive*, reprinted 1994 as *The Social and Economic Works of John Ruskin, 4*, Routledge/Thremmes Press, London.

Ruskin, J. (1885) *Praeterita*, George Allen, Orpington.

Sassoon, S. (1928) *Memoirs of a Fox-Hunting Man*, Faber and Faber, London.

Sawyer, P. H. ed. (1968) *Anglo-Saxon Charters: an annotated list and bibliography*, Royal Historical Society, London.

Sayce, R. U. (1942) 'Popular enclosures and the one-night house', *Montgomeryshire Collections* **47**, 2, 1–12.

Scargill, I. (1989) 'Social and Economic Trends' in *Rural Oxfordshire in the 1990s*, Oxfordshire Rural Community Council, Oxford.

SCR (various dates), *Sheffield Clarion Ramblers' Handbooks*, Sheffield.

Seaman, P. J. ed. (1988) 'Norfolk and Norwich Hearth Tax assessment Lady Day 1666', *Norfolk Genealogy* **20**.

Seaman, P. J. ed. (2001) *Norfolk Hearth Tax Exemption Certificates 1670–1674: Norwich, Great Yarmouth, King's Lynn and Thetford*, British Record Society Hearth Tax Series 3, British Record Society, London.

Seymour, S. (2000) 'Historical geographies of landscape' in eds B. Graham and C. Nash, *Modern Historical Geographies*, Prentice Hall, London, 193–217.

Sheail, J. (1970) 'Old grassland: a problem in conservation', *Area* **1**, 3, 79–80.

Sheail, J. (1982) 'Underground water abstraction: indirect effects of urbanisation upon the countryside', *Journal of Historical Geography* **8**, 365–408.

Sheail, J. (1985) *Pesticides and Nature Conservation*, Clarendon Press, Oxford.

Sheail, J. (1998) *Nature Conservation in Britain: The Formative Years*, The Stationery Office, London.

Sheail, J. (2000) 'Eric Duffey – an appreciation', *Biological Conservation* **95**, 123–8.

Sheail, J. and Wells, T. C. E. (1969) *Old Grassland: Its Archaeological and Ecological Importance*, The Nature Conservancy, Huntingdon.

Short, J. (1991) *Imagined Country*, Routledge, London.

Silvester, R. J. (2004) 'The commons and the waste: use and misuse in central Wales' in eds I. Whyte and A. J. L. Winchester, *Society, Landscape and Environment in Upland Britain*, Society for Landscape Studies Supplementary Series 2, Society for Landscape Studies, Birmingham, 53–66.

Simmons, I. G. (2003) *The Moorlands of England and Wales: An Environmental History, 8000 BC–AD 2000*, Edinburgh University Press, Edinburgh.

Simpson, C. (1927) *The Harboro' Country*, The Bodley Head, London.

Simpson, J. and Roud, S. (2000) *A Dictionary of English Folklore*, Oxford University Press, Oxford.

Sissons, D. ed. (2002) *The Best of the Sheffield Clarion Ramblers' Handbooks: Ward's Piece*, Halsgrove, Tiverton.

Smee, A. (1872) *My Garden*, Bell and Daldy, London.

Smee, A. (1875–6) 'Proposed heads of legislation for the regulation of sewage grounds', *Journal of the Society of Arts* **24**, 32–49.

Smout, T. C. (1970) 'The landowner and planned villages in Scotland, 1730–1830' in eds N. T. Phillipson and R. Mitchison, *Scotland in the Age of Improvement*, Edinburgh University Press, Edinburgh, 73–106.

Speight, H. (1897) *Romantic Richmondshire*, Elliot Stock, London.

Spencer, D. (2000) 'Reformulating the '"closed" parish thesis: associations, interests, and interaction', *Journal of Historical Geography* **26**, 83–98.

Spufford, M. (1974) *Contrasting Communities. English Villagers in the Sixteenth and Seventeenth Centuries*, Cambridge University Press, Cambridge.

Spufford, M. (1990) 'The limitations of the probate inventory' in eds J. D. Chartres and D. Hey, *English Rural Society, 1500–1800*, Cambridge University Press, Cambridge, 139–74.

Squires, A. and Jeeves, M. (1994) *Leicestershire and Rutland Woodlands Past and Present*, Kairos Press, Newtown Linford.

Stacey, M. (1960) *Tradition and Change: A Study of Banbury*, Oxford University Press, Oxford.

Stacey, M., Batstone, E., Bell, C. and Murcott, A. (1975) *Power, Persistence and Change. A Second Banbury Study*, Routledge, Kegan and Paul, London.

Stamp, D.L. (1955) *Man and the Land*, Collins, London.

Stenton, D.M. ed. (1934) *Rolls of the Justices in Eyre*, Selden Society 53.

Steven, H.M. and Carlisle, A. (1959) *The Native Pinewoods of Scotland*, Oliver and Boyd, Edinburgh.

Stewart, K.C. (1996) 'An occupied place' in eds S. Feld and K.H. Basso, *Senses of Place*, School of American Research, Santa Fe, New Mexico.

Stobart, J. (1998) 'Shopping streets as social space: leisure, consumerism and improvement in an eighteenth-century county town', *Urban History* **25**, 3–21.

Stobart, J. (2000) 'In search of a leisure hierarchy: English spa towns in the urban system' in eds P. Borsay, G. Hirschfelder and R. Mohrmann, *New Directions in Urban History*, Waxmann, Munich, 19–40.

Stobart, J. (2002) 'County, town and country: three histories of urban development in eighteenth-century Chester' in eds P. Borsay and L. Proudfoot, *Change, Convergence and Divergence. Provincial Towns in Early Modern England and Ireland*, Proceedings of the British Academy 108, British Academy, London, 171–94.

Strachan, G.R. (1904) *Report on the Beddington Irrigation Farm*, Croydon Corporation.

Surrey County Council Public Health Department (1923) *River Wandle, Report of the County Medical Officer of Health*, Kingston.

Sweet, R. (1997) *Writing of Urban Histories in Eighteenth-Century England*, Oxford University Press, Oxford.

Sweet, R. (2002) 'Topographies of politeness', *Transactions of the Royal Historical Society* 6th ser. **12**, 355–74.

Tansley, A.G. (1939) *The British Islands and their Vegetation*, Cambridge University Press, Cambridge.

Taplin, W. (1772) *Observations on the Present State of the Game in England*, London.

Tebbutt, M. (2004) 'Gendering an upland landscape: masculinity and place identity in the Peak District, 1880s–1920s' in eds I. Whyte and A.J.L. Winchester, *Society, Landscape and Environment in Upland Britain*, Society for Landscape Studies Supplementary Series 2, Society for Landscape Studies, Birmingham, 141–8.

Thirsk, J. (1978) *Economic Policy and Projects. The Development of a Consumer Society in Early Modern England*, Clarendon Press, Oxford.

Thirsk, J. (1994) 'William George Hoskins 1908–1992', *Proceedings of the British Academy* **87**, 339–54.

Thomas, C. (1967) 'Enclosure and the rural landscape of Merionethshire in the sixteenth century', *Transactions of the Institute of British Geographers* **42**, 153–62.

Thompson, F.M.L. (1981) 'Landowners and the Rural Community' in ed. G. Mingay, *The Victorian Countryside*, 2 vols, Routledge and Kegan Paul, London, vol. 2, 457–74.

Thompson, F.M.L. ed. (1982) *The Rise of Suburbia*, Leicester University Press, Leicester.

Thompson, F.M.L. (1988) *The Rise of Respectable Society*, Fontana Press, London.

Thompson, M.W. (1964) 'Reclamation of waste ground for the Pleasance at Kenilworth Castle, Warwickshire', *Medieval Archaeology* **8**, 222–3.

Tilley, C. (1994) *A Phenomenology of Landscape*, Berg, Oxford.

Tolhurst, P. (1982) 'The Vernacular Architecture of Norfolk. A Sample Survey', unpublished MA thesis, University of Manchester.

Tolhurst, P. (1993) 'Brick as an indicator of wealth 1450–1750' in ed. P. Wade-Martins, *An Historical Atlas of Norfolk*, Norfolk Museums Service, Norwich, 112–13.

Tolkien, J.R.R. trans. (1979) *Sir Gawain and the Green Knight*, Unwin, London.

Toman, J. (2001) *Kilvert: The Homeless Heart*, Logaston Press, Almeley.

Toman, J. (2002) *The Books that Kilvert Read*, Kilvert Society Publications, Leamington Spa.

Tubbs, C.R. (1968) *The New Forest*, David and Charles, Newton Abbot.

Tubbs, C.R. and Dimbleby, G.W. (1965) 'Early agriculture in the New Forest', *Advancement of Science* **22**, 88–97.

Turner, S. (2004) 'The changing ancient landscape: south-west England c.1700–1900', *Landscapes* **5**, 18–34.

Tyson, L.O. (1995) *The Arkengarthdale Mines*, Northern Mine Research Society, Keighley.

Upton, D. (1988) 'White and black landscapes in eighteenth-century Virginia' in ed. R. Blair St George, *Material Life in America, 1600–1860*, Northeastern University Press, Boston, 357–70.

Urry, J. (1995) *Consuming Places*, Routledge, London.

VCH (1907) *Victoria County History of Gloucestershire, vol. 2*, ed. W. Page, 2 vols, Constable, London.

VCH (1914–23) *Victoria County History of the North Riding of Yorkshire*, ed. W. Page, 2 vols, Constable, London.

VCH (1972) *Victoria County History of Oxfordshire, vol. 10*, ed. A. Crossley, University of London, London.

VCH (2003) *Victoria County History of Cheshire vol. 5 part 1: The City of Chester: General Survey and Topography*, ed. C.P. Lewis and A.T. Thacker, Boydell and Brewer, Woodbridge.

Wade Martins, S (2003) *The Model Farm: Building the Agricultural Ideal, 1700–1914*, Windgather Press, Macclesfield.

Wade Martins, S. (2004) *Farmers, Landlords and Landscapes. Rural Britain, 1720–1870*, Windgather Press, Macclesfield.

Wade Martins, S. and Williamson, T. (1999) *Roots of Change. Farming and the Landscape in East Anglia, c.1700–1870*, Agricultural History Review Supplement Series 2, British Agricultural History Society, Exeter.

Walker, G. (1814) *The Costume of Yorkshire*, Longman, London.

Walker, T. (1890) *Some of the Public Works of Croydon*, Association Of Municipal and Sanitary Engineers and Surveyors, District Meeting, Croydon.

Walsh, D. (1970) *Report of the Committee of Enquiry into the Arrangements for the Protection of Field Monuments, 1966–8*, HMSO, London.

Walvin, J. (2003) 'The colonial origins of English wealth. The Harewoods of Yorkshire', unpublished typescript.

Webster, F. ed. (1988) *Nottinghamshire Hearth Tax 1664:1674*, Thoroton Society Record Series 37, Thoroton Society, Nottingham.

Weiner, W. and Rosenwald, G. (1993) 'A moment's monument: the psychology of keeping a diary' in eds R. Josselson and A. Lieblich, *The Narrative Study of Lives*, Sage, London, 30–58.

Wells, T.C.E. (1968) 'Land-use changes affecting *Pulsatilla vulgaris* in England', *Biological Conservation* 1, 37–43.

Wells, T.C.E. (1985) 'The botanical and ecological interest of ancient monuments' in ed. G. Lambrick, *Archaeology and Nature Conservation*, Oxford University Department of External Studies, Oxford, 1–9.

Wells, T.C.E., Sheail, J., Ball, D.F. and Ward, L.K. (1976) 'Ecological studies on the Porton Ranges: relationships between vegetation, soils and land-use history', *Journal of Ecology* 64, 589–626.

Whelan, K. (1997) 'The modern landscape: from plantation to present' in eds F.H.A. Aalen, K. Whelan and M. Stout, *Atlas of the Irish Rural Landscape*, Cork University Press, Cork, 67–105.

White, A. (2004) 'Mary Isabella and Elizabeth Gascoigne, parallel lives. Philanthropy, art and leisure in the Victorian era' in ed. R.M. Larsen, *Maids and Mistresses: Celebrating 300 years of Women and the Yorkshire Country House*, Yorkshire Country House Partnership, York, 64–76.

White, P. (2003) *The Arrow Valley, Herefordshire: Archaeology, Landscape Change and Conservation*, Herefordshire Studies in Archaeology 2, Hereford Archaeology, Hereford.

Whyte, I. (2003) *Transforming Fell and Valley*, University of Lancaster, Lancaster.

Wiliam, E. (1995) '"Home-made homes": dwellings of the rural poor in Cardiganshire', *Ceredigion* 12, 3, 23–40.

Will, J.S. (1899) 'Underground water', *Transactions of the Surveyors Institution* 22, 255–320.

Willan, T.S. and Crossley, E.W. eds (1941) *Three Seventeenth-Century Yorkshire Surveys*, Yorkshire Archaeological Society Record Series 104, Yorkshire Archaeological Society, Leeds.

Williams, W.H. (1965) *The Commons, Open Spaces and Footpaths Preservation Society 1865–1965*, Commons Preservation Society, London.

Williamson, T. (1993) *The Origins of Norfolk*, Manchester University Press, Manchester.

Williamson, T. (1995a) *Polite Landscapes. Gardens and Society in Eighteenth-Century England*, Alan Sutton, Stroud.

Williamson, T. (1995b) 'Landuse and landscape change in the Norfolk claylands c.1700–1870', *Annual of the Norfolk Archaeological and Historical Research Group* 4, 44–58.

Williamson, T. (2002) *The Transformation of Rural England. Farming and the Landscape 1700–1870*, Exeter University Press, Exeter.

Williamson, T. (2004) 'Vernacular buildings in Norfolk: where next?', *Journal of the Norfolk Historic Buildings Group* 1, 53–9.

Wood, M. (2005) *Nancy Lancaster: English Country House Style*, Frances Lincoln, London.

Woudstra, J. (2003) 'The Planting of the Pleasure Gardens of Squerryes Court, Westerham Kent in 1718', *Garden History* 31, 34–47.

Wylie, J. (2003) 'Landscape, performance and dwelling: a Glastonbury case study' in ed. P. Cloke, *Country Visions*, Prentice Hall, London, 136–57.

Wylie, J. (2005) 'A single day's walking: narrating self and landscape on the south west coast path', *Transactions of the Institute of British Geographers* 30, 234–47.

Yaxley, S. (1995) 'Men of Fakenham versus Big H' in eds A. Longcroft and R. Joby, *East Anglian Studies: Essays Presented to J.C. Barringer*, Marwood Press, Norwich, 311–14.

Index

acts of parliament 25, 70, 81, 120, 123, 143, 148
aerial photography 2, 88, 102
aesthetic values 40, 43, 115, 118, 178
afforestation 46, 59, 86
agricultural depression 190
agricultural improvement 42, 43, 46, 58, 138, 147
agricultural landscapes 42, 43, 44, 45, 56, 58, 65, 67
   symbolism of 43
agriculture *see* farming
airfields 192–4, **196**
Alken, Henry, Senior 151, 153, 154, 160, 162, 166, 167
   The Leicestershire Coverts **157**, 160
amenity areas 119, 126–31
   acquisition of 126–30, 131
   management of 127–8, 130
Anglesey, Wales 55, 56, 116
Anglo-Saxon period, the 139, 142, 187, 195, 201
anthropology 3, 39, 199
AONBs 10, 149
Apperley, Charles James (Nimrod) 151, 155, 158, 160, 167
Appletreewick, Yorks. 15, 17
archaeologists xiii, 1, 2, 12, 54, 56, 59, 84, 86, 87, 88
archaeological evidence 2, 13, 18, 19, 39, 40, 44, 53, 68, 83,
   84, 85, 89, 187, 188
   preservation of 81
archaeology 1, 2, 18, 20, 85, 87, 88, 89, 139, 195, 201,
   202, 204
   commercial 2
   industrial 1–2, 3, 54, 83
   rescue 2
architects 107, 186
architecture 32, 81, 115, 118, 201
   as an expression of power 47
   polite 23, 43, 113, 114, 115
   vernacular 23–38, 113, 116, 118, 201
aristocracy, the 50, 70, 110, 152
Arkengarthdale, Yorks. 18, 19, 97
art 152, 160, 162, 163–6, 203
artists 154, 165
Askrigg, Yorks. 94, 95, 96, 97, 98, 99, 101, 104

Banbury, Oxon 185, 187, 189, 190, 194, 195, 196–9
Bath, Somerset 107, 115, 151

Beresford, Maurice 3, 80, 81, 89, 93
Birmingham 142, 149, 155, 197, 198
Black Death, the 1, 93
botanists 84
botany 83, 89
boundaries 10, 14, 17, 18, 22, 41, 46, 53, 55, 66, 70, 88,
   108, 111, 139, 172, 173, 183, 187
   markers **76**, 139
Bowen, Collin 85, 86, 88, 89
Brocklesby Hall, Lincs. 41, 45
Brodsworth Hall, Yorks. 40, 47
Bronze Age, the 14
Buckingham, dukes of 107
building *see* development
building materials 24, 30, 31, 32, 33, 34, 38, 64, 201
buildings 1, 2, 3, 40, 56, 57, 59, 62, 67, 81, 84, 99, 100,
   102, 103, 105, 106, 113, 116, 191
   agricultural 35, 37, 158, 191
   public 93, 114, 126
   vernacular 23–38
      landscape context of 23, 24, 33, 36, 37
      plans of 29, 30, 31, 32, 36
      rebuilding of 31, 33
      size of 26, 29, 30, 31, 32–3, 34
      social space in 37
      survival of 24, 25, 27, 31, 32, 33, 35, 37, 38
building styles 24, 119
building traditions 31, 32, 37
built environment 151, 152
Burlington, earls of 98
Burton Constable Hall, Yorks. 40, 48, 51
Bwlch, Powys 64, 65

Cambridgeshire 26, 27, 82, 84
Camden, William 9
cantref 58
Cardiganshire 57
Caribbean, the 50
Carlisle, Earl of 42, 47
Castle Bolton, Yorks. 102–3
Castle Howard, Yorks. 40, 42, **45**, 47, 48, 49
   Carrmire Gate, the 42, 43, **44**
castles 62, 113, 118

cathedrals 113, 114, 118
cattle 32, 74, 85, 89, 96, 97, 98, 99, 106, 143, 146, 157, 198
caves 141
chapels 70, 97
Cheshire 108, 109, 110, 111, 112, 114, 116, 117
Chester, Cheshire 108–18, 202
chimneys 30, 31, 32
churches 60, 61, 62, 67, 81, 97, 99, 116, 141
Civil War, the 32, 70
clergy 109, 170, 171, 172, 174, 182, 186
Clyro, Wales 3, 170, 171, 172, 173, 174, 175, 178, 179, 182
colonialism 41, 49–52
commerce *see* economics, economies
common land 35, 36, 45, 56, 57, 58, 59, 60, 61, 62 -3, 64, 65, 66, 67, 70, 138, 143, 144, 145, 146, 147, 148
common rights 29, 143, 147, 195
community, communities 3, 26, 27, 31, 32, 38, 41, 42, 44, 46, 47, 50, 56, 58, 67, 98, 111, 143, 146, 168, 190, 191, 199, 202
   ecological 81, 82, 87, 88, 89
conservation 81, 82, 85, 86, 87, 189, 199
continuity 35, 40, 46, 86, 133
Conzen, M. R. G. 107
coppice 68, 82
Cornwall 11
cottages 27, 29, 33, 47, 48, 53, 57, 58, 60, 61, 63, 64, 65, 103, 104, 144, 173, 183
Cotswolds, the 140, 169, 185
counties 108, 109, 111, 112, 117, 149, 197
country houses 40, 41, 49, 107, 115, 152
   approaches to 42, 43, 47
   demolition of 52
   relationship with estates 40, 41
countryside 3, 4, 52, 55, 80, 81, 84, 87, 89, 94, 107, 123, 130, 148, 151, 152, 162, 173, 174, 175, 177, 182, 185, 186, 191, 196, 198, 199
Countryside Agency, the 4
courts 93, 99, 108, 109, 121, 146
   assizes 108, 109, 114
   manorial 64, 65
   quarter sessions 108
county histories 111, 201
coverts 46, 53, 154, 155, 156, 158, 159, 160, 161, 163
Crickhowell, Powys 63, 64, 65
cropmarks 194
Crown, the 56, 57, 94, 99, 142
Croydon, Surrey 119–34, 202
cultivation 50, 58, 87, 188, 189
   of exotic plants 51–2
cultural geography 3, 173
cultural landscapes 4, 12, 39–40, 54
Cumberland 109
Cumberland, earls of 98
Currie, Chris 24, 35

deer 85, 145, 152
deer parks 42, 46, 138, 142, 145, 147, 152
defended sites 14
Defoe, Daniel 113, 137, 141, 155
demographics 46, 48
Denbighshire 109, 111
Derbyshire 3, 70, 85, 138, 143, 147, 150
Dersingham, Norfolk 29
Deserted Medieval Village Research Group 86
deserted medieval villages *see* settlement, deserted
designed landscapes 40, 41, 42, 43, 56
   architecture within 42
development 86, 108, 116–17, 118, 119, 126, 131, 189, 192, 196, 198, 199
Devil, the 137, 139–41, 143, 150
Devon 4, 83, 84, 150
Devonshire, dukes of 78
Dimbleby, Geoffrey 82
disease 47, 79, 121, 122, 123
Dissolution, the 40, 142
ditches 74, 158, 159, 167
documentary evidence 2, 13, 35, 37, 40, 48, 49, 53, 80, 82, 83–4, 85, 88, 89, 100, 102
dogs 69–70, 74, 144
Domesday Book 62, 159
Dorset 81
downland 85, 87, 88, 89, 126
drainage 19, 45, 72, 125, 167
Duffey, Eric 2, 81, 82, 86, 87, 89
dwellings *see* buildings

early modern period, the *see* post-medieval period, the
earthworks 1, 2, 14, 81, 85, 87
   experimental 87
East Anglia 34, 35, 81, 82
Eaton, Cheshire 115, 117
ecologists 86, 87, 88, 89
ecology 4, 80, 82, 84, 85, 87, 119, 120, 123, 202
economics, economies 1, 4, 10, 22, 23, 24, 25, 26, 29, 31, 32, 33, 34, 36, 37, 38, 39, 40, 41, 42, 43, 59, 81, 93–4, 97, 98, 104, 106, 107, 108, 109, 110, 113, 116, 117, 143, 151, 157, 158, 190, 194, 198, 202, 203
Edwards, Lionel 154, 156, 159, 160, 163, 166–8
   A Leicestershire Sketch Book 160, 168
   My Hunting Sketch Book 160
   Sheepthorns **156**, 159, 160, 167
   The Quorn, The Hoby Vale 1934 167
Emery, F. 189, 195, 198
employment 42, 47, 49, 190, 191, 198
enclosure 43, 44, 45, 55–6, 57, 58, 60, 65, 67, 70, 126, 145, 147–8, 154, 157–8, 195
   parliamentary 10, 36, 55, 63, 67, 68, 70, 145, 157
enclosures 58, 59, 60, 61, 147, 155, 156, 157, 167

encroachment 56–67
England 56, 59, 66, 78, 84, 94, 137, 140, 147, 169, 172, 174,
  185, 187, 190, 197, 201, 202, 203
  eastern 82
  northern 55, 110, 148, 196
  south-eastern 121
  south-western 55
English Heritage 4, 40
Enlightenment, the 51
environment 4, 23, 37, 50, 59, 82, 87, 89, 116, 117, 119, 120,
  133, 149, 150, 202
  improvement of 120
Essex 25
estates 3, 27, 40, 41, 43, 44, 45, 46, 47, 48, 49, 50, 51, 52,
  54, 57, 62, 63, 64, 65, 67, 70, 71, 74, 75, 78, 102, 142,
  144, 202
  break-up of 52
  improvement of 47–8, 98, 99, 105
  workers on 41, 43, 46, 47, 48, 49, 50
estuaries 82
ethnography 3, 172
Europe 40, 70, 123, 138, 153, 198
Everitt, Alan 66, 108, 111, 196
extraction see mining

fairs 94, 95, 96, 97, 99, 102, 103, 104
farmers 30, 32, 34, 35, 38, 43, 45, 74, 103, 152, 158, 175
farmhouses 30, 31, 32, 34, 35, 36, 37, 147, 151, 182
farming 24, 25, 32, 33, 35, 36, 38, 41, 42, 44, 49, 65, 82,
  109, 142, 147, 157, 158, 190, 191, 192
  arable 27, 31, 33, 34, 42, 43, 83, 98, 157, 190
  modernisation of 43
  pastoral 26, 30, 32, 34, 59, 147
  'sheep-corn' 27
farmland 57, 58, 60, 64, 82, 145, 152, 153
farms 23, 34, 35, 37, 43, 57, 65, 67, 172, 173
  size of 31, 34–5, 37
fashion 81, 110, 126, 154, 166
fences 153, 154, 155, 156, 158–9, 160, 161, 167
  wire 159, 167
fens, the 26, 29, 42, 139
Ferneley, John, Senior 153, 154, 160, 162, 166, 167
  The Hon. George Petre with the Quorn at Rolleston 1814
    166, **168**
  The Quorn Hunt Scurry at Billesdon Coplow **160**, 162
fertilisers 88
Ffawyddog, Powys 63–4, 65
field patterns 56, 58, 190, 191
fields 23, 45, 46, 53, 58, 59, 61, 65, 67, 74, 145, 147, 148,
  154, 157, 172
field systems 2, 67, 85
fieldwalking 1
fieldwork 2, 15, 19, 37, 82, 84, 85, 89, 199

Fiennes, Celia 112, 137, 138
First World War 74, 78, 125, 153, 162, 164, 201
fishing 122–3, 125, 133
Fleming, Andrew 14
Flintshire 109, 111
flint tools see lithics
flooding 59–60
floodplains 59
folklore 137, 139, 140, 142, 150
Forden, Powys 61–3, 66, 67
forest law 142–3
Forestry Commission 65
forests 50, 63, 64, 65, 66, 70, 85, 137, 138, 139, 141–2, 143,
  145, 146, 147, 148, 153, 187, 188
Fowler, Peter 87

game laws, the 70–1, 143
game birds 68, 70, 74, 78
gamekeepers 49, 70, 71, 74, 78, 126, 127, 149
  lodges 71, **72**, 75
gardens 37, 50, 51, 65, 103, 115, 123, 128, 129
  kitchen 51, **53**
Garton-on-the-Wolds, Yorks. 43, 44
gentlemen 35, 42, 69, 71, 146
gentry 56, 70, 108, 109, 110, 113, 114, 115, 117, 118, 202
Georgian period, the 117, 118
geography, geographers xiii, 84, 108, 184, 191, 199
Geographical Information Systems 4
geology 3, 10–11, 12, 15, 18, 19, 20, 24, 27, 29
  location of mineral veins 10–11, 13–14, 17
geomorphology 55
geophysical survey 2
Gilpin, William 138
Girouard, Mark 107
Glamorgan 56
Gloucestershire 84
Godwin, Harry 82
government 4, 34, 89, 114, 202, 203
Grassington, Yorks. 15, 17, 18, 19, 95
grassland 42–3, 45, 56, 68, 82, 86, 87, 88, 146, 147, 148,
  155, 156–7, 158, 160, 161, 162, 167, 172, 187, 190
grazing 27, 29, 32, 35, 56, 74, 85, 87, 115, 143, 156, 168 also
  see grassland
Great Rebuilding, the 106, 201
Greenhow Hill, Yorks. 13, 15, 17
Grinton, Yorks. 95
Grosvenors, the 109, 110, 114, 115–16, 117, 118
grouse 68, 69, 70, 71, 72, 74, 75, 78, 79, 145, 148
  drinking troughs for 75, **76–7**
guns 70, 71, 72, 74

habitats 79, 80, 83, 85, 87, 88, 150
  agricultural 82

Hampshire 162
Hardy, Thomas 81, 139
hares 70, 75, 78, 143
Harewood, Earl of 46
Harewood House, Yorks. 40, 46, 47, 51
Hawes, Yorks. 95, 97, 98, 101, 104
hearth tax, the 25–7, **28**, 29, **30**, 31, 97
    exemption from 25, 26
    evasion of 26
heather 68, 70, 72, 74, 75, 78, 126
    burning of 68, 70, 72, 74, 75, 79, 128
heathland 23, 60, 81, 82
hedgebanks 83
hedges 1, 2, 23, 37, 81, 83–4, 89, 158, 159, 161
    dating of 83–4
    origins of 84
    species in 83, 84
Herefordshire 58, 138, 139, 141, 172
heritage 4, 52
Hertfordshire 120
hillforts 14
hills 3, 9, 14, 20, 56, 58, 59, 65, 121, 126, 127, 128, 131, 137,
    139–41, 142, 146, 147, 148, 160, 172, 173, 179
    origins myths about 140–1
historians xiii, 12, 25, 26, 29, 34, 54, 56, 66, 71, 80, 81, 82,
    83, 100, 126, 186, 190, 195, 203
historical ecology, ecologists 2, 80, 81, 82, 83, 84, 85, 88,
    202
Historical Ecology Discussion Group 84, 85, 86
historical geography, geographers 3, 41, 54, 67, 85, 169, 189
Historic Environment Records 4
Historic Landscape Characterisation 4, 46
Hooper, Max 3, 83, 84, 89
horses 18, 19, 85, 96, 107, 110, 115, 151, 154, 157, 158, 162,
    164, 165, 166, 168
Hoskins, W. G. xiii–xiv, 1, 2, 3, 5, 9, 37, 38, 52, 55, 79, 80,
    81, 83, 89, 93, 94, 106, 107, 153, 155, 156, 157, 159, 167,
    182, 185–200, 201, 203
    anti-modern feelings 185, 187
hothouses 51
hounds 45, 75, 142, 154, 155, 162, 163, 166, 167, 168
housing stock 23, 24, 25, 26, 27, 32, 36, 37, 38, 114
hunting 138, 142
    of foxes 44–6, 68, 75, 151–68
        buildings associated with 151
        trades associated with 151
    of deer 152, 162
    hunts
        Belvoir 151, 162, 163
        Cottesmore 151, 166
        Fernie 151, 160, 161
        Pytchley 151, 155, 158, 160, 163, 165, 167
        Quorn 46, 151, 154, 160, 163, 168

huntsmen 142, 162, 163, 166, 167
Hurst, John 86

identity 3, 47, 58, 111, 117, 146, 174, 177, 180, 183, *also see*
    landscape and identity
    national 152, 153, 162, 163–4, 172
    regional 108
industrial landscapes 2, 3, 9, 148, 199, 203
industry, industrialisation 3, 9, 41, 54, 56, 113, 116–17, 118,
    120, 132, 147, 166, 192, 198, 202
    rural 30, 34
Ingold, Tim 3
Inspectorate of Ancient Monuments, the 81, 86, 89
Ireland 49–50, 93, 98, 104, 113, 114
    estates in 49
Iron Age, the 14, 159–60
iron production 3, 167

kennels 45, 75, 151, 166
Kent 27
Kent, Nathaniel 42
'Kilvert Country' 170, **171**
Kilvert, Francis 3, 170–84
    diary 170, 171–2, 173, 174, 175, 177–9, 180, 182, 183, 203
Kingswood, Powys 61–2, 66, 67

labourers 36, 43, 46, 66, 144, 179, 202
labour market 94
Lancashire 27, 109, 110, 111, 117
landholding patterns 46, 158
landlords 33, 45, 57, 95, 98, 102, 158
landowners 33, 41, 42, 43, 44, 45, 46, 47, 49, 51, 56, 57, 59,
    70, 71, 74, 78, 105, 116, 117, 120, 147, 149, 154, 202
landownership 41, 44, 64, 107, 126, 147, 158
landscape
    and identity 146–7, 169–70, 171, 177, 179, 181, 182
    as metaphor 171
    characterisation 4–5
    cultural significance of 169
    experience of 3, 39, 50, 169, 170, 175, 183
    human impact on 3, 4, 10, 56, 81, 82, 87, 89, 192, 203
    movement through 169, 170, 171, 173–4, 175, 177, 180,
        183
    of hunting 45–6, 152, 153, 155, 156, 158, 159, 161, 166, 167,
        168, 203
    perception of 3, 4, 53, 54, 163, 182, 202, 203
    preservation of 4, 190, 194
    representation of 153, 154, 159, 160–1, 169, 183
    rural *see* countryside
    symbolic role of 40, 41, 44, 169
    theoretical approaches to 169
    urban 107–34
    value of 4, 126, 131

landscape archaeology/history 1, 2, 4, 39, 54, 56, 75, 83, 169, 183, 200, 203
    empiricism 39
    theoretical approaches 3, 4, 39, 40
Landscape Character Assessments 4
Land Utilisation Survey, the 81
lanes *see* roads
lead ore 9, 10, 11, 12, 15, 17, 18, 18, 20
leases 14, 17–18, 19, 64
Leicester 155, 158, 167, 197
Leicestershire 1, 46, 93, 154–9, 160, 166, 167
leisure 44, 78, 113, 115, 121, 126–31, 148–9, 202
Leland, John 9, 95, 201
Leyburn, Yorks. 96–7, 98, 99, 102–3, 104, **105**
Liddle, Peter 1
liminality 139, 172
Lincolnshire 84, 85, 86, 185
literature 139, 140, 142, 143, 146, 147, 153, 160, 203
lithics 4
Llandrinio, Powys 60, 66
Local Boards of Health 120–9, 133, 134
locales 41, 44
London 99, 103, 107, 119, 120, 128, 130, 131, 155, 190, 196, 197, 198
lords, lordship 27, 41, 61, 66, 70, 71, 96, 138, 142, 143, 147, 202
lowlands 24, 59–65, 68, 86, 138
Lotherton Hall, Yorks. 40, 49

Maelienydd, Wales 58, **61**
Malvern Hills, Worcs. 138, 146, 148
manorialisation 30
manors 57, 62, 63, 69, 70, 93, 98, 99, 106, 148
maps 9, 18, 35, 41, 55, 60, 62, 63, 65, 66–7, 100, 103, 105, 112, 116, 160, 201
marginal land 66, 147
Market Harborough, Leics. 93, 151, 155, 202
market places 95, 96, 97, 99–102, 103, 105
markets 9, 93–106, 198
    competition between 94, 95, 96, 97, 104
    costs of establishing 95, 97, 99
    crosses 93, 95, 96, 99, 103
    objections to 94, 96, 97, 99, 102
    paving 93, 95, 99
    royal grants of 93, 94, 95, 96, 97, 98, 99, 100, 101, 104
    tollbooths 93, 95, 99, 100, 102, 103
    tolls 95, 97, 99
    unlicensed 94, 95, 104
marriage 49, 172
Masham, Yorks. 95, 96, 105
material culture 40, 49
meadows 29, 68, 107, 139, 180

medieval period, the 2, 9, 19, 22, 36, 37, 42, 46, 60, 61, 62, 63, 68, 81, 83, 93, 94, 99, 100, 102, 105, 106, 116, 137, 138, 141, 142, 145, 146, 150, 195
Melton Mowbray, Leics. 151, 155, 156, 163, 167
Mercer, Eric 3, 24
Merioneth, Wales 56
messuages 35, 37
Meynell, Hugo 154
Middle Ages, the *see* medieval period, the
Middle Barton, Oxon 189, **192**, 200
middle classes, the 71, 109, 110, 111, 114, 129, 130, 178
Middleham, Yorks. 95–6, 97, 98, 99, 104
Midlands, the 26, 45, 138, 142, 143, 145, 149, 151, 154, 155, 156, 160, 196, 198
millers 120, 122
mills 19, 49, 75, 98, 116
mineral resources 3, 12, 14, 18, 19, 56, 146
mineral veins 13, 14, 15, 18, 19, 20, 22
miners 10, 12, 14, 15, 19, 146
mines 12, 13
    bell pits 13
    'hushing' 14, 18
    infrastructure 12, 13
        levels 12, 19–20, 22
        shafts 12, 13, 17, 18, 19, 20, 57
    stopes **11**, 12, 13, **16**
mining 3, 9, 10–22, 26, 56, 57, 66, 146
    administration of 14–15, 17–18, 22
    chronology of 13, 14, 15, 17, 19, 22
    customary mining law 14–15, 17, 22
    gins 18–19, 20
    meers 14, 15, 17, 18
    of coal 13, 19, 47, 66, 146
    of iron 146
    of lead 9, 10, 66, 97, 143, 203
    pillar and stall 13
    prospection trenches 18, 22
    quarter cords 14–15, 17, 18
    spoil 9, 13, 57
modernisation 153, 154, 166, 167
modern period, the 2, 3, 4, 9, 35, 36, 37, 38, 39, 40, 41, 44, 47, 48, 49, 53, 54, 55, 56, 57, 58, 59, 60, 61, 65, 66, 67, 68, 78, 83, 118, 119–34, 148, 152, 153, 154, 162, 169, 170, 185–200
Moelfre City, Powys 58, **60**, 67
monarchs
    Edward VII 163
    Edward VIII 153, 163
    Elizabeth I 201
    Elizabeth II 163
    George IV 162
    George V 163
    George VI 163

Henry V 138
Henry VIII 150
Victoria 78, 162–3
Monks Wood Experimental Station 3, 82, 83, 84, 85, 86
Montgomeryshire 59, 60, 62
monuments 4, 39, 86, 139, 179
Moore, Norman 81, 82
moorland 68–72, 74–5, 78–9, 137, 145, 146, 148, 149
    management of 68, 71, 72, 74, 75, 78, 79
    value of 71
moral economy 43
Munnings, Sir Alfred 154, 163, 164–6
    Changing Horses **165**, 166
    Frank Freeman on Pilot **164**, 166
    Major General Seely on Warrior 164
    The Prince of Wales on Forest Witch **153**, 163, 165
mythology 139, 153, 154, 160, 203

National Parks 10, 149
National Trust, the 40, 79, 132, 148
Nature Conservancy 2, 81, 82, 86, 88, 89
nature reserves 81, 82, 87
    management of 82
Neolithic period, the 160, 188
New Forest, the 82, 85, 86
newspapers 111, 134
Norfolk 23–38, 163, 201
Norfolk Broads 2, 81
Norfolk, dukes of 75
Norman Conquest, the 14, 61, 62, 142
Northamptonshire 85, 158, 187, 197
Norwich, Norfolk 26, 29, 34
Nottinghamshire 27

Offa's Dyke 62
open fields 27, 42, 43, 45, 60, 83, 108
open space 119, 126–30, 131, 133
orangeries 51, **52**
Ordnance Survey xiii, 61, 66, 74, 88, 185, 187
ornamental landscapes *see* designed landscapes
Orwin, C. S. 190
Otmoor, Oxon. 185, 187, 195
Oxford 186, 187, 194, 195, 198
Oxfordshire 36, 185–200, 203

parishes 26, 33, 35, 47, 48, 56, 58, 59, 61, 65, 67, 97, 120,
    123, 126, 131, 156, 174
    'open' and 'closed' 46, 47, 189
parks 43, 107
    public 115, 130, 131
pasture *see* grassland
Peak District, the 68, 69, 70, 78, 79, 137, 139, 145, 146
peat 57–8, 81, 87

Penistone, Yorks. 99–100
Pennell-Elmhirst, Captain (Brooksby) 155, 156, 157, 158,
    159, 160, 167
pesticides 83, 88
Peterken, George 84, 85
phenomenology 3, 170
Picturesque, the 138
pillow mounds 58
place-names 46, 83, 172, 173, 201
'planned' countryside 55
planning 79, 107, 121, 189, 191, 192, **193**, 195, 199
plantations
    conifer 65, 68, 83, 145
    sugar 50–1
plant species 51, 52, 82, 84, 86, 87, 88, 123
ploughing 86, 88, 89
poaching, poachers 70, 71, 137, 143, 144
policymaking, makers 85, 86, 87, 189, 198
political control 14, 96
politics 1, 40, 41, 44, 47, 55, 104, 108, 109, 114, 115, 116,
    117, 172
ponds 120, 122, 139
poor rates 25
poor, the 26, 31, 32, 56, 65, 67, 129, 144, 148, 172, 179
population 25, 27, 30, 44, 45, 47, 56, 78, 79, 80, 84, 97,
    98, 121, 126, 129, 130, 159, 190, 192
post-medieval period, the 1, 2, 14, 31, 68, 100, 105, 107,
    108, 111, 202, 203
poverty 26, 96, 105
Powys 58, 60, 66
predators 68, 71, 79
prehistorians 12, 39
prehistoric period, the 3, 9, 14, 39, 59, 66, 68, 139, 142,
    146, 159–60, 187, 195, 197
Prince of Wales, the 153, 163, 164, 165–6
probate inventories 32, 34, 36, 109
public access 45, 46, 68, 78, 79, 126–8, 148–9, 202

rabbits 58, 75, 78
Rackham, Oliver 55, 82, 83, 85
Radnorshire 58, 59, 173
railways 78, 116, 117, 124, 148, 155, 167, 173, 185, 186, 195,
    196, 198
Raistrick, Arthur 9, 22
Rawding, Charles 41
recreation *see* leisure
recreation grounds *see* amenity areas
Reeth, Yorks. 95, 97, 99, **100–1**, 102, 106
regions 24, 33, 37, 38, 47, 108, 110, 111, 112, 139
relief *see* topography
religion 49, 109, 114, 137, 139, 141, 150, 172, 178
    religious houses 9, 138, 140, 142, 143
Repton, Humphry 51–2

Restoration, the 32, 70, 113
Reynolds, Fiona xiv
Richmond, Yorks. 95, 96, 97, 98, 102, 104, 109
ridge and furrow 42, 43, 81, 157, 160
rights of way 45, 126, 127, 148–9, 173
ritual activity 188
Rio, Elizabeth Zadora xiv
rivers see watercourses
roads 23, 64, 70, 72, 100, 126, 155, 173, 179, 180, **181**, 185, 186, 187–9, 191, 192, 195–6, 197, 198, 200
Roberts, Brian 55
Roman period, the 14, 195, 197
Romantics, the 139
routeways 37, 45, 189
Royal Commission on the Historical Monuments of England 2, 3, 85, 89
Royal Society for the Protection of Birds 79, 89
royalty 138, 142, 143, 151, 152, 160, 162, 166
Ruskin, John 126, 132
Rutland 158, 159
Rutland, Bob 1
Rutland, dukes of 70–1, 74, 75, 78, 79

Salisbury Plain 88
Sassoon, Siegfried 153, 160, 167
schools 48, 115, 128, 134, 180, 191, 192, 194, 196
Scotland 50, 75, 78, 82, 93, 98, 104
Second World War 85, 162, 190, 201
sense of place 23–4, 37, 38
service rooms 37
Settle, Yorks. 95, 98, 100, 102
settlement 1, 39, 46, 47, 48, 56, 57, 59, 60, 61, 62, 63, 64–5, 66, 102, 142, 187, 188, 189, 190, 196, 199
    deserted 2, 87
    dispersed 65, 66, 67
    nucleation 58, 62, 66, 67
sewage disposal and treatment 119, 120, 122–5, 133, 192
    opposition to 123–5
sexuality 180–2
sheep 27, 68, 74, 78, 89, 96, 107, 143, 146, 157, 179
Sheffield Clarion Ramblers 78
Sheffield, Yorks. 69, 71, 75, 78
Shires, the 153, 154, 155, 156, 158, 159, 162, 163, 164, 165, 168
shooting 68, 70, 71–2, 74, 75, 78, 79, 149, 161, 163, 202
    bags 70, 72, 74, 78
    battue, the 74, 126
    butts 68, 72, **73**, 74, 78, 79
    cabins **73**, 74
    clubs 71
    lodges 70
    rights 71, 127
    season 70, 71

shops 93, 99, 102, 192, 194, 196
Shrewsbury, earls of 113, 114, 117
Shropshire 58, 59, 110, 117, 139–40, 146, 148
Sites and Monuments Records 4
Sites of Special Scientific Interest 86
Skipton, Yorks. 95, 96, 98
slaves 50, 51
smallholdings 56, 65, 66, 146
Smee, Alfred 123
smelting 9, 19
Snowdonia, Wales 89
social conditions 22, 24, 31, 47, 112
social order 42
social status 23, 35–6, 67, 110, 164, 172
social structures 1, 24, 25, 26, 30, 31, 32, 33, 38, 39, 40, 41, 43, 46, 47, 49, 50, 53, 67, 110, 164, 166, 189, 198–9, 202
Society for Landscape Studies xiii, 204
socio-economic structures see social structures
soils 24, 25, 26, 27, **28**, 29, 30, 32, 33, 38, 42, 58, 82, 86, 88, 89, 138, 155, 156
Spufford, Margaret 26, 27
Squire Osbaldeston 161, 163, 167
Staffordshire 69
Staverton park, Suffolk 85
Steeple Barton, Oxon. 185, 186, 187, 189, 192, 194, 200
    vicarage 185, 186
Stewart, Katherine 3
Stiperstones, the, Salop 139–40, 142
stock-keeping see farming, pastoral
Stubbs, George 166
suburbs, suburbanisation 114, 117, 119, 120, 123, 125, 130, 133
Suffolk 25, 26
Surrey 123
surveys 15, 19, 41, 57, 58, 63, 64, 69, 84, 88, 106, 190–1, 198, 199
Sussex 88
Swaledale, Yorks. 9, 14, 17, 18, 95, 96, 97, 99, 104

tai unnos 57, 67
Tansley, A. G. 82, 88
Taylor, Christopher xiv, 1, 2, 86, 189, 200
Temple Newsam, Yorks. 40
tenants 35, 41, 43, 45, 46, 47, 48, 49, 103–4, 126, 134, 147, 152, 158, 202
tenure 1, 30, 35, 50, 70, 103
territories 14, 84, 108, 111, 117, 173
The Making of the English Landscape xiii, 1, 2, 3, 5, 9, 55, 80, 185, 186, 187, 189, 191, 200, 201, 203
Tilley, Chris 3
tithe surveys 58, 61, 63, 88
topography 3, 17, 19, 23, 49, 58, 60, 61, 64, 139, 170, 201
tourists 179

towns 4, 34, 36, 43, 80, 81, 93, 94, 96, 97, 98, 99, 103, 106–12, 114–18, 120, 122, 123, 126, 131, 151, 156, 173, 192, 196–9, 201
    as administrative centres 108, 113
    as cultural and social centres 110, 111, 113, 115, 116, 117, 118
    as economic centres 93, 110, 111, 113, 118, 202
    built environment of 107, 108, 113, 119, 201, 202
    county 108, 112
    cultural interpretations of 107
    economic interpretations of 107
    elites of 113, 114, 116, 117, 151, 165, 199
    functions of 108–9, 114
    hinterlands of 107–14, 116–18, 197
    new 93, 94, 194, 202
    plans of 107, 112, 114, 116, 202
trackways 1, 57, 59, 74, 187–9
trade 93, 94, 96, 97–8, 104, 110, 112, 113
trade directories 110, 112, 116
transport 2, 3, 23, 110–11, 118, 155, 174, 191, 198
travel 78, 94, 110, 137, 138, 192
trees 42, 51, 115, 123, 15, 159, 160, 164, 165
Tubbs, Colin 85

UNESCO 4
uplands 24, 55, 56, 57, 58, 59, 66, 67, 68, 85, 96, 98, 131, 138, 139, 143, 146, 149, 185, 187
urbanisation 104, 110, 111, 118, 123, 132, 189, 202

valleys 19, 20, 29, 50, 58, 59, 61, 62, 63, 65, 66, 67, 75, 96, 126, 132, 133, 139, 143, 145, 136, 173, 187, 194
Van Dyck, Sir Anthony 165
    Charles I on Horseback 165
Vernacular Architecture Group 3, 202
Victorian period, the 68, 117, 119–34, 170, 171, 172, 174, 178, 183, 185, 189
villages 1, 4, 30, 33, 50, 65, 93, 99, 100, 101, 102, 109, 110, 111, 160, 172, 180, 190, 191, 192, 194, 196, 198
    model 47, **48**

Wade-Martins, Susanna 31
Wales 55–67, 78, 109, 110, 111, 112, 113, 114, 117, 145, 147, 170, 171, 172, 173, 203
warrens 75, 144
Warwickshire 26, 187, 197
waste 56, 58, 66, 67, 68, 70, 138, 142, 143, 147, 149, 179
water 3, 14
    groundwater 119, 120–1
    power 18, 50
    quality of 121, 122
    rights to 119
    supply 119, 120–1
    towers 120

watercourses 17, 29, 58, 59, 60, 61, 63, 65, 87, 99, 103, 109, 116, 119, 122, 124, 125, 138, 139, 143, 150, 187
    amenity value of 120, 122
    artificial 18, 109, 116, 185, 187, 195, 196, 198
    Cherwell 187, 194
    Derwent 75, 150
    pollution of 119, 122–3, 125, 132, 133
    Severn 59, 61, 62, 66, 67, 139, 141, 143
    Usk 63, 64, 65, 66, 67
    Wandle 120, 121, 122, 123, 126, 130, 131–2, 133
    Wye 59, 138, 139, 150, 173
wealth 26, 27, 29, 30, 32, 34, 43, 67, 106, 109, 110, 114, 117, 126, 131, 151
weaving 30, 34
Wells, Terry 84, 88
Wensleydale, Yorks. 95, 96, 97, 104
Wensley, Yorks. 95, 102
Westmorland 109
wetlands 82, 139, 185, 187
Wharfedale, Yorks. 17, 95
Wharram Percy, Yorks. 86
Wilberforce, William 52
wilderness 137–50
wildlife 81, 82, 83, 85, 87, 88
Williamson, Tom 1, 31, 34, 36
Wiltshire 86, 87, 88, 171
Winchester, Marquis of 98, 102–3
woodland 23, 46, 50, 59, 63, 64, 65, 82–3, 85–6, 87, 138, 143, 145, 147, 149, 152, 154, 159, 160, 187
    clearance 189
    clear-felling of 83
    management of 82
    preservation of 83
    primary 86
    secondary 86
wood pasture 26, 34
Worcestershire 138, 141, 143
Wordsworth, William 138, 179
workforce, the 43, 192
    migrant 47
    proletarianisation of 43
working class, the 78
World Heritage Sites 4
Wrathmell, Stuart 55
Wrexham, Clwyd 110, 112
writing 9, 15, 49, 52, 80, 83, 89, 94, 139, 147, 160, 167, 171, 174, 175, 176, 177, 179, 180, 181, 185, 203
writs *ad quod damnum* 94, 96, 99

yeomen 29, 30, 32, 34, 35, 36, 71, 158
Yorkshire 9–22, 26, 40, 44, 51, 70, 109
    Dales 9, 10, 13, 14, 17, 19, 22, 68, 94, 105, 106, 203
    Wolds 43